The Female Archangels

"*The Female Archangels* stands in harmony with the return of the Divine Feminine energies to our planet. For many years, we've been taught about the male aspects of the Divine souls assisting us, and we're now ready to connect and embody the unconditional love that the female aspects bring to us. Calista's unique, powerful, and beautiful book is written from direct experience with the Archeiai and will fill you with authentic guidance that is much needed on Earth right now!"

—**Tim Whild,** ascension expert
and co-author of *The Archangel Guide to Ascension*

"Calista is a rare and radiant angelic light . . . who will help you connect to your angels and find within yourself the loving courage to truly shine."

—**Theresa Cheung,** dream expert
and author of *The Sensitive Soul*

"At last, an angel book with a difference! Highly recommended if you wish to awaken and step into your Divine light. Calista's connection to, as well as her experience with, the angels is evident from the start, as the power of pure angelic energy pours straight from the pages. Through her beautiful healing words and unique teachings, you'll naturally tap into the truth of your higher wisdom, receive your own ethereal wings, and experience deep heart expansion to connect with all that is Divine Love. This book is a healing process by itself and a must-read for all who wish to bring angels fully into their life. Time to soar with the angels, who are lovingly waiting for you to reclaim your power!"

—**Flavia Kate Peters,** Angel Energy Practitioner® founder
and author of *Way of the Faery Shaman*

T0274176

"In *The Female Archangels,* Calista revolutionizes the way we see, relate to, and work with the angels. It's packed with profound new information on the nature and origins of the Archangels, aiding in a more inclusive and, therefore, holistic understanding of them. Through the attunements, exercises, and direct messages from the female angels, you'll not only get to know them but also truly feel them in your being and life."

—**George Lizos,** intuitive healer
and author of *Lightworkers Gotta Work*

THE *Female* ARCHANGELS

Empower Your Life with the Wisdom of the 17 Archeiai

CALISTA

Illustrated by Marie-Joe Fourzali

FINDHORN PRESS

Findhorn Press
One Park Street
Rochester, Vermont 05767
www.findhornpress.com

Findhorn Press is a division of Inner Traditions International

First edition published in 2020 by That Guy's House as *The Female Archangels: Evolutionary Teachings to Heal and Empower Your Life*

Revised and expanded second edition published in 2023 by Findhorn Press

---

Disclaimer

The information in this book is given in good faith and intended for information only. Neither author nor publisher can be held liable by any person for any loss or damage whatsoever which may arise from the use of this book or any of the information therein.

Cataloging-in-Publication data for this title is available from the Library of Congress

ISBN 978-1-64411-841-2 (print)
ISBN 978-1-64411-842-9 (ebook)

Printed and bound in China by Reliance Printing Co., Ltd.

10 9 8 7 6 5 4 3 2 1

Edited by Nicky Leach
Artwork by Marie-Joe Fourzali
Text design and layout by Richard Crookes
This book was typeset in Adobe Garamond Pro, Baskerville, Snell BT, Helvetica

To send correspondence to the author of this book, mail a first-class letter to the author c/o Inner Traditions • Bear & Company, One Park Street, Rochester, VT 05767, USA and we will forward the communication, or contact the author directly at **www.calistaascension.com**.

For Rowan, Eden, and Amaya,
and all the other New Earth pioneers here
to stir it up!

This book is dedicated to you,
Shining Ones.

CONTENTS

PREFACE
TO THE SECOND EDITION

Much has changed on and around our beautiful planet since the release of this book back in March 2020. Ironically, the publication date fell on the first day of the UK lockdown—something I didn't plan for, yet the angels did! They foresaw how humanity would awaken their potential during the "great global reset", a time when many people felt powerless and were looking for ways to exert more empowerment in their lives. Enter the Archeiai, the Divine feminine angels! Heavenly luminaries who have been focusing their Light on Earth since 11/11/11 and are now reaching out to those ready to spark creative change and build a brighter New Earth.

The birth of *The Female Archangels* came about as the result of my meeting and working with the Archeiai and introducing others to them over the last 15 years. It is the first book to solely profile who these blessed angels are and how we can partner with them to positively learn, change, and grow.

Before sharing how the second edition differs from the original, I just want to say thank you to those who've taken the time to say how much the book has changed your lives, and how inspiring it's been to see the Archeiai featured and represented in the works of other angel authors, especially those who initially discredited their existence. It's another reminder to stay fluid in our beliefs, for there is always more to learn about Creation, more to rekindle and embrace.

Seeing the Light of the Archeiai shared across social media via artwork and the art turned into an oracle deck is a dream come true! As are all the messages that serve as confirmations as to how meaningful this work is, such as Michelle's note following:

"A personal thank you for creating your beautiful book and oracle cards. It's such a joy to start my spiritual awakening by going through each card, and at specific ones I find myself saying, 'oh, I know you!' The tears and truth-bumps that come as names are put to the energies that have been helping me for so long, but just out of my sight. Thank you, what a gift!"

Changes You Can Expect

Along with a brand-new cover (thank you, Archeia Grace), changes from the original include the addition of six new chapters, profiling **Archeiai Hope, Harmony, Strength, Victory, Radiant,** and **Joy,** and their teachings from the Angel Healing® therapy system, plus, their full-colour illustrations, an updated A–Z Angel Healing® Prescription Guide, and new handy reference tables. Each chapter has also been upgraded with more on-purpose content for our ascending age, including unpacking the importance of spiritual discernment, how to build stellar-like resilience, the art of angelic feng shui and angelic breathwork, how to see and sense angels more easily, and ways to work together to create fulfilling relationships, exuberant health, and financial freedom.

Alongside the crystal allies associated with each angel, you'll also find the plant allies. Blessing your space with these crystals and plants, working with their consciousness, and ingesting them as essences (where and when appropriate under the guidance of a licensed crystal/ flower therapist) will close any perceived gaps between you and your angels, for crystal and flower essences work on the soul and Spirit body to bring about a deeper Resonance to our Divinity, and consequently, our angels.

Whether this is your first dance with the Archeiai or you walk with them already, may this book provide a portal for the personal transformation you're ready for, and then some!

Open your wings. It's time to fly!

Calista

INTRODUCTION

This book speaks to where we are as a collective human tribe. For eons, we've lived within a masculine-dominated society, where everything feminine is viewed as less worthy than its male counterpart. This has nothing to do with physical gender and all to do with our inner feminine and masculine qualities. The inherent feminine gifts of the unshackled heart—*being, feeling, nurture,* and *flow*—have been considered inferior to those qualities associated with the masculine ego: *action, control, logic,* and *structure,* creating an imbalance. Yet, suppressing the feminine is to deny our Divinity, for the feminine always gives birth to the masculine. We can harmonize our lives and help the world come into balance by integrating the feminine with the masculine, allowing both to be equal but unique in their strengths.

A New Way to Connect with Angels

As the Divine Feminine within all of us is asking to be empowered, so too is the Sacred Masculine ready to rise. The female archangels (aka the Archeiai) are responding to both needs. In 2020, a new seven-year ascension cycle began, in which the central theme is integration: coming into Divine union with all that we are. In this age, the masculine will come into peace and return to its sacred role of holding space for the feminine to move and create, while the feminine will no longer feel she needs to hide or act like a man to be heard. She'll feel free and will honour the masculine fully, so they can unite and live in Divine balance within and without. In practice, the masculine and feminine inner wounds and stories we've been carrying will continue to emerge to be heard and transformed. This is nothing to be fearful of, for we're ready to hold this in wholeness with all of life.

In this guidebook for personal and global change, you'll discover the parts of your being that feel out of sync with Source, and use tried-and-tested ways to bring yourself back into harmony. The Archeiai will help reveal where dis-ease (and its root cause) is showing up in your world, and together you'll go on many inner journeys to reconcile what's needed. You'll come away with a better understanding of yourself and others, and how these energies play out within the world at large, all for the purpose of bringing about balance for all of Creation.

An Angelic Evolution

As more Sleeping Beauties awaken to the knowing that there's more to life than what can be perceived physically, the nature of consciousness is shifting. Slowly but surely, the masculine hierarchy of the last Piscean Age, and its 2,000-year-old reign of interpreting God (aka, Source/Creator) as a singular, external entity, is dissolving. Emerging in its place is a vaster inner realization of the multi-dimensional and multi-universal nature of God. Many self-aware souls are now choosing to side-step limiting patriarchal beliefs to not just know Source but to *feel* Source as Source. Despite our entering the new Aquarian Age on 11/11/11, the transition from Pisces to Aquarius has been felt for many years and may yet be experienced for years to come. This is because everyone is on their individual path of Ascension.

The angels are here to assist everyone in better understanding these changing times. Some are experiencing the shift into the Aquarian Age as a struggle, while for others it's a joy. Yet, the angels have no hesitation or judgement in guiding those who are willing through this period of unprecedented growth. As we advance onward, so too is our perception of angels evolving. Archangels, who have come to humanity's aid since the dawn of time, are now appearing alongside their feminine twin flame counterparts.

Archeia Who?

From the beginning, the predominant portrayal of angels has been in masculine form, for God has been viewed as being in the image of man. Similarly, in Christianity, the understanding of God as the Son has been exemplified by the symbol of Jesus Christ. In other religions, such as Buddhism, God is seen as the masculine form of Buddha, yet all the while there exists within the consciousness of an angel a feminine aspect.

What I'm introducing here has nothing to do with biological gender (given that angels are non-physical beings), but more to do with the energetic vibration of an angel, which can emanate—and be sensed through our Awareness—as either male or female. Much like how a coin has two sides but is still one coin, an angel has two sides, too.

The feminine quality of an angel represents the seed of Creation, while the masculine is the flower that develops from this virtue, shaped through will and action. The Archeiai are therefore the existential essence of each Archangel; their inner, energetic potential, or as it is sometimes referred to, their "twin flame". Since 11/11/11, the Archeiai have been focusing their Light on our planet to help humanity birth into higher states of Awareness as we come into wholeness with all that we are. These universal angels reflect the great potential and worth we're all born with and, as such, are masters at helping us to empower our feminine energy, no matter the gender, culture, or creed we identify with.

To date, there's only a sprinkling of information about the Archeiai in other books, and much of this has been lifted from misconstrued religious doctrine. What you'll learn in this book (or more precisely, *remember*) has been experienced first-hand through connecting with these incredible luminaries. And so, **please get to know the Archeiai directly, drawing your own conclusions from the many experiences you enjoy together.** Talk to them. Question them. Channel them. Embody them. Ask them how you can support their evolution. Creating mutual intentions will foster a closer resonance between you both, while catalyzing the shifts you want to see in your life.

In most instances, the Archeiai complement the Divine attributes of each twin Archangel, and vice versa. Neither is a separate being, but each reflects the other, which means inviting one aspect always gives rise to the other. Yet, there's something altogether magical in inviting the Archeiai in solely. You'll know what I mean in practice!

To make your connection easier, in Appendix I, you'll find two tables that summarize the 17 Archeiai profiled within this book, including who their masculine twin is, the spiritual rays of Light they serve on, their colour manifestations, their energetic influence, their key message and affirmation to connect to them, and their crystal and plant allies. To partner with the angels further and bolster your well-being journey, you'll find the Angel Healing® Prescription Guide in Appendix II. This multipurpose directory is based upon a decade of Angel Healing® practitioner and client breakthroughs and includes close to 400 dis-ease symptoms and the best angels to resolve them.

Bringing Angels to Life

Each chapter (except the first and last) profiles a different Archeia. You'll learn intimate ways to connect with them and the means to attune with and embody their Light. A depiction of each Archeia crowns their corresponding chapter. If you're like me, you'll want to flick through the book now and have a look-see! I teamed up with my Lebanese soul sis'star and Angel Healing® Practitioner Marie-Joe Fourzali to create the artwork.

We had so much fun channelling the Archeiai. Each one touched our lives in magical ways. Some illustrations, like that of Archeia Constance, the angel of Universal Ascension, took over a month to produce due to all the personal shifts she kept inspiring! In total, it took us six years to produce the artwork to convey and portray the vibration and consciousness of the angels. Each image has layers of Spiritual Rays and alchemical angelic fires of coloured light, sacred geometry and Ascension codes, crystals, and animals associated with each angel, plus sparkly nuances and light codes to bring the angels to life! We invite you to meditate with these living, breathing works of art, so you can equally experience the magic. Be prepared, though—it'll be an adventure in and of itself! Please do screenshot the Archeiai images and share/follow on social media using the hash tags **#TheFemaleArchangels** and **@TheFemaleArchangels**. We'd love to connect with you.

How to Fully Juice This Book

How many times have you read a high-vibe book but skimmed its exercises? Perhaps you had every intention of going back to do them later, but life got in the way, or you felt you didn't have the time—

as a working single mama of three young children, I feel you! Yet, dear sis'star/brother, when you prioritize gifting yourself with what awaits, this uplifting book turns into a life-changing catalyst to spark all you've been calling in and, together with your angels, you'll create that juicy life you've always imagined.

So go get a journal and pen, if you don't have one already. Enjoy the ceremonies, meditations, and magical "me-time" moments, the *Rise Like an Angel* exercises that ask you to pause and speak directly with each Archeia. The more time you dedicate to this process of self-healing and empowerment, the greater will be your transformation. Trust me when I say, **positive change is inevitable when you make your joy a priority**. Plus, the moment you invite the Archeiai into your life, your reality will rise!

Within this book, you'll also find the staple of Angel Healing®: the attunements. Light-codes, light-language, angelic activations—all are trendy buzzwords in the modern spiritual arena, yet the angel attunements throughout this book have an ancient origin and are encoded (as the artwork is) to transport you to a special room in Heaven, reserved for passing on Angel Healing® attunements only.

These energetic transmissions, whereby the consciousness of the angels blends with your own, create a bond that by its very nature is healing. Receiving attunements supports Divine remembrance and helps you reclaim soul and Spirit fragments, much like a jigsaw puzzle coming together, enabling the corner pieces and the picture of who you are and why you're here to be revealed. As attunements are a vibrational experience, I highly recommend you get in touch to receive a free audio download created to escort you into Heaven or access this at www.CalistaAscension.com.

And so, Shining One, let's begin! Divine alchemy awaits in the most miraculous of ways! Prepare for your deepest power to be evoked, stirred, poked, and prodded as you shatter limiting paradigms and create space for Source to flood in. Let go of the old, let in the new, embrace the change, embrace You!

Chapter 1

RECEIVING YOUR WINGS
"I AM ready to fly"

We've all experienced the moment of standing on a precipice with the opportunity to leap into a new way of being and seeing. Life has caused us to change direction, and in doing so, we're faced with the chance to either evolve and explore a new landscape or stay the same and continue to cycle only what we know. The question is whether we'll leap consciously. Life will invariably cause us to jump at some point, but do we jump on our own terms, or do we fumble forward because we feel pushed by an external circumstance? Expansion occurs either way, but oh, is conscious leaping far more thrilling and fulfilling!

My First Step Forward

Prior to becoming spiritually aware, I felt more pushed at these inception points than empowered to jump of my own accord. This was okay, because I didn't know any alternative. More accurately, I'd forgotten, for as a child, I knew angels had my back.

My gran raised me alongside my mum. I loved staying at my gran's house, as she was the best baker and she always let me lick the cake bowl! She was kind, grounded, and had a magical affinity with Mother Earth. If she wasn't in her kitchen, she was in her garden, tending to her veggies. The only aspect I didn't enjoy about staying at my gran's house was sleeping there, for her house was haunted.

Two hundred years prior, the garage that adjoined the bottom bedroom of her long cottage had been part of a grain store. Her home was haunted by a gentleman who hanged himself in the store. Even though my gran wasn't interested in the world of Spirit like her sisters and mother were, she still felt the presence of this man and would often have the covers pulled back from her while she slept. Her friend and spiritualist medium—who was known to me as "Mrs. Gourlay"—stayed at my gran's house to help move on the spirit of the troubled man. Mrs. Gourlay was able to release the presence from the top half of the house after staying awake for two days and nights in spirit communication, but she never returned to resolve the bottom half of the house where I slept.

Despite it being a stone-built cottage, the bottom bedrooms were always freezing! Bless my gran, she always placed a hot-water bottle in my bed and made sure I had plenty of blankets, yet the room temperature always felt icy. My dog at the time, Scruffy, used to curl himself behind my legs, but even his shaggy warmth couldn't take the edge off the chill or help remove the presence of the departed man, who would often manifest in my room. (Years later, I realized there was nothing to fear about this man—as shared in Archeia Serenity's chapter—but as a young child, my fears felt very real.)

The first time I felt him, I shut my eyes so hard and prayed for help. I'd heard of angels before, but didn't know what they were, yet something instinctual called to them from within me. Before realizing what I was saying, I asked the angels to protect Scruffy and me. No sooner had my request been sent out than the heaviness began to lift, until it completely vanished! I peeked out of the corner of one eye and saw a light more brilliant than anything I'd seen before. It was like looking directly into the Sun, but without any of the discomfort. In fact, it was the most comfortable, safe, and soothing feeling I'd ever felt. I opened both eyes and watched in awe as this form of Light began to deepen into a soft, shimmering gold, before enveloping Scruffy and me in a large, luminous bubble. To this day, I can still feel the peace of that moment. There was no sound, no fear; just a velvety calm that sent me straight to sleep.

Conscious Leaps Propel You Higher

As I grew up, my interest in angels and spirituality waned, as my focus was taken up with academic studies. I received an honours degree in Medical Biotechnology and began a career as a cancer research scientist. Even though my passion was great for helping others to have a better quality of life, the longer I worked within pharmaceuticals, the more I wanted nothing to do with it. I wondered if doing a Ph.D. or starting a family with my then fiancé would replenish the emptiness that was filling within me, but life presented a better option!

I began learning reiki, and applying its wisdom, started to meditate in my spare time. I met many angels this way, including Seraphime (my main guardian angel), who was the same angel who comforted me as a child. Seraphime guided me to become a reiki teacher and a practitioner of different angelic modalities.

Through consciously partnering with Seraphime, my life began to reshape. At every opportunity, I gave myself reiki and angelic self-healing treatments, even in the bathroom at my work! My research friends scoffed at what I was doing because my belief in alternative healing was a joke to them, but I didn't care what they thought anymore. Up until that point in my life, I'd always given my power away to others by valuing their opinion of me over my own, but it was time to change that story, and as I did, the passion for my then fiancé also waned. He was a caring soul, yet a cynical academic! When I told him of my desire to leave science and become a professional healer, he tried to understand, but he couldn't rationalize it.

After ending our relationship and leaning more towards leaving my job, illness after illness manifested in my body. All the inner mental doubts I was holding onto began to mutate in my external reality. At one point, I lost the sight in one eye—body-speak for doubting the path ahead.

My body was right: I was scared—terrified of leaving all I knew. I was stepping into the unfamiliar, and despite my heart telling me, *Just jump!* my ego countered with, *How is this going to work? How are the bills going to get paid? Who will physically support me?* along with a thousand more mental melodies on repeat. Our inner being never provides the specific steps we need to take in our lives before we take them, which is frustrating in the moment of reaching for the evidence that moving forward is the *right* thing to do! Through the eyes of Source, there isn't a "right" or "wrong" way to do anything; there's only our choice. Either we're choosing to move forward in the direction of feeling good, or we're staying the same, which, over time, will make us feel "less than".

Why do we feel bad when we hesitate or stagnate in opposition of our dreams for too long? Because at the core of our being, we're driven by expansion. To expand and take life beyond what it's been before is central to all our earthly and spiritual desires.

If we realize that a new desire has developed within us, we must know we have the wherewithal to create the physical manifestation of it. As we embody this Truth, we cannot fail. I'll say that again: **When we trust that the greater part of ourselves is always supporting us to move forward in the direction of what feels good, we cannot fail.** All we need to do in these moments is trust that when we naturally sync with Source's stream of wellbeing, the leaps will present themselves. In practice, this means moving forward in the knowing that everything is going to be okay before the evidence of this shows up in our reality.

Leaps don't have to be scary or big. Small actions are still momentum as we move towards what's important to us. As Seraphime said to me when I needed help taking the conscious leap to leave science that led me being here with you now, beautiful soul:

Follow your heart all-ways and in every way, for your heart will always guide you towards feeling good. When you feel good, know you are on the right track. Trust this exhilaration. Use it as the wind beneath your wings to take you to vaster heights and perspectives, as you soar into a landscape of your own creation.

Oh, was she right! I knew in my heart that leaving science was the right path for me, and that the details would fill in after I'd jumped. Turning down the mental chatter and clamour of external judgements and opinions about what I *should* be doing with my life, my inner guidance found its groove again. Finally, after six months of this self-inflicted struggle, I flew! One moment I was teetering on the edge of a life that was bringing me no joy; the next, I was soaring into the unknown, where yes, all the details hadn't manifested yet, but it didn't matter. I was awake! I was aware! I was free! Faith moved through me like breath, and all I needed to do was lean forward and enjoy the ride.

Rise Like an Angel

For a moment, let's pause. Any time you see *Rise Like an Angel* in this book, it's an invitation to stop and move through a self-reflective doorway (often to meet and share with a different Archeia). These contemplative "me-time" moments create strong angelic bonds and bring understanding and inspired action to take the leaps you're ready for. And so, please journal your answers to the following:

◊ "Where do I feel stagnant in my life? What's preventing me from making a change?"

◊ "Breathing into this resistance, what are the core limiting beliefs here?"

◊ "Am I ready to let these go and take a leap of faith into a new way of being and seeing? If not, what needs to be reconciled?"

Listen, Apply, Leap!

The angels guide you to trust the first response that comes to you after asking each *Rise Like an Angel* question. This is because the initial reply comes directly from your inner being, reflecting the unconditional Truth in the moment. The second voice/sense you receive is often the conditioned self, aka the aspect of your ego that doesn't want you to move forward. Acknowledge this aspect, and have a wee laugh, as often what our ego says is ridiculous in the grand scheme of Source! In these instances, say aloud: "Thank you for sharing, but I'm only interested in following my Truth."

The voice of your inner being is the pure Awareness of Source that lives within you, blended with the sage counsel of your guardian angels and multi-dimensional spirit guides and facets. As such, your inner being is completely devoted to you and is always focused on your highest wellbeing and joy. Your inner being wants you to live a life that not just fulfils and thrills you but is constantly evolving and expanding as you take Creation beyond where it's been before.

You'll know when your Divinity speaks to you, for the voice will be clear, direct, and positive and will give you a sense of expansion as it replies to your query. Likewise, you'll know when you're following the voice of your Divinity, for the direction of your life will feel good and will flow easily. Although challenges may arise, you'll recognize them as opportunities to grow, and thus respond to them through inner enquiry rather than reacting outwardly.

Conversely, you'll know when your ego speaks to you, for the voice will be critical, judgmental, and negative and will give you a sense of contraction as it replies to your query. You'll know when you're following the voice of your ego, for you'll be preoccupied with focusing on what others are doing/not doing, or what they have that you don't have, while experiencing a lot of drama, doubt, and fear in your life as your highest needs are not being addressed.

Know that your inner being only seeks expansion through the joy of being; it doesn't harbour personal ego, judgement, doubt, or condemnation towards you or others. This means that if you feel negativity or criticism coming from your guardian angels when, for example, you're chatting with them, know that you're not in a conversation with an angel, or your fearless and unbounded Spirit for that matter. In these moments, all you need do is to pivot your vibration back into alignment. To do this, invite in Archeia Faith (who you'll meet in the next chapter), and ask her to first cleanse your energy field of egoic influences and connect you wholly to Source as you envision this happening. Imagine a bright column of golden Light streaming down from Heaven, connecting you with the centre of Mother Earth and then the centre of the Sun. See yourself held within this column of LoveLight, as you breathe in gold and breathe out gold. Breathe this pure "Source Breath" in and out until you feel centred again.

Now that you know what true Divine guidance feels like, and how to trust it, pop this gem into your toolbox: **listen, apply, leap**. Listen to what your inner being shares, apply the inspired action that follows, then leap without hesitation. Leap as you leave the past behind, with the doubts, dramas, excuses, and stories that have been holding you back. Keep following what feels good; you'll keep flying higher.

F.L.Y.

No matter where you feel you are in your life right now, trust in your own capabilities to be, do, or create anything that's meaningful to you. You cannot fail in life, for it's your own creation to do with as you please. Your guardian angels, who you'll meet shortly, and all the Archeiai who await, will continue to bolster you as you make all the leaps that your inner being is ready for, but they want you to remember an acronym before we go any further: **F.L.Y. (First Love Yourself)**.

After leaving science, I read this on a sign, and its sentiment has never left me. First, love yourself. Simple, isn't it? Yet, its meaning is so profound. In order to fly and take leaps in life, of course we need to love ourselves enough to believe we're worthy to seize our dreams. We could swap the word and meaning of "Source" or "God" with Love, for it's all the same essence. All comes from Love and all returns to Love, and our journey of life is the adventure of moving from Love embodied (our state of being before we physically incarnate) to love forgot (the sleepy state we navigate through following our birth), and then back to Love embodied (either through our re-emergence back into non-physical, or through awakening our Awareness during our earthly lifetime).

As I began to accept myself as a being of Love—accelerated by inviting angels into my life—the natural ease of spirit connection I experienced as a child rekindled. I could see clearly again, realizing there was more to reality than my body, my senses, and the limiting stories I'd been empowering. One by one, I consciously met my spirit team, the non-physical guides who assist us all to express our path, power, and purpose on this physical plane. Knowing our guides gives us a knowing of our inner being, which, like our spirit team, is Infinite and ever-changing. Yet, we all have guides that remain fixed throughout our physical life, such as our guardian angels.

Angels Reflect the Love of Who You Are

Angels aren't beings separate from you and me, but instead are reflections of our highest capacity to love and be loved. They remind us of our Divinity; that we have the wherewithal to enjoy radiant health, overflowing abundance, and magical spiritual connections, no matter our background or beliefs. Similarly, angels are non-denominational. They exist as universal Source consciousness and act as Divine messengers, supporters, and eternal friends. Although there are many different types of angels, your guardian angels are your closest angelic allies.

I'm often asked, do we have more than one guardian angel? Yes, we can have many. From around 12 weeks in utero, we're all assigned a main angelic guide who helps us birth into being, assists us in our everyday reality, and escorts us as we merge back into non-physical.

As noted in the Introduction, angels are genderless ethereal beings. As our Awareness consciously evolves and we better understand what consciousness is, our skill in perceiving different frequencies of vibrational Light is being refined, too. Coupled with this, the unintegrated parts of our masculine and feminine psyche are emerging for us to realize, heal, and love. Our spirit guides are responding to this evolution by presenting aspects of their consciousness that are a match to what is being resolved. In practice, this means you may sense your main guardian angel as now having two aspects that you can communicate and work with, often a Divine feminine and masculine presence, just like the Archeiai and their Archangel counterparts.

Are Guardian Angels Masculine or Feminine?

As a result of 15 years of teaching Angel Healing® in 70+ plus countries, I've recognized that the more an individual is awake to their spirituality and open to reconciling the inner feminine and masculine stories that have been holding them back, the more they sense their guardian angel as having two expressions: one feminine and one masculine. Depending on what needs to be addressed in the moment, they can sense the feminine aspect of the angel with them, while the masculine aspect stands back to hold the space of the connection, or vice versa.

Equally, when they give and receive Angel Healing®, their guardian angel can bring a more feminine or masculine vibration into the session in order to meet the needs of the client. These findings serve to confirm why many angel readers, healers, teachers, and authors sense certain Archangels as being more "feminine", such as Archangels Gabriel, Ariel, and Jophiel. I believe that they are perceiving the presence of the

Archeiai Hope, Strength, and Clarity (respectively) without realizing the deeper intricacies of angelic expression that the teachings herein explore.

No matter how we perceive our closest angel allies, they are forever with us; however, they'll not insert themselves into our reality unless we ask them to, as we have free will. Under extenuating circumstances, and in alignment with our inner being, they can intercede for our highest and best interests, and do so under a spiritual law called the Law of Grace.

Often, the term "guardian" can instil a sense that these angels protect us from something "negative", but looked at through their eyes, all is Source; it's only the beliefs we carry that determine whether we believe we need to be protected. Angels help us alight from the limiting beliefs we've accepted as fact in order to reveal the Truth, separating it from the dross. They do this easily because they are neutral, loving beings who exist beyond the plane of earthly duality. If you ever feel you need protection, for whatever reason, please lean into your guardian angels for peace of mind. Likewise, if you ever feel in doubt about moving forward in your life, ask your angels to give you that extra boost of faith and resilience.

Intention Is Everything

When you make leaps in your life, and equally, when you ask for the support of your guardian angels, intention is everything! Bring to mind and heart what you'd like help with. Stay in the good feeling place of trusting that the best possible outcome is manifesting, and you'll keep open to allowing them to appear.

Likewise, the more you acknowledge and thank the angels, the more they'll show up in your reality—either directly, as you've invited them in, or through their many reassuring signs, such as white feathers, repetitive number sequences like 11:11 or 22:22, familiar scents, or coloured orbs appearing around you. Accepting and appreciating the loving support of your angels builds trust in your shared connection, while raising your angelic frequency.

As Seraphime shared with me when we began to consciously connect with each other:

To know an angel is to become an angel. Remember, the only difference between humankind and angel-kind is a physical body. We are equal to you, for we are all reflections of Source.

Angels guide us to see beyond the fear and worry of modern life, so we can understand that we're beings of pure Love. They do this by dropping guidance into our Awareness to keep us aligned in our hearts, while assisting us to embody the virtues they reflect, such as compassion, faith, hope, and unity, to name but a few. As we invite such virtues into our life, we become virtuous. Likewise, as we walk with angels, we become angelic, for they literally inspire our "angelic presence" to radiate out. And as we emanate our authentic Self, we help others to remember who and what they are. In this way, we become *earth angels*.

What Do Angels Look Like?

The human mind tends only to trust information that appears physical versus vibrational, so angels often manifest as physical-seeming forms, and historically, they have done so in masculine bodies. It's true that angels are unified Source consciousness, but they understand that by revealing more of themselves (that is, their feminine side), we in turn acknowledge and express our Divine femininity, too—the aspect that has been personally and collectively suppressed since the Golden Age of Atlantis, some 13,000 years ago.

In general, angels will always appear to us in a way we're most comfortable with, for they can tune into our inner being and shape themselves accordingly. In my experience of helping many people meet angels, some see them as "old friends", as their vibe feels so familiar. Others sense angels having wings, illuminated halos, cloaks, manifesting as/with sacred symbols, geometry, alchemical fires, as a colour emanation with/without the Source Ray they serve upon, or perceive their presence via an inner knowing, sound, vision, and/or sense.

Through teaching Angel Healing®, I've found that many students want to see angels as they've been depicted in art and literature. For example, one student said he wanted to see Archangel Michael (twin of Archeia Faith) in his full regalia of body armour, shield, and sword before he would believe in his existence. Even though Michael has been depicted in this way, he also presents in other forms, and even as a physical man! So, if Michael had knocked on the door of that class-room door to show himself to the student, I'm sure the student would have said, "Go away. I am waiting for Archangel Michael!"

An exaggerated point, but I've seen this many times over, where people are carrying a narrow idea of what an angel is, and all the while their angels are saying, "Hello, I am here with you!" We must realize that the nature of our consciousness *is* changing and, therefore, so is our perception of consciousness. Staying narrow in our views only narrows the path. If we can instead let ourselves be empty in our beliefs, Heaven will fill the space, and all the proof and presence will rush in.

Do All Angels Have Wings?

When developing the Angel Healing® modality with Archeia Virtue and her counterpart, Archangel Raphael, I asked if all angels have wings. Raphael shared that all angels have wings, and then went on to say:

> Angels choose their form to match their role, just like all beings of Creation. Our wings represent our ability to raise humankind to new heights, and to help all see from a perspective of Love. Like you, we are universal uplifters, and we use our wings to envelop souls when they feel in need; to provide warmth when they feel no light burns within, and to foster strength through times of unrest. Our wings are not physical, yet they are an extension of our collective heart and the emanation of Source's Love in flow. For those who need to see them, they appear. Know, however, that every human being has wings, too!

Since Angel Healing® was launched in 2009, during each attunement ceremony, as students align their consciousness with the 17 Archeiai and 17 Archangels of the system, they not only meet their guardian angels but also receive their etheric wings!

How to Receive Your Wings

Let's go on a heart-expanding journey to receive your wings and meet your guardian angels, who are eager to connect with you, especially if this is your first conscious meeting. To best prepare for this journey, ensure you're first relaxed. Set aside any expectations or judgements about meeting your personal angels, especially if you've already met them. Be open to letting your connection evolve so as to allow new experiences to unfold. Equally, if you've never met your angels before, don't worry if you don't sense them. Your intuition is like a muscle, so if you haven't used it for a while (or ever), it'll take time and practice to build it up.

Have a journal at hand to note down insights from your angels, and please drink some water before you meditate to raise your vibration. If you're choosing to meditate at the end of your day, please also rinse the back of your neck with cold water. The occipital ridge (where the base of your skull meets your spine) is a major point for Source consciousness to enter your body. When you feel tired or out of kilter in your mind and emotions, rinsing this point resets the nervous system and brings you back into your Self.

Receiving Your Wings

◊ Find a comfortable place where you won't be disturbed. Sit upright with your hands on your lap, palms facing upward. Close your eyes, and take your attention inward to the centre of your heart. Breathe through your heart for a count of five. Suspend your breath for a count of five and then exhale for five. Repeat this pattern two more times. As you inhale, breathe in a sense of Love. Let that Love fill you as you hold your breath and then exhale Love into your space.

◊ Allow your face and body to soften, breathing Love into any areas of tension, and then choosing to let go of any concerns. This is time for you; time to connect with your angels. With every breath in, feel your vibration rising. If any thoughts appear, witness them, then take your attention back to your breath, using the inward and outward flow as a touchstone to keep you present.

◊ Imagine you're held in a column of rose-gold Love, with sparkles of diamond Light within. This LoveLight from Source pours into your being from your crown and then into your chakras, organs, limbs, and cells. Absorb its warming purity on your inhale, and emit its blissful glow on your exhale. With every "Source Breath" you're raising your vibration to merge with the frequency of your angels. Connect the LoveLight (through you) to the centre of the earth and then to the centre of the Sun.

◊ Sense yourself atop a mountain on a warm summer's day. The air is fresh and clear, and from this vantage you can see all of Creation. Ask your guardian angels to make themselves known to you now. Breathe in their presence as they come into your energy. Relax, and allow your angels to fully manifest as a form, colour, light, or feeling now. As one or more angels approach you, you may feel a deeply loving recognition with them.

◊ Ask your main guardian angel to face you, becoming aware of whether they feel male or female or a unified blend of both energies. As their unconditional Love wraps around you, allow your vibration to merge with theirs. Ask your angel to tell you their name, trusting the first answer you receive. Ask what the highest and best guidance is for you at this time.

◊ Your angel now places their hands on yours and asks you to bring to the surface anything you want to let go of—anything that's causing you to feel dense, heavy, or tired. Sense these energies (plus, their cords, roots, and webs) pass through your hands and into your angel, who instantly transforms them. Breathe out, and let go into your angel's presence and then breathe in, and let their Love replenish you.

◊ Now, take your awareness to your heart, for your angel is ready to gift you your wings! Your wings stem from your heart, and as your angel touches you here, your heart begins to expand. Feel into this expansion as your chest opens at the front, at the sides, above, and below. As your heart opens at the back, feel the angelic LoveLight warming your spine and shoulder blades in preparation for your wings unfurling. As they emerge now, feel into the type of wings you have. They might be feather, faery, animal, or Light-based wings.

◊ Stretch and shake your wings. Feel how good it is to free them fully! Notice the vibration of confidence and ease that rushes in when your wings are open, and the comfort and peace you feel as you wrap your wings around you now. Let yourself be cocooned in the healing energy of your wings. Feel their soft, soothing safety pressing onto your brow, heart, and belly. Any lingering density that you might have been carrying melts away in their tender embrace. Feel yourself being strengthened by your wings.

◊ Now fuelled up, hold hands with your guardian angel. Breathe in their Love, and know that your guardian angel is your wings. Lean into your wings to know and express your Divinity and to take the leaps you're so ready to take. You cannot fail, for you are infinitely supported. Keep opening your heart, and send Love out into the world and then feel Love return to you.

◊ Thank your angel for gifting you your wings and then feel the LoveLight sparkling in your eyes as you open them now.

◊ "My guardian angel(s) appeared to me as . . . "

◊ "Their guidance for me was . . . "

◊ "My wings looked and felt like . . . "

◊ "I'll use my wings and get to know my guardian angel(s) more by . . . "

Ways to Use Your Wings

Sometimes, the development of our wings as they extend from our heart centre can give rise to discomfort in our back and shoulders. If you're experiencing this following the meditation, dab a drop of frankincense essential oil on your heart, plus any other areas of discomfort, to alleviate the "growing pains". You can also ask your guardian angels to lift any tenderness, too.

Throughout the book, you'll discover many ways to use your wings to further your spiritual path and supercharge your everyday life. In summary, these ways fall into three categories:

◊ **For Empowerment**—to boost self-confidence, focus, and strength, as you open your wings fully; e.g., Archeia Faith's Wild Winged Breath exercise in Chapter 2, page 42.

◊ **For Healing**—to cleanse, heal, and purify your energy, as you fan your wings to release unwanted attachments; e.g., Archeia Purity's attunement in Chapter 5, page 104.

◊ **For Comfort**—to bring a sense of safety and love when moving through periods of distress by wrapping your wings around yourself (or another); e.g., Archeia Charity's Love Yourself Ritual in Chapter 7, page 151.

Chapter 2

ARCHEIA FAITH
"I AM ready to trust"

The Origin of Angels

Angels help us trust our choices, while nudging us to take the leaps that'll propel our earthly life forward and our spiritual path upward. But where do angels come from?

In 2007, Archeia Faith and her twin counterpart, Archangel Michael, inspired me with the vision to create the Angel Healing® modality. Becoming their student, they certainly put me through my paces!

Every day, either Faith, Michael, or a unified blend of their consciousness would come forward and give me a task to do. In retrospect, they were preparing me to become a teacher, but back then, I literally was a babe in the woods, so naive about the angelic realm and my purpose within it. I had studied Angelic Reiki and other similar therapy systems, as I transitioned away from science, but found that nothing compared to learning from the angels directly.

One day, I asked Faith and Michael about the origin of angels and why angels exist. I believed in angels from meeting them as a young child and was now experiencing them first-hand in my adult life, but I wondered how long they'd been around. To this day, Faith and Michael are by far the "chattiest" of angels I've encountered, and there's never a question they haven't answered directly or indirectly through inspiring inward enquiry.

Just like consulting your inner being, when you pose a question to an angel, trust the first response you receive, for this is the angel speaking to you. You may receive your reply as hearing their words inwardly

35

or outwardly, and likewise, you may see, sense, or know their response and feel the air of reassuring Truth as it accompanies their guidance. Often, when you ask angels something, even before you finish, they'll reply. **So close is their connection with us that as soon as we create the question, they've inspired the answer to emerge!**

Before I finished asking Faith and Michael about the origin of angels, a whole scene manifested as an inner vision, as if watching it on a screen. They showed me Creation as an infinite and luminous spiral of Awareness. There was no end nor beginning, just a series of inter-connected networks that moved in rhythmic unison with one another. I watched in awe as tiny sparks of light cascaded in and out of the spiral. So radiant were the sparks of light that I could hardly stand their brilliance, yet to this day, this is one of the most beautiful sights I've ever seen. Michael said:

> The sparks of Light are the original angels of Creation, what humankind refers to as Elohim. The Elohim are pioneers and architects of Source, who gave birth to the stars, planets, and heavens.

I wondered what period this was, and in response to my thoughts, Michael shared that this scene reflected the dawn of linear time as we mark it upon Earth. He explained that from Source perspective, time is non-linear (that is, it doesn't have a beginning or end) and simply spirals, creating more of itself through an inherent drive to expand. Yet, from physical perspective, time appears linear. The Elohim were petitioned to oversee the birth and development of humanity upon planet Earth, and using the elements of earth, air, fire, water, and ether, and the support of the elementals (the nature beings), they sculpted the planet into being.

As with all angelic beings, the Elohim don't have free will as human-ity does; they are driven by Divine Will. There are 12 great cosmic beings who comprise the Elohim Council of Light, including Archangel Michael and Archeia Faith, who help bridge the Love of Source between all realities and dimensions of being in our Universe. While Michael's focus has always been towards Earth, bringing his power and grace into the many energetic grids that surround our planet, as well as coming to our aid, Faith's focus has been maintaining the universal grids of

Light until now. Like all the Archeiai presented in this book, she began to bring her presence into the earthly planes from 2011. Her role is to connect with the hearts and minds of the awakened human souls who are here to help bring in the next Golden Age, or "New Earth" as the angels call it.

Returning to my vision, the more I watched the birth of humanity, the more I found myself within its weave. I was there, amongst the original angels as a pulsing pure Light. Each Light animated a different colour frequency, which Faith later defined as the "Source Rays", the means by which angels bridge and travel from one reality to the next, doing so simultaneously.

Am I truly here? I thought.

"Yes, Calista, you are here, dear one!" the angels collectively answered. *"It is time to fully awaken and remember your Elohim Self—you have quite a journey ahead. Know that we all come from the stars. We are all made from Source, as Source. You are one of us, and we, You."*

Tears of Truth ran down my face in recognition. My ego would have had a field day with what was being experienced, but my vibration was too high for its muddy grasp. My heart had been opened, I rested in the warming remembrance that ensued, knowing that my world would never be the same again.

Believing Your Truth

I knew that if I was to embrace my path as a spiritual teacher and create Angel Healing® and the other modalities that followed, I first had to fully believe what the angels had shown me: I had to believe in my Truth. Yes, part of me was/is Elohim. But if you're reading this now, know that you are part angel, too. **As Archangel Michael shares, 80 percent of humans have angelic souls.**

As an angelic soul, part of your purpose in this lifetime is to awaken your Divine heritage and use your gifts to shape New Earth. You may already feel part angel, and also remember being a Priest, Priestess and/ or what's not often mentioned, a "Presti", a being of unified gender, in other lifetimes. The process of remembering and embodying our Divine blueprint is being catalyzed by the Archeiai so that we can easily hear what our feminine, masculine, and unified selves need in order to become healed and empowered.

As you journey through this book, allow your inner Priestess, Priest, and Presti to emerge, as you let go of any separation wounds, stories, or limitations that have been holding you back. Likewise, allow your inner angel to shine as you marry with all that You are.

Have Angels Lived Physical Lives?

A misguided belief about angels is that angels have never lived a physical life. I once bought into this idea, but Archeia Faith helped me to fully understand why this isn't true. In her words:

> As more souls awaken their Awareness, they are realizing their multi-dimensional origin, and with this comes the remembrance of their angelic lifetimes both on and off Earth.
>
> Religion, which once was a touchstone for helping souls connect to their Divinity, has been misconstrued and is now falling away in favour of going inwardly to seek Truth. There are many valuable stories, lessons, and accuracies in religious texts, such as the Bible, but much has been misinterpreted, especially when it comes to the nature of angels.
>
> Yet, what is Truth? Remember, Truth is never fixed; it moves and changes depending on the perspective of the beholder. There is room for all perspectives in Creation, yet if you wish to emulate Creator's Truth, embody yourself as Creator. Likewise, if you wish to know angels, you must recognize yourself as angelic in turn. In practice, let yourself be empty in your beliefs, so you can be full of Love. Then, and only then, will you be living your Truth and allowing others to live theirs. So, yes, angels have walked and are walking the physical plane because, dear one, you are part angel!
>
> Invite me to help you understand all that is ready to be discovered. And if you would like to know of your celestial origin and learn more about your valued purpose in the weave of Creation, come with me on a journey of remembrance now . . .

The more you connect with Archeia Faith, the more you'll begin to understand who and what you Divinely are. Whether you feel you've given away, lost, or someone or something has taken your power from you in your current or other lifetimes, your sovereign authority will be regained with Faith by your side. Moreover, if you currently feel suppressed or burdened in any way, lean into Faith. She'll help you let go of anything or anyone that's constricting you, so you can regain control of the reins of your life.

Rise Like an Angel

Please pause and look at Archeia Faith's image. Breathe in her powerful presence, and wrap yourself in her sapphire-blue and golden Light. Ask Faith to be with you now and to reveal your celestial origin, affirming aloud:

Loving Archeia Faith,
Thank you for showing me now my first angelic lifetime, and
for awakening all aspects of my being that are angelic.
Thank you, and so it is.

Relax into a meditative state with Faith now. You may feel "truth-bumps" as Faith reveals your origin. (Truth-bumps are energetic goose bumps! The means of your body responding physically to the recognition/remembrance of a Divine Truth you're witnessing in the moment.) After meditating together, please ask Archeia Faith to step out of your energy field, give thanks, and journal about the following:

◊ "Archeia Faith helped me to see that my angelic origin is . . . "

◊ "Experiencing this remembrance was significant because . . . "

◊ "I will continue to honour my angelic aspect by . . . "

Archeia Faith Revealed

Archeia Faith, whose name is derived from the Latin *fidere*, meaning "to trust", serves on the Blue, Gold and Sapphire Ray of Divine Will, Power, and Protection with her counterpart, Archangel Michael. Other names for Archeia Faith are "Lady Faith" and "Mikaela".

Archeia Faith has a healing influence over our throat chakra but also helps open and align our third eye and heart centre to Source.

In her depiction, Archeia Faith asked to be shown as having the presence of a Norse Valkyrie blended with the softness of the Universal Mother. She asked for a holy sapphire crystal to be placed on her third eye, for this connects her to Michael, along with the royal blue cloak she often wears. Faith asked for "less armour" in her depiction, as opposed to what Michael often wears in his portrayals, for her unwavering belief in the goodness of Creation is her protection. Her heart is open to All, for she, like you, beautiful soul, is All. **She reminds us that what we focus on, we become. If we focus on uncertainty, this will become our experience, and likewise, if we focus on self-belief, we'll live with greater confidence**.

From a religious vantage point, faith has been defined as believing in something we cannot see, but Archeia Faith is here to help our understanding of this virtue to evolve. She defines faith not as a belief in something unknown but rather, an intrinsic knowing.

Therefore, we could further define faith as believing in ourselves unconditionally; in who we are beyond the doubts that we or others have placed upon us, and doing so in the knowledge that we are

———————

Note: In Appendix II, Angel Prescriptions for the Spiritual Body, you'll find a summary of the angels that support each chakra. Cited is the 13-chakra system used in Angel Healing®, as this incorporates the seven main chakras and the higher-dimensional centres that become active as we expand our Awareness. Running from below the feet to above the head, these comprise the *earth star, base, sacral, navel, solar plexus, heart, higher heart, throat, third eye, crown, causal, soul star,* and *stellar gateway* chakras. The angels are helping us open and integrate these chakras (and the many more that exist) to accelerate the path of Ascension.

infinitely supported. For Source *is* faith and, in every way, believes in our intrinsic capabilities. Just like Archeia Faith, we too can be all-knowing beings if we are willing to align with the fullness of all that we are.

Sometimes, we can feel we've lost our way in life, but has our faith truly disappeared or have we just covered it up with crap? (Crap being the distractions, excuses, and negative self-talk preventing us from realizing our full potential.) I empathize, for there are still moments when I feel lost, even amidst writing this chapter on faith! This is par for the intrepid course with the Archeiai: As soon as we invite their powerful feminine force into our lives, they incite the learning we need to embody in order to move ourselves forward and upward.

Having just two months to write the first edition of this book, and just a month to complete the second edition, I felt under pressure, but bolstered by the confidence and soft nurture of Archeia Faith, all was finished on time.

If you ever feel your hair being stroked or ever-so-gently tugged, turn your focus from what you're doing to the angelic presence who is with you. Invariably, it'll be your guardian angels or Archeia Faith trying to gain your attention.

In these moments, listen. What higher guidance or inspired action is here for you? When I experienced Faith's nudges while writing this chapter, it was often a sign to take a break in nature. She knew, as my inner being did, that sequestering myself indoors to write without breaks drained my energy, and that going outside would refuel me.

Faith's Way of Conquering Doubt

As well as helping us to feel better in the moment, Archeia Faith can help us uproot personal doubt. She excels at this, for she understands the guts and focused love it takes to alight from loops of negative thinking, a love that's real, raw, and in every way honest.

Using focused intention and the strength from your angel wings, the following meditation can help you burst through rigid worries, fears, and blocks, plus built-up karma and identities that may be causing you to feel uncertain in your life. Just as a flower can emerge through hardened earth, so too can you break through storied versions of truth and arise stronger.

This journey also draws from a powerful energy stream that the Council of Galaxies—the highest vibrational councils of Light—gifted humanity with in 2016. If you've attended my live events, you may have heard me speak about this Ascension tool, the Universal Code of Communication, and how it can be used to connect with every human being on Earth. Throughout the book, we'll be using this sacred satellite signal to transmit different wavelengths to one another. As we send out, so too do we receive, instantly and simultaneously. The purpose of this celestial tool is solely the joy of uplifting everyone, but every time we use it, we raise the frequency of Earth.

I can wholeheartedly say, this meditation is life-altering! It takes only a few minutes to do, but its positive effects are long-lasting. Make it your daily practice for 21 days and watch how your self-belief soars.

Wild Winged Breath

◊ Sitting in a comfortable place where you won't be disturbed, bring your hands into Gyan Mudra (a hand posture that stimulates knowing by bringing Heaven into Earth) by touching the tip of each thumb to the tip of each index finger while keeping the rest of your fingers straight. Rest your hands on your knees, and close your eyes. Take your attention inward and upward to your third eye. Breathe through this seat of intuition for a count of eight. Suspend your breath for a count of two and then exhale for four. Keep repeating this breathing pattern to keep focused.

◊ Sense yourself held in a column of swirling sapphire-blue and gold Light. Breathe into this blended Source Ray . . . and breathe it out. Intend it to fill every part of you, including your aura and wings, and then sense yourself (through this Light) connecting to the centre of the Earth and the centre of the Sun. Feel your guardian angels standing on either side of you.

◊ Invite in Archeia Faith, and ask her to demystify all negative perceptions within and around you now. As she comes into your presence, sense your wings opening wide. Dip the base of your wings into the ground and then focus on the top points of them. Connect each point to your third eye centre now, feeling the triangulation that takes place. A laser-like beam of blue-gold Light is created. As it radiates outward into Infinity, open your heart to merge with the stream.

◊ Life will always ebb and flow, but your wings forever have your back; they can stabilize and harmonize you in any storm. Feel the unwavering certainty of this Truth as you rejoice in the knowing that you're forever supported.

◊ Now, send this comfort to everyone on Mother Earth using the Universal Code of Communication. Affirm aloud, "Universal Code of Communication, I now send Faith to all of humanity." Breathe in, and feel the essence of faith (trust in action) fill you, and as you exhale, beam it out through your laser-like focus. Breathe in Faith . . . breathe out Faith. Appreciate the Oneness you're experiencing, as you send out Faith and feel it return to you.

◊ Bring into your laser-like beam any doubts that may still be surfacing. Watch as they transform into greater confidence now. Likewise, sense all your chakras clear and align to Source, especially your throat and heart chakras. Ask Archeia Faith to remove any energetic shrouds, collars, or chains from these areas, so you can be fully seen, heard, and felt. The awareness of other energetic wounds may also surface. If this happens, hand everything over to Faith as you become clearer and brighter. Now, ask for the bliss you're feeling to be increased 10 times, then 100 times, then 1,000 times!

Step into your invincibility as you proclaim aloud:

Yes! I am here. My heart is open,
my trust is strong, and my faith is unshakeable.
Thank you. And so it is.

◊ Breathe in Faith . . . breathe out Faith, as you close the
meditation. Thank all concerned, and feel the LoveLight
sparkling in your eyes as you open them.

Rise Like an Angel

◊ "Using my wings in this way felt . . . "

◊ "I'll continue to use the Wild Winged Breath for helping
with . . . "

The Source Rays

Before revealing more ways to connect with the power and potency of
Archeia Faith, let's unpack the "Source Rays".

The Archeiai want us to feel tuned into the fullness of all that we
are in every moment, not just when we meditate. This is becoming
increasingly important in our digital age, as the draw to check in with
our mobile phones is overshadowing the draw to check in with ourselves. Yet, we can ground our spirituality into our everyday experience by connecting with the alchemical Source Rays, fractals of Source
Light that were created for Source to experience and expand itself.

Source exists as clear Diamond Light, but when life animates
through Source, just like when sunlight moves through a clear crystal,
the colours of the rainbow emerge. Many angel books share that there

are only seven angelic rays that correspond to that of a rainbow, or the seven-chakra system, but in Truth, there are an Infinite number of rays that exist, and more are revealing themselves in response to the Archeiai manifesting upon Earth. Throughout this book, we'll explore the seven base spectrum colors of *red, orange, yellow, green, blue, indigo,* and *violet* as well as the *black, copper, gold, magenta, pink,* and *silver* rays, plus the gem rays of *diamond, emerald, ruby,* and *sapphire* for some extra sparkly goodness!

Each ray is an energetic stream of transformative Light but can also be defined as an alchemical fire or angelic flame. The rays are shaped through conscious thought and Divine will and exist in constant motion. Angels can serve (that is, express their Presence) on one or more rays. They use the rays as the means to bridge and travel from one reality to the next simultaneously. Therefore, when you invite in, for example, Archeia Faith, if you've developed your clairvoyance (clear intuitive seeing), you may see her Blue, Gold, or Sapphire Rays as she appears to you. The Archeiai tend to express the finer aspects of each ray, while the Archangels express the deeper, more intense aspects.

In their non-physical form, the rays are pure and activated, but when we bring them into our body with loving intention, such as for the purpose of healing, we must consciously activate them.

In practice, this means expanding our vibration to match the frequency of that ray. I say "expanding" in favour of "raising" our vibration here, for this is what Ascension is. As we make a conscious choice to connect with the Source Rays, our vibration expands at a glandular, cellular, and energetic level, as we literally "anchor" greater quotients of Light within us.

The greater and finer the frequency of Light we can consistently embody, the more we'll naturally in-lighten, adjusting our vibration and awareness of experiencing ourselves as a reflection of Source. This is often accompanied by the realization that Ascension isn't a mystical event, a mode of spiritual travel, or a heavenly staircase we need to climb, but simply a process of anchoring into and exploring our own Infinite Awareness; therefore, **receiving and expressing the many light-codes within the rays *is* the activation of them**.

As you meet and merge with the rays, ever enhanced with interacting and partnering with the angels of this book, you'll naturally embody them.

Faith and the Sapphire Ray

As the Diamond Light of Source delineates into frequencies of itself, it first creates what are known as the "Gem Rays", and from these the base spectrum colours manifest. The Sapphire Ray is one of the main jewelled lights, which holds the Blue and Indigo Rays. As a collective energy, the Sapphire Ray can help you develop confidence and innate leadership qualities of integrity, compassion, and decisiveness. Consciously asking the Sapphire Ray to be made manifest in your body or seeing yourself ablaze in Sapphire fire will help you stay aligned with Source, assisting you to truly shape the life of your dreams.

Seeing through Faith's Eyes

◊   When you can't see a situation clearly, place your hands on your heart, and relax your breathing for a few minutes. Ask Archeia Faith to be with you, seeing yourself enveloped in her bright sapphire fire. Any heaviness you're holding onto, especially in your throat/voice, surrender into the fire for purification now.

◊   Ask yourself, How can I bring (or be) Faith in this situation? What do I need to let go of and move into for this to happen?

◊   The act of letting go means surrendering the situation and the way it's making you feel. Hand over the problem and the reaching for its solution to Faith, so you can breathe, refocus, and realign. This will help the best outcome to naturally unfold without further worry on your part.

◊   Bring your hands together into prayer pose by pressing your palms together at your heart centre, thumbs touching your chest. Appreciate that your questions have been heard and answered before thanking Faith for revealing what you needed to know.

Faith and the Gold Ray

Before the Diamond Ray splits into the gem frequencies, it radiates as three main expressions of itself: *black, silver,* and *gold*. The Black Ray represents the void of all potential. It's the internal (and eternal) womb space of Creation from which all is birthed. The Silver Ray signifies the feminine manifestation of Creation, and as such connects us with the deep feminine within us and in Mother Earth. The Gold Ray signifies the masculine manifestation of Creation, and so connects us with the Sacred Masculine within us and in Great Central Sun (aka, the core of our physical Sun), which is also the celestial home of the Gold Ray.

From the perspective of Archeia Faith, the Gold Ray represents Divine will and Divine wisdom. It's the same Light that's often referred to as "Christ consciousness", and although Jesus did channel this ray to help others heal themselves, its origin predates man-made religion.

All angels carry a golden frequency, yet some express this spiritual Light more than others. When you connect with Faith, don't be surprised if you sense gold infusing into your auric field. This is happening to help you bridge Heaven and Earth, so you can become more attractive (vibrationally speaking, but for sure it'll give you a physical glow!) to angels and enjoy a clearer communication with them. The Gold Ray can also help you merge your earthly life calling with your cosmic soul calling when you consciously channel its energy. Likewise, **each time this ray is invited in and applied practically, everything in the vicinity becomes blessed**.

The following practice is something I've found myself doing along with the assistance of the elemental kingdoms to usher in our New Earth. It's best done at sunrise and in bare feet. Archeia Faith guides that if we all take up this practice, it'll create great, positive shifts for our planet.

Birthing New Earth

◊   Face the Sun, or imagine the Sun is beaming at you.
Take a few moments to bask in its warming glow. Now,
intend to connect with the Great Central Sun, feeling
yourself merge with its cosmic heart.

◊   On your next inhale, and upon every one that follows,
sense you're breathing the Gold Ray from the Great
Central Sun through your third eye, down through your
body, and out through your feet into the ground.

◊   Let the Gold Ray spread its LoveLight in all directions
as it fills everything in nature, including the waters,
landscapes, and atmosphere of our planet. See
everything illuminated, renewed, and filled with golden
energy.

◊   Then see the golden energy move into the heart of
Mother Earth. Along with the elementals, she sends her
appreciation back to the Great Central Sun and then
back to you, as received upon the sunlight. Experience
the bright, cyclical flow of this golden Love.

◊   In this moment, realize that you're literally birthing
Heaven on Earth! Affirm aloud:

> *I am the heart of Creation and one with Earth.*
> *As I breathe in Gold, I give Gold to all.*
> *Heaven is now created.*
> *Thank you. And so it is.*

◊   Envision your version of New Earth. Experience how you
want it to look and feel for you and the generations to
come.

Building Greater Trust

One of the greatest gifts the Archeiai have helped me realize is my ability to bridge the realms of Creation, and to do so for the purpose of helping people attune to the many races of ethereal beings. Over the years, I've attuned thousands of souls to angels, crystals, elementals, Light councils, sacred geometry, and the wisdom of civilizations—really, whatever was Divinely guided in the moment. It took me a while to trust in this ability, but it became easier once I got out of my own way.

Attunements are energetic exchanges, which blend the consciousness of one being with another (for example, merging your vibration with that of an angel). This ancient form of soul retrieval activates aspects of ourselves that we may not have been consciously aware of and/or brings back parts of ourselves that have felt missing or lost. Attunements are a way of using our intention to unite our humanity with our Divinity. They help us understand ourselves better, while reconnecting us with our soul's gifts and talents. Furthermore, attunements can be life-altering, for they can catalyze deep healing.

With your consent (and with the angels holding space), I'd like to attune you to 17 of the most on-purpose Archeiai for our ascending age, beginning with Archeia Faith. These energetic transmissions will connect you intimately with the Archeiai, so you're forever linked with them and can channel their energy, teachings, and virtues for the benefit of all concerned. It will also strengthen your existing angelic relationships.

From witnessing the extraordinary expansion of those who've received similar attunements in Angel Healing®, I hope you'll feel as held by Creation and, from that loving certainty, enjoy greater trust and flow in your life.

Attuning to Archeia Faith

Although attuning to angels is a magical, high-vibe experience, it's also deeply grounding! There's nothing to fear if you've never received an attunement before, for they are always given as an unconditional positive for your Truth and experience. The angels may also deliver healing while attuning you. This helps alleviate any sudden shifts in your vibration and physical body during the attunement process and lifts any blocks that have been hindering you in your life.

Your guardian angels will help you relax as each Archeia comes forth to gift you with their Light and energetic virtue(s), which, as time progresses, you can grow at a deeper level. By receiving the angelic virtue—for example, receiving "faith" from Archeia Faith—you align fully with its root essence (trust in action) and, in turn, become a template of trust for others.

Everyone experiences attunements differently. For some of you, the sensations will feel subtle, while for others, the flow of energy will rise and fall within and around you. If you feel yourself getting too hot, ensure you're grounded by visualizing tree roots growing from the base of your heart down through your feet and then connecting with the heart of Mother Earth. Likewise, if you're guided to move your body, flow with this, especially when giving yourself healing as directed during the attunement. Always rest after attunements to help your body acclimatize to the new energies, and drink plenty of water, too.

Trust that you deserve to be linked to these luminaries of Light. The Archeiai represent Divine virtues and support humanity, but your role is equally important. Angels exist beyond the constraints of time and space, so can be with many people simultaneously. You don't need to worry about taking them away from something, for they are eager to assist you.

How to Prepare for Attunements

Each attunement takes between 20 minutes to an hour to receive, so it's best to give yourself plenty of time. You can record the attunement to play back or access the free audio to attune to all 17 Archeiai and their Archangel counterparts at **www.CalistaAscension.com**. If you're guided to repeat any of the attunement ceremonies, please keep open to a new experience each time, for the more you align with the angels, the more they can impart.

◊　When you're ready to receive your attunement, sit in a comfortable place where you won't be disturbed. Have some water at hand, along with your journal and the picture of the Archeia you're attuning to, which you'll find at the start of their chapter. Open your heart to her and breathe in her presence and then exhale any doubts or expectations, letting them go as you enter the ceremony.

◊   Bring your hands into prayer pose, and intend your wings to open wide. Invite in your guardian angels, affirming aloud:

"Loving guardian angels, may you now come forward to hold sacred space for this attunement to Archeia _____. Please ensure that everything that comes to, through, and from me is only unconditionally positive for my Truth and experience. I am ready to align to Archeia _____ and affirm this attunement perfect for me. Thank you. And so it is."

◊   Surrender the sense that you should be doing something or feeling something; just enjoy this beautiful experience.

Archeia Faith Attunement

Feeling centred, sense yourself held in a column of swirling sapphire-blue and golden Light. Breathe this blended Source Ray in and out. Allow it to fill every part of you, including your aura and wings, and then see it connect through you to the centre of Earth and the centre of the Sun. Feel your guardian angels standing on either side of you, radiating their Love, which expands your Light even more. When you're ready to invite in Archeia Faith, affirm aloud:

"Loving Archeia Faith, angel of Divine Will, Power, and Protection and master of the Blue, Gold, and Sapphire Rays, may you now attune me to your vibration and consciousness, so that I am forever linked with you. Please assist me in channelling your energy for the benefit of all concerned, and help me embody your qualities of confidence, leadership, self-assurance, and seeing the best in myself and others. Help me

unite with my angelic presence, and release me from any attachments, contracts, cords, hooks, vows, and webs of uncertainty within my life and within the world. Support me to unplug from fear-based agendas and limiting stories, so that I may live the Love of who I am. Thank you. And so it is."

Breathe in Faith, and breathe out Faith, as you allow this Divine angel to blend her consciousness with yours. Notice the shifts that are taking place within your mind, heart, body, and energetic field now. Ask Archeia Faith what the highest and best guidance is for you at this time, and if there's anything you can support her with.

As you continue to attune to Archeia Faith, you can also channel her healing Light. If there's a part of your body you'd like to heal, bring your hands to that area now, or gently cup your hands around your throat—the area Faith influences the most. Sense Faith's blue-golden Light moving into these areas now. As you receive healing, ask yourself: Where am I hiding in life? Where am I keeping myself small? What is stopping me from fully believing in myself? Let these questions melt into you, and listen as their answers arise. Feel yourself held in Source's Love as Archeia Faith reminds you: "You have wings, dear one, use them! Listen, apply, leap. Now is the time to SOAR!"

Bask in all the realizations that emerge, and when you feel the energy beginning to wane, intend the attunement to be complete. Thank your guardian angels and Archeia Faith, before opening your eyes and drinking some water to ground yourself.

Rise Like an Angel

◊ "Attuning to Archeia Faith and receiving her guidance is meaningful because . . . "

◊ "As I stop hiding myself from life, I've reclaimed trust and . . . "

◊ "I'll continue to invite in Archeia Faith to support me with . . . "

Daily Affirmation to Connect with Archeia Faith

"I rejoice in knowing that my life is by my design."

Crystal Allies

Elestial sapphire andara, golden topaz, Labradorite

Plant Allies

Frankincense, sunflower, tall mountain larkspur

Invite In Archeia Faith for . . .

Self-belief; self-assurance; protection; leadership; unmasking doubt, fear, and self-judgement; confidence; and knowing wholeheartedly that angels are always supporting you.

Chapter 3

ARCHEIA VIRTUE
"I AM ready to heal"

Going Deeper

While Archeia Faith and Archangel Michael helped me trust in myself and my capabilities for birthing Angel Healing®, Archeia Virtue and Archangel Raphael gifted much of the system's content.

Each day with Virtue and Raphael was a page of understanding from a book that felt so familiar. I wasn't learning about angels; I was remembering what I already knew about them, unveiling experiences with the Archeiai, the elementals, and the Elohim. Even though my ego still found it challenging to accept the possibility of living angelic lives, when I relaxed in meditation, my mind became neutral and began to widen its perspective. I thought to myself: *If the trillions of cells in our body hold the memory of all our ancestry, and are themselves ever-changing, then surely, it's possible that we can consciously remember all our incarnations, and not just those as a human being.*

Just like the spiritual rays, the angels showed me that my soul and Spirit, like yours, is both multi-faceted and multi-dimensional, containing within it myriad different colours of vibration, all existing at the same time.

Until this point of daily meditation with the angels, I hadn't heard of the term "Archeia" before. There were no books about the Divine feminine angels, and only a brief allusion to what might have been them had been made in the Hebrew text *The Book of Zechariah* (verse 5:9). And so, I turned to the angels to teach me more than what little was known about the Archeiai, and angels in general.

Just as we, as humans, originate from Source and ultimately return to Source, angels follow a similar path of creation—the only difference being that angels don't experience any of the veils of amnesia or illusions of separation that humankind does. Angels know their Divine heritage, unless of course it's part of their purpose to temporarily forget it (for example, if they are what mankind has termed a "fallen angel"). In most cases, however, angels courier the essence of Love across all realities, and do so by projecting and expressing aspects of who they are as a masculine and/or feminine entity. Again, this has nothing to do with gender, but all to do with the vibration of the consciousness they are expressing in the moment.

The Angel of Healing

If you've connected with an angel, you might have felt their presence as male or female, or as a neutral blend of both vibrations. How we perceive an angel depends on the type of support they're providing. For example, when my focus was learning about spirituality, Archangel Raphael manifested in my meditations, and when my intention was more healing-based, Archeia Virtue appeared.

For so long, **Raphael has been regarded as the main angel of healing, but the evolved Truth is that Virtue is the underlying weave of wellbeing that flows through all acts of healing**. So, if you've asked Raphael for healing before, know that Virtue has also been present. Often, she will infuse her soft pink Light into the emotional and mental bodies of all concerned, to heal through the freedom of honesty and forgiveness. This focus marries perfectly with the emerald Light that Raphael brings in to restore the physical body, all for the purpose of aligning the individual with their innate state of health.

Like all the Archeiai, Virtue's feminine presence gives birth to the masculine, helping us realize that we're more than just what we see physically; we are Creation and Creator expressing through form in every moment. Our earthly purpose, as we expand consciousness and raise our Awareness, is not just to bridge Heaven and Earth but to bring Heaven *through* Earth by way of our physical bodies, which we can easily do by partnering with angels. Angels help us embody both our humanity and Divinity, so we can enjoy the radiant health that is our birthright.

Be Real to Heal

As Virtue revealed the therapeutic techniques that would become the mainstay for Angel Healing®, I became the test subject! Ever the scientist, I wanted to know that the techniques worked, and also, by that point in my life, I had pushed down experiences of sexual trauma, self-harm, and bulimia that were ready to come to the fore for healing.

No matter how many times I gave myself Angel Healing®, Virtue always guided me to be real with my feelings by asking myself if I was fully ready to let go of the dis-ease and forgive those associated with it. She said:

> We angels, like your inner being, forever hold the immaculate vision of you as healed and empowered. If you are not ready to live this reality, there is nothing we can do to improve your state of being. That power is yours, dear one.

I asked Virtue to explain what the practical steps are for uniting with the vision of radiant health, and she replied;

> First, be honest with yourself and the feelings you are experiencing. Let them come to the surface, one by one, to be felt and acknowledged. Give credence to your emotions, for they are the indicators of your state of vibration; they are always reflecting whether you are aligned with your inner being or not. Let them rise, so you can hear and feel them. Appreciate their underlying message and the medicine they are carrying.
>
> Ask yourself: Who and what do I need to forgive that's associated with these feelings—myself, others, the circumstance, and/or the environment? Acknowledge that healing requires forgiveness on some level. By being honest with yourself, the pathway of wellbeing will open for you.
>
> Now ask: Am I ready to let go of feeling less than I Divinely am? Am I ready to let go of the symptoms and stories of dis-ease from my inner and outer conversations? Am I ready to envision with my angels and inner being my perfect health? Am I ready to feel better in every way?

If the answer to all of these is yes, acknowledge how you want to feel, dear one. What does perfect health look and feel like to you? Imagine and envision this. Breathe life into this with all your being. Then, be easy with yourself, as the parts of you that were not in alignment with Source unify. Believe in a better reality for yourself, as you breathe and create this vision into form.

Remember, no matter the diagnosis you or others define, the prognosis is within your control, for you hold all the keys to radiant health. You are the master of your own temple. We angels and your inner being can hold a template for your healing, for we see you always in your highest Light, but you must trust in the perpetual stream of wellbeing, which you originate from and are in each moment. Let yourself sync with this stream as you become it once more.

Rise Like an Angel

◊ Whatever dis-ease you're experiencing in life right now, please pause and look at Archeia Virtue's image. Gaze into her soft, unguarded eyes, and feel the LoveLight that radiates from her heart to yours. Breathe in her warming presence, and breathe it out into your space.

◊ Reread the previous section, Be Real to Heal, and answer the questions Virtue poses through journaling. Be completely honest with yourself as you go into deep meditative space. Make note of any additional insights that Archeia Virtue shares.

The Law of Healing

Angels understand that life as we perceive it to be through our senses is not always sunshine and rainbows! Yet, no matter the sh*t storms that may fill our world, and how we feel while we are in them, we must remain true to ourselves. When we are real with ourselves and how we are feeling, it becomes easy to communicate with our inner being and arrive at the heart of what's making us feel "less than".

If we run from or deny our feelings or hold onto the density of them without being willing to consciously engage, we're only side-stepping the opportunities for growth that emerge for us to embody. By listening with honesty, we can see clearly—perhaps for the first time—all perspectives of the presenting dis-ease and its associated circumstances that have caused us to feel powerless, or to feel overly special (for example, when we wear dis-ease as a badge of honour).

As we find the strength to forgive, we lay ourselves bare, and through our transparency, inner struggles cease and the momentum of density subsides. We move from repeating to ourselves and others the symptoms of "our" dis-ease to detaching from that identity. Then, the Light of hope can move through us, rousing appreciation for everything the dis-ease evoked. As hope grows, dis-ease lessens and eventually loses its grip on us.

Self-destructive behaviours that were associated with feeling powerless/overly special stop when our true power is reclaimed. Then, we can begin to envision clearly how we want to feel by pivoting our vibration towards feeling better and deliberately choosing better-feeling thoughts and behaviours. Our inner shine returns, as there's nothing to cloud its radiance, and our heart and wings open as we're free to move in rhythmic unison with our inherent stream of wellbeing, which eternally propels us forward rather than backward. If we ever doubt what Virtue terms this "Law of Healing", we only have to lean into her, and she'll help us soar upon her wings until we remember that we have wings, too.

Drawing from the certainty of this law, whatever healing you're ready to see show up in your life, act upon it, for the only thing that stands in your way, beautiful soul, is you. I say that with love, being a seasoned veteran on this path! Virtue has helped me piece my life back together on so many occasions, from moving through divorce to navigating loss; from liberating chronic dis-eases (which, by doctors' prognosis, I should still be enduring) to empowering myself through postnatal depression; and the universal challenges we all face in our human experience from Love forgot to Love embodied. If you take nothing else from this book, remember that radiant health is your innate state of being. **There's nothing you cannot heal, no matter who tells you otherwise, for the prognosis is always in your power**. Lean on Virtue to help you know how supported you are and to let health flow anew.

Archeia Virtue Revealed

Archeia Virtue, whose name is derived from the Latin *virtutem*, meaning "goodness", serves on the Green, Pink, and Emerald Rays of Healing, Truth, and Divine Love with her counterpart, Archangel Raphael. Within the emerald gem frequency is the Green Ray, which represents healing on all levels of being. The Pink Ray is born from the Ruby Ray, and it stands for compassionate love and understanding. Virtue also carries within her consciousness the Gold and Violet Rays, so you may see these colours when you connect and channel her energy. Other names for Archeia Virtue are Lady Virtue and Mareia. Although Archeia Virtue has a healing influence over our third eye, her main focus lies in empowering our heart and higher heart centres.

For her depiction, Virtue asked for a trinity of doves around her head, to help us sooth mental worries and blocks that oppose the belief that we can heal ourselves. As peace of mind is regained, our bodies can regenerate easily from the inside out, as reflected by the DNA helix that Virtue asked for in her dress.

Many angel books refer to Mother Mary, who gave birth to Jesus Christ, as the twin of Archangel Raphael. Throughout the physical lifetime of Mother Mary, Archeia Virtue did act as one of her main spirit guides, to assist her in becoming the Divine Mother that she chose to be before incarnating, but Virtue and Mary are not the same being. Like her namesake, Archeia Virtue carries all the Divine Virtues of human and cosmic consciousness within her vibration, and so was able to assist Mary in conceiving and birthing Jesus with unwavering love and conviction. Virtue also helped Mary to raise Jesus, so that he could accept his Divinity and ascend into his highest calling.

When we embrace the teachings and Light of Archeia Virtue in our life, we become a Divine Mother, too, irrespective of whether we are male or female in body. We learn how to parent through learning what it takes to love ourselves enough to value all that we are and then to express through our being all that we came here to be in this lifetime and beyond, without a semblance of hesitation or censure. Archeia Virtue also acts as a midwife for souls that are either going through their spiritual awakening or just about to start.

Open to Forgiveness

Archeia Virtue guides that all acts of forgiveness absolve us from the emotional hooks, triggers, and traumas that incite dis-ease. We can never change past events, but we can change how we respond to them. Likewise, we can't change what others have subjected us to, but we can remove ourselves from their energy by ceasing to relive past experiences with them as we take our power back.

It's part of the Law of Healing that we'll return to feeling good when we're willing to be real with ourselves, real with our feelings, real with our choices, and real with who and what we need to forgive in order to move on. Practically speaking, Virtue supports us to do this by making peace with all that has hurt us, whether this includes forgiving ourselves, others, the environment, and/or circumstances associated with the dis-ease in mind.

Around the time of writing this chapter, I taught a three-day Angel Healing® Teachers retreat. On the morning of the third day, I broke my toe. I was trying to do many things at once and just before the soon-to-be teachers arrived, I hit my toe on one of the workshop chairs, and it bent right back! The pain was excruciating, but thankfully, as soon as I started channelling the angels to deliver the course, the discomfort vanished until everyone had left for the day. Then, I invited in Archeia Virtue for healing, saying the following:

Loving Archeia Virtue, may you now channel your healing energy through me and into me for my highest and greatest good. Please focus your Light into my toe as I hold it now. I affirm, I forgive the chair I hit my toe on, and how busy I felt,

and anyone and everything concerned. I'm grateful this happened for the reminder to keep grounded and present in my
awareness, but now let go of all discomfort. I am ready for my
toe to be healed. Thank you. And so it is.

Change the wording to suit what is ailing you right now, then allow the
Light of Virtue to move through you and into you as she blends her
healing with yours. If you stay in the moment, you'll know what to say
and who and what to forgive.

Don't be surprised if you find yourself forgiving things you wouldn't
normally even think about when working with the emotional detec-
tive that's Archeia Virtue! In the past, after forgiving surface-related
circumstances, I've found myself forgiving all the women in my life,
then all the men, then the patriarchy as a collective entity, then Mother
Earth, Father Sky, and everything in between! Our inner being and
angels always help us heal associated cords, roots, and webs of disharmony, but we must first come into a space of allowing.

Another important key here is affirming that what we're healing
has returned to health and vibrancy. Granted, my toe was still broken
and badly bruised after channelling Virtue's Light into it, but the pain
quickly subsided, and I found myself feeling better about the situation. In fact, Virtue helped me laugh at what happened and appreciate
the excuse to put my feet up! She inspired me to move from pain and
blame into comfort and gratitude, and from this higher vibe no dis-
ease can thrive.

Seeing Is Believing and
Believing Is Seeing

As we collectively realize that we can heal ourselves and our lives—
ever more so by partnering with angels—healings will become instant.
Perhaps you've experienced, or have been witness to, instantaneous
healing before? I remember lifetimes in Atlantis when we re-grew limbs
through our conscious focus of seeing the limb already renewed.

From visiting lifetimes in other golden times, a common thread
that repeats is how we all have the wherewithal to heal our bodies and
bring peace to our lives by seeing any parts of dis-ease (and in general

our whole being) as healed, healthy, and radiant. This ancient knowing is now surfacing in the hearts and minds of awakened souls and filtering into mainstream science.

I'm a big fan of American author Gregg Braden and his pioneering work bridging science and spirituality. Gregg also believes that through our conscious focus we can create healing.

For example, in his DVD *Science of Miracles*, Gregg shows video footage of a lady healing a 3-inch tumour in less than 3 minutes. Her bladder cancer had been deemed inoperable by conventional medicine, but Gregg shares how this woman went to a medicine-free hospital in Beijing, where she discovered alternative ways to change her lifestyle, nourish her body, and stimulate her chakras, as is the case with Angel Healing®.

The DVD footage shows this lady undergoing a procedure while awake to remove the tumour. Using a split-screen ultrasound monitor that was filming in real time, three energy-healing practitioners chant a word that reinforces the feeling of her already being "healed". As they chant, the footage clearly shows the cancerous tumour disappearing in less than 3 minutes!

Gregg reckons that her body responded to the sense of wellbeing the practitioners were embodying for her. Just like Jesus did, and many aware masters before and after him, the energy healing practitioners didn't focus on the cancer itself but on this lady being in perfect health. Yes, she could have healed herself on her own, but when an energy healing practitioner holds the "energetic space" for another (that is, sees them fully aligned with all they are and affirms them to be already healed, happy, and holy), as the angels and our inner being do, they renew faster.

Why? Because we believe in the healing that's being positively influenced for us, thereby catalyzing our inbuilt recovery process. As shared in the *Angel Healing® Prescription Guide* (Appendix II), only we can heal ourselves, but when we open to the energetic support of our inner being and angels (and believe in the template of health and wellbeing they hold for us), we feel the innate upliftment and so regenerate quicker.

Letting in Compassion

To help us trust that we always have the wherewithal to renew ourselves, let's lean deeper into forgiveness, a practice that can be best understood by its application through our heart centre. When we listen with our heart, we hear the presence of our inner being and realize that forgiveness, whether focused outwardly or inwardly, is a compassionate gift we give ourselves. As Mark Twain wisely wrote, "Forgiveness is the fragrance that the violet sheds on the heel that has crushed it." In other words, as we forgive, we project a Love so powerful, it softens all wounding while helping everyone concerned to move forward.

The following forgiveness ceremony was given to me by Archeia Virtue many years ago. It goes a lot deeper than what she's already shared, and it was the soothing balm I used to find compassion for those I felt had wronged me in my past. Through this powerful practice, Virtue taught me to value the contrasts in all life experiences for the expansion and wisdom that each event can provide. She also reminded me that it takes more energy to hate and hold a grudge than it does to love and forgive. In her words:

Stay in an aura of Compassion, and extend the Light of this Divine virtue to all concerned. This will help you look through the eyes of others and understand their vantage, instead of fighting them on the battlefield of your mind and emotions.

I am forever in appreciation for this teaching that **to love fully, we must be able to forgive fully**. And so, I hope this exercise, which is blessed by the unconditional compassion of the Pink Ray, brings you as much liberation.

Even if you feel you have nothing or no one to forgive, gift yourself this meditative ceremony anyway. It'll purge any underlying blame, shame, guilt, and pain, plus any other emotional, mental, or physical hooks from your subconsciousness that have been making you feel less than worthy. Having witnessed the incredible breakthroughs of clients who've done this ceremony, I will say: Don't be surprised if you feel amazing afterward! I've seen many people free themselves from dis-ease and density, open to Love again, heal existing relationships, and overall recognize the goodness that lives and breathes within them.

Forgiveness Ceremony

◊ Sitting in a comfortable place where you won't be disturbed, bring your hands into Shunya (Heaven) Mudra, a hand gesture to help you listen to your feelings, consisting of bending your middle finger until it touches the base of your thumb. Press down on your middle finger with your thumb while keeping the rest of your fingers straight. Do this with both hands at the same time, then rest your hands on your knees and close your eyes. Take your attention inward, and rest your focus in your heart centre. Breathe in for a count of eight, and exhale for a count of eight. Keep repeating this breathing pattern to keep centred throughout.

◊ Imagine a seed of brilliant pink Light in your heart. With each inhale, breathe life into this seed, and with each exhale, watch as it grows, until it surrounds you completely in a halo of pink Light. Breathe in this Source Ray, and breathe it out. Intend that it fill every part of you, including your aura and wings, and then sense yourself (through this Light) connecting to the centre of Earth and the centre of the Sun. Feel your guardian angels standing on either side of you.

◊ Invite in Archeia Virtue to be with you, and ask her to bring your awareness to anyone or anything you feel you need to forgive. Acknowledge the memories, feelings, and circumstances that arise (without identifying with them), as well as the people who step forward. Sit with it all for a few moments, as you witness who and what is appearing. Stay present as you watch this process, remaining in the compassion of the Pink Ray as it envelops all concerned.

◊ Accept that whatever you're recounting from your past served you in some way, but you don't need to hold on or identify with your past or re-live any of its heaviness anymore. It's time to heal and reclaim your power—time to let go of all blame, shame, guilt, pain, and regret, and anything else that's been making you feel less than whole or worthy.

◊ Intentionally choose to forgive. Breathe in for a count of eight, as you decree yourself Creator of your reality, and exhale for a count of eight as you release anything that refutes this Truth. Affirm aloud:

I forgive on all levels of time, space, dimension, and being, everything that has come forward to be absolved. I choose forgiveness. I choose health. I choose Love. I choose me. Thank you. And so it is.

◊ Now bring all concerned into your heart, and wrap your wings around yourself. Encase everything and everyone in pure, loving goodness. If any dense feelings still rise, address them one by one. For example, if guilt is present, affirm aloud:

I release myself from guilt, as I breathe Innocence into me.

◊ Let the virtue of Innocence completely fill your being. Likewise, if shame remains, breathe in Worthiness; if hurt remains, breathe in Wholeness; if anger remains, breathe in Peace; and if fear remains, breathe in Love. Always breathe in the opposing virtue to whatever density arises to best help yourself move forward.

◊ Bask in the positive, loving shifts you're experiencing and then amplify this bliss 10 times, then 100 times, then 1,000 times!

◊ Sense, know, and feel yourself to be completely free now. This ceremony has not only cleansed and transformed what was holding you back but has brought healing to both your maternal and paternal bloodlines, positively impacting seven generations back, and enabling greater liberation for your future descendants. What you've been able to resolve is a gift that will keep on giving, creating ripples of purity throughout time and space. Breathe into this knowing and all the goodness it stirs . . . and breathe out deeply.

◊ As the ceremony draws to a close, see everyone and everything exit your energy field and connect to Source, including yourself. Thank all concerned, then journal your insights, and drink some water to ground your energy.

Rise Like an Angel

◊ "This ceremony was deeply healing for me because . . ."

◊ "By choosing to forgive, I feel better in myself and have greater trust in . . ."

If you feel there are residual energies or attachments to others that don't feel good following the ceremony, write a letter addressed to the circumstance and/or people concerned, airing what you feel needs to be said before you can fully move on. Be real with your words, and if you feel you need to swear, scream, or cry, just let loose without editing or judging yourself. Empty yourself of all ill feelings without staying in their vibration for too long.

Remember: Through this exercise, you're bringing Light into all the dark corners of your subconsciousness for the purpose of laying to rest buried burdens and negative memories.

As you allow yourself the grace to let all emerge without censure, remind yourself that you're doing this exercise to feel better and to live in greater ease. You're allowing yourself the freedom of surrendering all the mental, emotional, and psychic hooks that have been holding you back, whether these were known consciously or subconsciously. Once you have transcribed these energies into your letter(s), burn them safely outside to symbolically shed the past. Let the elemental forces of nature transform this energy back into life-renewing prana. You've created a positive new timeline. Celebrate this moment—you did it!

To become One with Archeia Virtue and receive direct guidance from her, please enjoy the following. I recommend to first read "How to Prepare for Attunements" in Chapter 2, page 50.

Archeia Virtue Attunement

Feeling centred, sense yourself held in a column of swirling emerald-green and pink Light. Breathe in this blended Source Ray, and breathe it out. Allow it to fill every part of you, including your aura and wings, and then see it connect through you to the centre of Earth and the centre of the Sun. Feel your guardian angels standing on either side of you, radiating their Love, which further expands your Light. When you're ready to invite in Archeia Virtue, affirm aloud:

"Loving Archeia Virtue, angel of Healing, Truth, and Divine Love and master of the Green, Pink, and Emerald Rays, may you now attune me to your vibration and consciousness, so that I am forever linked with you. Please assist me in channelling your energy for the benefit of all concerned, and absolve me from all emotional hooks, triggers, and traumas that have been causing dis-ease in my reality. Help me see that while I can't change past events, I can empower myself by staying true

to who I am in the moment. Help me see that I can heal myself no matter the external diagnosis, while being a template of overflowing health and vibrancy for others. Allow me to embody my loving, compassionate heart, and to let Love guide me always. Thank you. And so it is."

Allow this Divine angel to blend her consciousness with yours, and ask Archeia Virtue what the highest and best guidance is for you at this time, and if there's anything you can support her with.

As you continue to attune to Archeia Virtue, you can also channel her healing Light. If there's a part of your body you'd like to heal, bring your hands to that area now, or rest one hand on your third eye and the other on your heart (areas that Virtue influences). Sense Virtue's emerald-green and pink Light filling these areas now.

As you receive healing, ask yourself: *"Would my life improve if I were easier on myself?"* If yes, then ask: *"Where do I need to soften?"* . . . *"What would it take for me to be more compassionate towards myself and others?"* . . . *"How can I improve my health and life now?"* . . . Let these questions melt into you, and listen as their answers arise. As they do, Virtue reminds you that positive change abounds when you deliberately choose thriving over surviving.

Breathe in Goodness . . . breathe out Goodness. Bask in all the breakthroughs that are taking place. When you feel the energy starting to wane, intend the attunement to be complete. Thank your guardian angels and Archeia Virtue before opening your eyes and drinking some water to ground yourself.

 *Rise Like an Angel*

◊ "Attuning to the softness of Archeia Virtue felt like . . . "

◊ "In order to be easier on myself, the action I need to apply is . . . "

◊ "I'll continue to invite in Archeia Virtue to assist me with . . . "

Daily Affirmation to Connect with Archeia Virtue

*"It is safe for me to open my heart to love and
be loved in return."*

Crystal Allies

Emerald, petalite, rhodochrosite

Plants Allies

Daffodil, hyssop, willow

Invite In Archeia Virtue for . . .

Spiritual awakening and development, opening the heart, healing, honesty, forgiveness, detoxification, comfort in dark/dense moments, and for instilling peace and understanding.

Chapter 4

ARCHEIA HOPE
"I AM ready to connect"

Making an Angelic Connection

In Angel Healing®, in order to become certified and receive support, practitioners are asked to enjoy and journal 34 meditative conversations and/or healing sessions with the angels of the system. They follow tried-and-tested steps that make angelic connection a breeze. Inspired by Archeia Hope, the angel of communication who bridges both trust and a strong belief in our guardian angels, we'll explore these steps, along with an evolved way of working with angels directly.

Inviting versus Invoking

Angel communication can often be overcomplicated, when it can be as simple as talking with a friend—for, of course, angels are our friends, and just like being with a loved one, respect is key.

If you're an existing angel therapist, or have read other angel works, you may have learned to "invoke", "call in", or "summon" an angel. Yet, we can't hold dominion over an angel, just as we wouldn't wish to dominate our friends. Archeia Hope helps us to better understand this way of spiritual etiquette that is becoming more important as the veil between the physical and non-physical world thins.

To connect with an angel, we only need to invite them to be with us. Before the thought of inviting them forward has fizzled away they will invariably be present, but the angel will appreciate the respect taken and the air of gentle kindness lent by "inviting" versus "invoking". Moreover, as the overall vibration of humanity has been raised, no formal prayers or ceremonies are needed to prepare yourself to speak with an angel; all that is required is an open, loving heart and a clear intention of what you'd like assistance with to enjoy easeful connections.

A True Angel Connection

After inviting in an angel, you may sense them and receive their Divine guidance in a variety of ways—perhaps through your vision, hearing, smelling, thoughts, feelings, or instinctual knowing. When you become friends with an angel without forcing or willing the relationship, a loving bond is able to grow.

If you ever doubt that you're speaking with an angel, ask Archeia Hope to confirm the connection, and look for the following signs:

A True Angelic Experience Feels:

◊   Loving and positive, instilling a sense of empowered expansion

◊   Safe, secure, and supported

◊   Like there is a change of air temperature or pressure

◊   Like a loved one is touching your head, hair, or shoulders

◊   Real and natural, with a sense of "coming home"

◊   Overall certain, as you receive repetitive and consistent gut feelings, thoughts, and signs to make a definite life change, or to take a certain step.

A False Angelic Experience Feels:

◊   Cold and negative, instilling depressive and contractive feelings

◊   Unpleasant, uncertain, and discouraging

◊   Like the experience is "not real" deep down

◊   Like you're forcing or willing the experience or guidance to happen

◊   Random and unrelated to your intentions. Messages feel deliberately confusing and ever-changing.

False angelic experiences happen when we overly control or judge the connection. By staying in this egoic, low vibe we can also align with non-physical entities or thought-forms posing as angels. Most angel texts don't talk about lower-level energies, or if they do, it's only to say that such things don't exist.

Source can be a rainbow but also a muddy puddle, too! As New Earth pioneers we're ready to burst the fear bubble and allow dualistic beliefs to evolve, for **everything in Creation stems from Creation, and therefore has a purpose**.

We'll unpack this subject more throughout the book, but for now, if you're ever worried about "false angels or guides", see yourself and the space you are in ablaze in Violet and Diamond fire. Intend that all that is less than Love is cleansed and connected with Source, then ground yourself by moving your body.

The Four Essential Steps

You may already talk with your angels every day and invite them in to support a co-creation in the moment. To take your communication to the next level, I recommend using the following Four Essential Steps. Together, this tried-and-tested methodology, crafted from over 15 years of partnering angels, is the cornerstone of all Angel Healing® treatments. The steps will not only raise and expand your vibration to meet the angel you'd like to chat with but also ensure you're fully in your body, aligned in your Divine Awareness, and open to clearly receive Divine guidance. The steps (otherwise known as: BCGC) consist of:

Step 1—Breathing

Breathing is our life force: It sustains us and is the bridge between the physical and non-physical planes. When we breathe deeply and fully, there's a natural settling down of the mind and body, and as relaxation takes place, the sensitivity of our subtle energy body heightens. Any limiting beliefs and concerns can easily exit on our exhale as we create the space to receive the connection.

And so, I invite you to begin your more in-depth angel conversations, healings, or readings by simply breathing. Let's practice now…

◊ Take a few deep, conscious breaths. Breathe from your navel as your stomach expands out and air comes in and up your body. Hold at the top of your inhale for a few moments while relaxing the muscles around your eyes and jaw. Breathe out any tension, and feel how your navel and stomach draw in towards your spine. Focus on the in-and-out rhythm of your breath, and contemplate how the *prana* (the life force of the breath) is revitalizing your physical body, and in turn, rouses your energetic body. Observe all, as your breath naturally heightens your Awareness and guides you into the moment.

Step 2—Centring

The act of centring means placing oneself in the middle of something else. In practice, this means to bring our focus to our heart, the mid-point of our being, and consciously link our heart with Source.

The more we regularly "heart-link" with Source, the easier it becomes to live in harmony with all of Creation. Limiting beliefs (existing more at a subconscious and unconscious level) readily resolve, making it easier to translate Divine guidance and integrate the wisdom into our world.

Many healers skip this step of centring into pure Awareness, and instead, invoke forms of "protection" prior to connecting with angels. Yet, affirming we need to protect ourselves against something else perpetuates fear, as in:

"If I am protecting myself, then from what? What is there to fear? Am I doing the right thing?" And so on.

As Archeia Hope guides, when we assert ourselves fully in our heart we're inherently "protected", for like attracts like in our ascending Universe. Denser entities do exist (as we shared earlier), but interacting with angels through the lens of our heart instead of the lens of mental duality ensures that we align with an experience that's unconditionally positive for our Truth and experience. Remember: The limits of our mind represent the limits of our reality; change the way we think, and we change (and open up to) new realities.

◊ Following on from step 1, if you'd like to centre yourself now, please take your focus to your heart. Imagine you're breathing in … and out … through your heart. If your mind wanders, welcome the thoughts without resistance. Observe them, then let them go as you return your attention to your heart. Intend that your heart be fully open … and the flow of *prana* is radiating out in all directions … and then returns from all directions back into your heart. Enjoy a sense of expansion as you feel yourself as the centre of all Creation.

Step 3—Grounding

Grounding (or, as it is sometimes called, earthing) is the holistic practice of connecting to the earth. It's the easiest and most transformative means to improve health, reduce stress, and bring one into electromagnetic resonance with the energy (and Love) of the planet.

While we can ground physically by walking barefoot on the earth, to best serve the purpose of meditation we can hold the intention of grounding energetically to the centre of Mother Earth, a practice that's equally beneficial.

By slowing down and enjoying this step, we assert

ourselves in our physical body and open to becoming a doorway, platform, and channel for the angelic frequencies to move through without opposing judgement or expectation.

Popular ways to ground in meditation are to imagine tree-like roots extending from the bottom of the spine, feet and/or from the earth star chakra into the centre of the earth. Here, I invite you to try an alternative way of grounding from your heart, a practice that Archeia Hope introduced in the later years of Angel Healing®.

As Hope guides:

Your heart is a portal to pure, loving Awareness. Centring your attention here and consciously expanding your heart's radiant frequency will free all ego interference through a complete separation of Awareness from the consciousness of self. After awakening to pure Awareness as your original state of being, you can emulate Source by expanding Awareness to the limits of time and space, of this and all dimensions. Upon achieving this, you are no longer individual, a being separate from Source or anything else.
Now you emulate Source in being a reflection of Awareness with everything inside of you.

◊   Continuing from steps 1and 2, to ground from your heart centre begin to imagine upon each inhale that you're breathing in the Gold Ray, the golden consciousness of Heaven. Breathe in Gold … breathe out Gold. Imagine your heart is filling with this golden Light just like water fills a vase.

◊   When your heart can't contain the Light anymore, golden threads begin to grow from the base of your heart. Sense them as they move down the central channel of your body, enlivening your chakras and flowing through your legs and out through the soles of your feet.

◊ As the golden threads connect with the physical earth, they expand around planet Earth, before moving intelligently to the crystalline heart of Mother Earth, where they unite with all the Love of the Divine Feminine.

◊ Open your Awareness to being here, and draw up earth energy into your heart upon each inhale.

◊ To bring in balance, let's also ground upwards, into the cosmic heart of our Universe, into the Great Central Sun.

◊ Sense golden threads begin to grow from the top of your heart. They move up the central channel of your body, enlivening your chakras and flowing out through your head and higher crown chakras.

◊ As the golden threads connect with the physical Sun, they expand around it, before moving intelligently to the vibrational heart of Father Cosmos, where they unite with all the Love of the Sacred Masculine.

◊ Open your Awareness to being here, then draw down solar energy into your heart upon each exhale … As the Golden Ray marries with your Awareness and the Love of the Divine Feminine and Masculine, you are unbecoming the consciousness of your individual self and all egoic interference. Moving seamlessly into the last step of connection, becoming a pure reflection of Source existing everywhere and nowhere, as everything and no-thing—Creation One with Creator.

Step 4—Connection

By this stage it's lovely to just be in silence and enjoy the feelings of Bliss at being the embodiment of pure loving Awareness. Through silence, we can connect to the finer vibrations of Source, and more readily recognize and translate Divine guidance as it flows in from our inner being, guardian angels, and Archeiai.

Moving into step 4, as your highest and most expansive Self, affirm:

I am pure loving Awareness as a reflection of Source.
I invite my guardian angels forward to hold the space of this
meditation/healing/reading high and invite in _____
[saying the name of the angel you wish to connect with]
to align with me for the intention of _____.
I affirm this connection to be unconditionally positive
for my Truth and experience.
Thank you. And so it is.

Although the BCGC steps may seem like a lot to remember, in practice, they become seamless and automatic and can level up any energetic experience, whether communing with angels, enhancing your breathwork practice, or enjoying better sex! They'll support you to stay present, at One with Source, and empty of egoic doubts, expectations, and judgements.

Deepening Your Angelic Connection

You may wish to incorporate the Four Essential Steps above with the following template to gain the most from your angelic connections. This guide can be easily adapted for hands-on, planetary, and remote healing, meditation, card readings, or channelled dance, yoga, art, and angelic writing, which we'll now explore.

Template Guide for Angelic Communication

◊ Relax in a quiet place where you won't be disturbed. Decide upon the Archeia (or Archangel) you'd like to connect with.

◊ Follow the Four Essential Steps, and as you sense the angel stepping forward, breathe in deeply their angelic resonance in order to merge with them fully.

◊ Enjoy being in their company, chat with them, pose a question, invite their healing energy to flow through you, or bring in another intention. Trust the first sense, answer, knowing, gut feeling, or creative action, insight, or guidance that emerges from the angel.

◊ Invite the angel to stay with you for a specific time frame, depending on your intention. Continue to dialogue with them, and observe (through your senses) their unique energetic signature so you can recognize them in future.

◊ When it's time to close the connection, reverse the Four Essential Steps; that is, disconnect from the angel by asking them to gently step out of your energetic field, ground yourself (and anyone else involved), centre your Awareness back in your heart, and breathe deeply as you thank the angel.

Angelic Channelled Writing

To bring this together in practice, with the help of Archeia Hope, let's explore one of the most profound ways to speak with our angels: angelic channelled writing. Often called "automatic writing", "spirit writing", and "psychography", this practice involves connecting with an angel and allowing them to write through you words you've not consciously written yourself. Despite sceptics saying this is nothing more than an unconscious muscular reflex, from witnessing the meaningful messages that pour through students directly from the angels over the last 15 years, I can wholeheartedly say this technique is real.

As you align your energy with that of an angel for the purpose of receiving written insights from them, you may witness long passages flowing through you onto the page, or perhaps see yourself draw pictures, symbols, or light-encoded geometry. If nothing emerges on your first try, that's okay; channelling angels is an artform in and of itself.

The key to this technique—and all forms of Spirit communication—is to step out of the mind, which tends to rationalize and judge what is and isn't flowing, and step fully into your heart so you can simply be the perfect Divine conduit you already are. **Remember, you are Spirit, too, and your Spirit is not in your body, your body is in your Spirit**. The more your perspective embraces this Truth, the smoother this technique will become.

Practise angelic writing (adapting the following process) with all the Archeiai of this book, and see how your confidence and connection grow! With practice, you can refine this skill to channel angelic energy through your voice and your body for the purpose of healing.

Writing with Hope

◊ Gather your journal and a pen, or if you'd like to use this technique to enjoy a channelled art session, gather your art supplies! Feel into a non-specific question—for example, *What guidance best serves me?*—so you're not overly attached to the answer. With practice, you can ask more intricate questions, but to begin with, keep your questions and intentions broad. Write at the top of your page, for example:

*Archeia Hope, thank you for sharing the best
guidance for me at this time, and for
effortlessly channelling through me.
Thank you, and so it is.*

◊   Now, put down your journal and pen. Close your eyes and enter a meditative state by following the Four Essential Steps switching the affirmation in step 4 to reciting aloud the following:

I am pure loving Awareness as a reflection of Source. I invite my guardian angels forward to hold the space of this channelling high and invite in Archeia Hope to channel through me the answer to my question and any other meaningful insights that flow in the moment. I affirm this connection to be unconditionally positive for my Truth and experience. Thank you. And so it is.

◊   Sense your guardian angels with you. As Archeia Hope steps into your Awareness, notice the way she appears and how it feels to be in her company. Invite Hope to step fully into your body now, so that your arm becomes her arm, your hand becomes her hand.

◊   Softly open your eyes (staying aligned with Archeia Hope), and pick up your pen, laying it on the page. Allow your hand and pen to move when you feel the impulse to do so. Observe what's taking place as if you're outside your body watching this experience. Try not to consciously read the words or interpret what's flowing through you until you feel the message is complete. If one word, symbol, or pattern appears, or a long passage, or nothing at all, just stay present and enjoy "being" Archeia Hope, as she blends her Light with yours.

◊   When you feel it's time to close the connection, reverse the Four Essential Steps by asking Archeia Hope to gently step out of your energetic field, ground and centre your Awareness back in your heart, and breathe deeply. Thank Hope and read the insights she shared.

Rise Like an Angel

◊ "Channelling Archeia Hope in this way felt like . . . "

◊ "Archeia Hope's insights for me at this time are . . . "

◊ "I'll continue to explore channelled writing by enjoying a session with . . . for the purpose . . . "

Archeia Hope Revealed

Archeia Hope, whose name is derived from the Old English word *hopian* meaning "positive expectation", serves on the White and Crystalline Rays of Harmony, Purity, and Communication with her counterpart, Archangel Gabriel. Hope also carries within her vibration the Pink and Pale Blue Rays, so you may see these colours when you connect with her and channel her Light. Other names for Archeia Hope include "Lady Hope" and "Annunciata".

Archeia Hope has a healing influence over our heart and supports the higher development of our navel and base chakras. Often, she talks to us through our ear chakras. If you notice ringing, light whispers, or sound vibrations in your ears (while reading this chapter and during her attunement), know that Hope is talking to you. She shares that you can turn up the sensations for greater clarity or ask for the transmission to be turned down when needed.

The angel of Hope epitomizes "innocence in flow". Equally, being the strength behind Gabriel, she helps us tap into our inner power. Hope walks on water to reflect that anything is possible; that we have the capability to make miracles our everyday experience. As Jesus once said, "Greater things I have done you will do." Archeia Hope's halo magnifies this impenetrable certainty, helping us believe in our gifts and expect only the best for ourselves, our world, and the legacy we're here to create.

Hope reminds you that your word is power. That Source gave you a voice, a gift to share with the world. Your voice can equally build worlds or tear them apart. By choosing your words and being intentional with how you speak, express, and act you can bring your version of Heaven to Earth.

For example, while writing this chapter, I found myself in the morning affirming aloud the type of day I was going to have, often saying: "Today, I'm going to be loving towards myself and loving in every choice I make."

This kept me aware in choosing the most loving breakfast for myself, the most loving activities for that day, and often pivoting to the most loving thought when I ventured off into empowering a limiting one. What a difference these days were compared to those when I slipped back into making unconscious, habitual choices.

Archeia Hope truly supports us to expect the best by consciously choosing the best for ourselves. Washing away anything that's been getting in the way so we can spiral upwards into hope, into thinking and feeling as Source, for hope isn't something to gain but a vibration to raise into. Meditating, being in or near water, and bringing white lilies (Hope's flower) into your space are great ways to raise your vibration into hopefulness and create a more loving, and conscious reality.

To embody the effortless flow of Archeia Hope and deepen your connection with her, please enjoy the following attunement. I recommend to first read "How to Prepare for Attunements" in Chapter 2, page 50.

Archeia Hope Attunement

Feeling centred, sense yourself held in a column of sparkling white crystalline Light. Breathe in this Source Ray, and breathe it out. Allow the Light to fill every part of you, including your aura and wings, and then sense it connect through you to the centre of the earth and the centre of the Sun. Feel your guardian angels standing on either side of you, radiating their Love, which further expands your field. When you're ready to invite in Archeia Hope, affirm aloud:

"Loving Archeia Hope, angel of Harmony, Purity, and Communication and master of the White and Crystalline Rays, may you now attune me to your vibration and consciousness, so that I am forever linked with you and may channel your energy. Please assist me in receiving Divine guidance easily. Help me understand that I am One with Source and, therefore, One with Source's wisdom and strength. Thank you for inspiring me to always expect the best outcome of every situation and to reach for a higher-feeling thought during change and challenge. With you by my side, apathy and procrastination dissolve, for you bring all to Light. Thank you for helping me to see all, face all and dissolve all that stands in my way. And so it is."

Breathe in Hope, and breathe out Hope, as you merge with this Divine angel. Then ask Archeia Hope what the highest and best guidance is for you at this time, and if there's anything you can support her with.

As you continue to attune to Archeia Hope, you can also channel her healing Light. If there's a part of you you'd like to empower, bring your hands to that area now, or rest your hands on your navel (the chakra that Hope influences the most). Sense pure white and crystalline Light moving into your navel and filling the rest of your being.

Breathe in feeling good . . . breathe out feeling good. Sense yourself within a bubble of optimism as strong as Hope's Divine halo. Bask in how good it feels to be alive in this moment—aware, connected, with Infinite possibilities and pathways open to you. Imagine the most hopeful version of you. Sense what you look and feel like. How do you live your life? How different is your vibrational state and mindset? Step into this hopeful you. Rejoice in knowing that all pathways of opportunity are open for you. And if obstacles seem to be in the way, know that hope will find a way through them. Breathe in . . . become this most confident You; breathe out . . . thanking Archeia Hope as the energy begins to wane. Intend the attunement to be complete and open your eyes and drink some water to ground yourself.

Rise Like an Angel

◊ "Attuning to the optimistic Light of Archeia Hope felt like ..."

◊ "By consciously stepping into my most expectant, hopeful Self on a daily basis, the miracles that'll flow into my life include . . . "

◊ "I'll continue to invite in Archeia Hope to co-create . . . "

Daily Affirmation to Connect with Archeia Hope
"I am a lover of life and its Infinite possibilities!"

Crystal Allies
Aquamarine, blue calcite, chrysocolla

Plant Allies
Calendula, trumpet vine, white lily

Invite In Archeia Hope for . . .
Calm and easeful angelic communication, development of the navel and base chakras, inner child healing and empowerment, letting the Light of Source in (aligning the self and Higher Self), optimism, and raising vibration, especially to receive inner/Divine guidance.

Chapter 5

ARCHEIA PURITY
"I AM ready to cleanse"

Maintaining a Consistent Connection

Knowing how to focus our intention and open to feeling good by incorporating the teachings of Archeiai Faith, Virtue, and Hope helps us raise our vibration, but how can we maintain a steady connection with our inner being when the world around us is in constant motion?

In every moment, our energetic field (comprised of our aura and radiant light body) interacts with both wanted and unwanted frequencies transmitted by others and the environment. When we have a handle on our vibration, we know what is our energy and what is being projected from others, therefore knowing if there's anything in our field that's not serving us. If we haven't learned how to hone this innate sensitivity, or if our field has been weakened through neglecting ourselves, it's easy to draw unwanted influences into our life, which can lead to us snowballing in directions we'd otherwise not go.

How can we be an empath in the world without feeling the whole world in the process? Or as one nonconformist student asked me once, *"How can I be a badass empath in a world full of f*ckers?!"* I know—it made me laugh, too!

Let's be real. As shiny souls, it certainly feels like our Light attracts those who would otherwise like to see it diminished. We'll uncover this and so much more, as we explore the fiery clarity of Archeia Purity!

What Is an Empath?

While researching this subject, I was interested to learn that the word "empath" was coined by fellow Scots author James Murdoch MacGregor in 1956. James modelled the word empathy from telepathy, defining it as the ability to identify with the attitudes, feelings, thoughts, and overall energy of others.

Do you believe that you are an empath or have empathic qualities, as many awakened souls feel they do? If you're unsure, please read through the following exercise, Ten Signs You're an Empath. If you resonate with three or more of these signs, the likelihood is that you have this gift of heightened sensitivity and intuition.

For some, however, such a "gift" can feel more like an affliction. I've seen many talented souls shy away from fully expressing who they are in favour of living a hermetic lifestyle, because they haven't learned how to manage their empathy. Sadly, this often leads to them shutting down other spiritual skills and living with dis-eases, which they've often imprinted from others.

Ten Signs You're an Empath

Please take a moment to read through these tell-tale indicators of being an empath, feeling for the "truth-bumps" as an extra confirmation.

1   You pick up on the feelings and thoughts of others, and do so without them telling you how they're feeling or what they're thinking. If you're not grounded in these moments, you can absorb these energies and assume they are yours.

2   You're a human lie detector! Bull-sh**ters beware, as you can pick up on the teeniest social cues to read a person's true intentions and motives, even if they're trying to hide them from you.

3   You sense the vibe of the room, as you can interpret the emotional feel of a space and translate it through your body and field. This, in turn, means you like your home to be calm and organized versus loud and messy.

4   You mimic emotional reactions, and do so automatically if you're not fully centred. For example, if someone cries, you easily well up, too! Among a group of people, you can also feel overwhelmed by sudden emotional charges.

5   People love to be around you, as you understand where they're coming from, especially if they can't express themselves physically or emotionally. Babies, small children, and animals will gravitate towards you because your extra-sensory perception means that you can understand their non-verbal cues.

6   Spirit communication is easy for you, because you're a translator of non-physical energy. You often speak with your angels, crystals, "graduated" loved ones, and ethereal guides.

7   You're drawn to helping others thrive, as well as the planet, as connection and heartfelt relationships are very important to you.

8   You feel drained often, because you haven't learned how to master your empathy. This happens from absorbing the energies of others and taking on their problems when they come to you for help and advice.

9   Intimate relationships can be challenging, as even the slightest irritations can feel huge if you're not feeling good and centred in your Light. If your partner doesn't honour your need for personal space or has narcissistic tendencies—empaths are like catnip for narcissists, and vice versa—then relationships can easily break down.

10   You're a healer or caregiver, as you can pick up on areas of discomfort and dis-ease in others. If you've learned how to hone your instinctual empathy, you'll see this as a gift and work with it. If not, this can feel more like a burden, as you can often be imprinted by their symptoms and experience them as if they were your own.

I believe that most spiritually aware souls are empaths, for we relate to one another in a way that Sleeping Beauties do not. Not only can we pick up on one another's body language but we can pick up on vibrations, too. The key to honing our sensitivity is to get a grip on our vibration, so we can interpret if the thoughts and emotions we're experiencing are coming from our inner being or if we're relaying them from an outside source.

Archeia Purity guides that we can never "pick up" anything that isn't already active within us, because we live in an attractive- and creative-based Universe. This means that **nothing can insert itself into our Awareness unless we're a match to it vibrationally**, or we've consciously/subconsciously brought it into our reality because it's the basis of a growth lesson we need to experience.

I understand how challenging to rationalize this may feel, especially in a moment of feeling drained by another person or weighted down by "stuff" that doesn't appear to be our own! If we can take time to breathe and pause at these inception points and accept that what we've picked up is also within us, the underlying wisdom of what's presenting will be revealed. As we acknowledge what we need to know about ourselves, the other person, and/or the environment, we can easily pivot and turn our vibration towards feeling better. This process helps us to have a consistently pure vibe, no matter the outside circumstances. It just takes practice and discernment to master.

Applying Discernment

Discernment always determines our state of vibration, for even as we choose, our choice mirrors our reality back to us. This means that if we're continuing to let people and circumstances into our life that we know don't serve us, especially after discerning their "stuff" from ours, we'll continue to experience disharmony. As empaths, we need to feel okay about choosing who and what we let into our energy field. This includes everything from the foods we eat to what we watch and listen to, to the conversations we join, and how we decide to interact with the world at large.

As Archeia Purity shares:

As an empath, be aware of the opinions, judgements, and density of others as they come into your field. Stay vigilant, and empower only what feels true to you. If anything feels like it's weighing you down, strengthen your boundaries so that you are letting in only what inspires and delights you. Having boundaries does not mean you have to separate yourself from the world. Having boundaries is honouring who you are, and the means of recognizing and nurturing the integrity of your energy to ensure your cup is always full. As an empath, your heart is wide open—you have so much to give! Only give when you are full enough to give the best of yourself, and only give to those who have asked for your support. Not everyone needs or wants help, despite you thinking or feeling they do. Remember, enabling another always disables their own growth. You can positively influence them by caring enough for your own alignment first. Whether they choose to follow suit is their choice. The key is to honour yourself, so that you can be empathic without feeling empty, drained, and weighted down by discordant attachments. This empowered path awaits you, Dear One, if you are ready to choose it.

Being Aware of Your Choices

While writing this chapter, I had to pause and take some time out for myself. My dad transitioned into Spirit, the kids were pinballing one illness after the other to each other, my then toxic relationship with my fiancé was coming to an end, and I was experiencing daily migraines from the lack of sleep and good nutrition. Long story short: I was in a real funk! The more I affirmed how drained I was, the more life mirrored this back to me. Feeling swamped by it all, and too tired to meditate, I asked Archeia Purity to enter my dreams and give me some practical advice.

Upon waking, I had a strong urge to compile two lists: one titled Energy Drainers and the other Energy Raisers. Under Energy Drainers, Archeia Purity said to write everything I felt was wearing me down and making me feel less than my Divine Self. Like Archeia Virtue, Purity asks us to be real with our feelings, so we can use them to pull us out of funks rather than drowning in them.

And so, I wrote down everything that was depleting me, from loops of negative thinking to feelings of hype and drama picked up from others that I hadn't reconciled within myself, to destructive behaviours like emotional binge-eating, which felt soothing in the moment but left a hangover of pain and shame.

For the second list, I wrote down all that lifts and fuels my energy, and in doing so, realized why Archeia Purity inspired this exercise!

Angels, like our inner being, never judge the way we think or behave, yet they are always on hand to shake us out of limiting states.

Firstly, this exercise shook me out of stagnancy, which I'd been blaming external circumstances for inciting, and secondly, it brought me home to my Awareness, so I could take my power back. As I remembered that the content and design of my reality is my own creation, I felt empowered to choose my thoughts and behaviours more deliberately.

Reading the Energy Raisers, it was apparent how far I'd ventured from putting my needs first. The things that renew my cup, such as yoga in the morning, prioritizing a daily walk in nature, and asking for childcare help, were all within my reach; I'd just neglected to choose them. As a result, my energy field felt weak. I was picking up on everybody else's stuff, and their misalignment was mirroring my own. This exercise, which Archeia Purity invites you to do now, isn't an opportunity for self-judgement or punishment; it's the means to set you free!

No one can adjust our vibration or see through our perspectives. Sure, we can be influenced when others hold a loving space for us, as we explored in Chapter 3, but ultimately, we lead our own life and vibration. When we dwell in what we perceive as the "drainer" column of life, that becomes our experience, because we punish ourselves the most during these times of limitation. While Virtue helps us be real with our feelings, Purity goes a step further, to help us face what we define as our inner demons, so we can begin to cleanse them.

When I asked Purity to help me with what I was moving through personally, her Light filled me with such buoyancy! I felt more tuned in, tapped in, and turned on to my inner being than ever before. I was more alert with what was and what wasn't serving me vibrationally, and bolstered by her warrior-like presence, it was easier to make informed choices that helped me stay empowered.

After this exercise, there followed another insightful dream. This time, Purity guided me to look at my home and intuitively feel into any areas of blocked energy. Upon waking, I was inspired to unblock my shower, which I'd been putting off doing. As I cleared it, the migraine I'd been experiencing for days left me! Encouraged by Purity, I walked around my house, asking her to show me where the energy was stagnant. She guided me to fix other things I'd been putting off, and to clean my windows inside and out to let light in.

"Everything in your outer environment reflects your inner one," she said, as she nudged me to clear my cupboards of things we both knew that I'd never use!

Energy Raisers and Energy Drainers

Please look at Archeia Purity's picture. Gaze into her eyes as you connect your heart with hers. Imagine that you're wearing her holy amethyst necklace, which provides a portal into her cleansing and purifying power. Begin to breathe in her Violet fire . . . then breathe it out into your space. Repeat this sacred breath twice more. As the vibration within and around you begins to lift, invite Archeia Purity to be with you, affirming aloud:

Loving Archeia Purity, please reveal to me what I need to know and apply in my energy field, choices, actions, relationships, and home space to better enjoy a consistently pure, high, and expansive vibration. Thank you. And so it is.

◊ Feeling Purity with you, pick up your journal and create two columns: Energy Drainers and Energy Raisers. In column 1, write down everything that's currently weighing on you, including the habitual behaviours, cycles, and addictions you're ready to rebirth. In column 2, write down everything that lifts your spirit, including any new routines, affirmations, and activities you're going to bring into your life. Don't think too much about this; just let the words flow as you did when writing with Archeia Hope. Be honest—no one needs to read this but you—while staying curious so that Purity can reveal more to you in the moment. **It is time to start living the life you've always imagined for yourself**.

◊ For the next seven days, before you get out of bed, affirm aloud:

> *Thank you for this new day, a new way to be,*
> *a new way to see! I am awake, I am here—at One*
> *with Source and crystal clear.*

◊ Consciously choose three things from your Energy Raisers column to bring into your day, and later, check in with how you're feeling before you go to bed. Keep incorporating what fuels you into each day, and you'll find the draining activities will naturally begin to fall away.

◊ Within the seven-day period, fix what you've been putting off in and around your home, or begin to make in-roads towards their repair. Unblock any drains or pipes, clean your windows inside and out, clear any clutter (especially around windows and doorways), give away or sell unwanted items, and bring flowers, crystals, and other beautiful things into your space. (And to add extra sparkling goodness into your space, incorporate the angelic feng-shui principles explored in the next chapter with Archeia Victory.)

Rise Like an Angel

◊ "This exercise helped me become aware of . . . "

◊ "After seven days of prioritizing a bright, clean vibe, I feel . . . "

◊ "I'm going to continue to uplift my home and workspace by . . . "

As soon as you invite Archeia Purity into your life, she'll bring up the vibe to where it's needed. She may inspire you to sift through areas of stagnancy in your beliefs, actions, or behaviours, so you can begin to free yourself from limitation and alight from the influences that have been hypnotizing you to think and act in a certain way. Purity may ask you to reflect upon, *Am I living life on my terms? If not, what would it take for me to do so?* She reminds us that we're all born with the same potential, but it's our choice whether we choose to stay in limitation and feel the discord or decide to break free and feel better. Like everything in life, practice makes perfect. But with Archeia Purity by our side, we cannot fail!

Archeia Purity Revealed

Archeia Purity, whose name is derived from the Old French word *purete*, meaning "truth", serves on the Violet Ray of Transformation and Surrender with her counterpart, Archangel Zadkiel. Other names for Archeia Purity include "Lady Purity", "Holy Amethyst", and "Amethystia". Archeia Purity has a healing influence over our Sacral, Crown, and Soul Star chakras, as well as our Auric Field.

In her depiction, Purity wears a holy amethyst crystal that connects her with Zadkiel, and a cosmic diamond that connects her with Source. She is the keeper of mysteries and queen of the spiritual rays; her energy is fiery and enigmatic. Although Purity serves on the Violet Ray, she is also connected with the Silver, Gold, Magenta, and Diamond Rays, as reflected in her image. As with all the Source Rays, within each one exist sacred flames. Within the Violet Ray exists the "Violet Flame of Transmutation", which purifies and raises consciousness every time it's brought in. In her portrayal, Purity holds the Violet Flame in one hand and releases feathers of freedom in the other, to reflect her innate powers of Divine alchemy, a power she can help us master.

In recent years, the Violet Flame has revealed more of itself by radiating the colours of Purity's other aspects (Silver, Gold, Magenta and Diamond) within its fire. The Silver aspect connects us with the Divine Feminine and the heart of Mother Earth. The Gold aspect connects us with the Sacred Masculine and the heart of the central Sun. The Magenta aspect connects us with our soul and our soul's highest calling, so that we may express and expand upon it in our lifetime. And the Diamond aspect connects us directly with Source, so that we may embody our Divinity all ways and in every way. Due to the dynamic nature of Archeia Purity, don't be surprised if you never see her in a physical-seeming form. Know, however, that she's by your side when you seek assistance to transmute anything that is less than Love.

Archeia Purity helps us face our feelings instead of fleeing or denying them. Amid density, she guides us to ask, "What is the positive learning and understanding to this feeling/situation?"

Once we realize the silver lining, we can pivot in our perspective and make the appropriate changes by being conscious in our choices. If we don't do this, the same limiting patterns and dis-ease will return, but with different faces and places.

Likewise, our angelic sister reminds us to take time to tune in to ourselves daily so were not only tapping into the frequencies of others. She guides us to take everyone we're connected with through the day out of our energy field before sleep using the Mirror Technique (described on page 281) and prioritize keeping our Light bright with the Violet Flame Cleanse that follows.

This form of spiritual hygiene will keep your aura shiny and help you see through the eyes of Source. The cleanse draws from the alchemical fires of the Violet Flame and is best enjoyed monthly, or when you feel heavy within yourself. You'll know when you've picked up something from another person, place, event, or object, such as an antique, as negative thoughts or unkind prompts will come into your mind. Cleanse them away with the help of Purity's Violet Flame.

To best prepare, have a think about what's been coming up in your reality lately. Have certain loops of negative self-talk been replaying in your mind? Have there been dramas in your home or workspace? Does your overall health or financial wellbeing feel in need of a boost? This meditative cleanse can renew these areas while assisting you to create unsullied boundaries and a crystal-clear empathy . . .

Violet Flame Cleanse

◊ Come into a meditative state with your spine straight so your energy can move freely. Close your eyes, and sense your entire spinal column. By focusing here, any imbalances within your mental and energetic body will begin to harmonize. Breathe in for a count of five . . . hold for five . . . and exhale for five. Repeat this breathing pattern twice more and relax deeper.

◊ Invite in your guardian angels and Archeia Purity to be with you and facilitate the highest and purest healing for you. Ask them to kindly reveal if there are any entities, earthbound spirits, psychic imprints, or lower-level energies in your energy field. You may get the sense if there are any "hitchhiker" frequencies in your aura, too.

◊ Now say aloud with conviction:

I ask that the Violet Flame is made manifest within my body now.

◊ Breathe in, as your being fills with Violet Fire . . . then breathe out Violet Fire into your space. Sense yourself become ablaze, feeling the flames lighting up your entire spinal column, body, and auric field. Affirm aloud:

I give permission for all energy that's not unconditionally positive for my Truth and experience to return to Source now. Thank you. And so it is.

◊ Breathe deeply as this release takes place.

◊ As the Violet Flame purifies all density within and around you, transforming it into *prana* (life force energy) you can use, the fires of Magenta, Silver, Gold, and Diamond begin to fill you. Sense them infusing your physical, emotional, mental, and spiritual bodies, cleansing all that has been making you feel less than worthy, and any subconscious limitations or behaviours you're ready to resolve.

◊ Know that everything that's purifying is having a healing effect on your ancestry, influencing 10 generations backward and forward in your timeline. The Violet Flame is dissolving the ancestral wounds, habits, and behaviours that have been holding you back in your life. Breathe deeply as this healing takes place . . . Now, sense the people in your current life who aren't serving your joy being lifted out of your field, as the Violet Flame cleanses these and all your relationships. All your earthly relationships are now revitalizing, including the one you share with money. Breathe deeply, sensing everything reconnecting to Source.

◊ Archeia Purity now directs the Violet Flame to purify your cosmic ancestry. Here, the Light flows beyond the concept of karma, as it cleanses any beliefs of cosmic debt or density you may have been holding onto. Any heaviness, negative E.T. influences, false spirit guides, and/or 3D control agendas within your field now purify on all levels of being, time, space, and dimensions. Breathe deeply, sensing everything reconnecting to Source.

◊ Imagine yourself looking at your home now. Ask the elemental spirits of the land if you have permission to bring the Violet Flame into the earth and into the space of your home. If you sense a "yes" as their reply, sense the Violet Flame washing the land under and around your home. Sense the foundations, walls, rooms, and everything these spaces have absorbed being cleansed on all levels of being, time, space, and dimensions. Intend the furniture, plants, crystals, animals, and other people (under the Law of Grace) associated with this space being energetically washed, too, as all reconnects to Source.

◊ Do one last sweep of the Violet Fire through you, as old versions of you that no longer resonate with the path you're on and the life you've imagined burn away. Let them go into the fire now . . . As they are dissolved, breathe into a new YOU . . . bright, shiny, beautiful You. All that was blocking you from fully expressing your human, soul, and Spirit calling in this lifetime has been liberated into the sacred fire.

◊ Feeling different, vaster, welcome in all the life-renewing *prana* in exchange. Experience the Joy that rushes in after transforming the old. Ask for this Joy to be amplified 10 times, then 100 times, then 1,000 times! See yourself as Archeia Purity, as you breathe in Truth . . . and breathe out Truth . . . Affirm how healthy and strong your boundaries are, as everything and everyone in your life is connected to their wellbeing and no longer needs to take anything from you. Rejoice in how safe, supported, respected, and valued you all are.

◊ Feel the space you've created within yourself and the positive ripples of Joy you've brought to the world. Give thanks to all concerned, and feel the LoveLight sparkling in your eyes as you open them now. Have some water to ground yourself and keep well hydrated for the next 24 hours to assist the detox process.

Rise Like an Angel

◊ "This meditation was deeply healing for me because . . . "

◊ "I'll continue to invite in the Violet Flame for . . . "

To deepen your connection with Archeia Purity, please enjoy attuning to her. I recommend to first read "How to Prepare for Attunements" in Chapter 2, page 50.

Archeia Purity Attunement

Feeling centred, sense yourself held in a column of bright Violet Light. Breathe this Source Ray in and out. Allow it to fill every part of you, including your aura and wings, and then see it connect through you to the centre of Earth and the centre of the Sun. Feel your guardian angels standing on either side of you, radiating their Love, which further expands your Light. When you're ready to invite in Archeia Purity, affirm aloud:

"Loving Archeia Purity, angel of Transformation and Surrender, and master of the Violet Ray, may you now attune me to your vibration and consciousness, so we are forever One, and allow me to channel your Light for the greatest good of all concerned. Help me to continue to create strong, energetic boundaries that serve me to live my fullest integrity in this lifetime. Gift me your talent of transparency, so I may see the underlying Truth in all, while liberating unwanted attachments, psychic binds, and entanglements that I may not be aware of, so renewed vitality can flow into my life. Thank you. And so it is."

Breathe in Purity . . . and breathe out Purity, as you merge with this Divine angel. Begin to fan your wings to release anything from them, and from your mind, body, or energy field that you're ready to let go of. Affirm three times:

"I am clear. I am free. I am Divinely me!"

Ask Archeia Purity what the highest and best guidance is for you at this time, and if there's anything you can support her with.

As you continue to attune to Archeia Purity, you can also channel her Light. If there's a part of your body you'd like to empower, bring your hands to that area now, or place one hand on your crown chakra and the other on your sacral chakra (the chakras that Purity influences the most). Sense Purity's bright Violet Light moving into these areas and filling your aura. The Magenta, Silver, Gold, and Diamond Rays also envelop you, as they bring their gifts of healing. Breathe them in . . . then breathe them out, seeing Earth bathed in them, too. Envision those willing to receive these rays as thriving in truthful ease and grace.

When you feel the energy beginning to wane, intend the attunement to be complete. Thank your guardian angels and Archeia Purity before opening your eyes and drinking some water to ground yourself.

 *Rise Like an Angel*

◊ "Attuning to the fiery Light of Archeia Purity felt like . . . "

◊ "Archeia Purity's guidance for me at this time is . . . "

◊ "Having better boundaries, practising discernment, and making deliberate decisions helps me keep my energy shiny and . . . "

◊ "I'll continue to invite in Archeia Purity to co-create . . . "

Daily Affirmation to Connect with Archeia Purity

"Keeping my energy bright and buoyant empowers me to create and live my best life."

Crystal Allies

Auralite 23, sugilite, violet flame opal

Plant Allies

Lavender, St. John's wort, yarrow

Invite In Archeia Purity for . . .

Strengthening boundaries, the auric field, and soul star chakra; revealing underlying Truth; mastering empathy; justice and legal issues; energy transmutation; and cleansing all forms of hype, drama, and density.

Chapter 6

ARCHEIA VICTORY
"I AM ready to align"

Raising the Vibration of All

Archeia Purity and the Violet Ray are the best allies for leaning into personal detoxification; however, when space cleansing is the intention, as well as aligning every aspect of your multi-dimensional Self, including making your home sacred, Archeia Victory and the Diamond Ray are best to welcome in . . .

Archeia Victory Revealed

Archeia Victory, whose name is derived from the Latin word *vincere*, meaning "to overcome", serves on the Diamond Ray of Universal Ascension, Magic, and Wisdom with her counterpart, Archangel Raziel. While Raziel is the magical professor of Heaven, inviting us through his charming obscurity to stay curious about life, Victory is the underlying wisdom of Raziel, forever nudging us with ways to further our spiritual understanding by staying open and aligned to Source.

Archeia Victory has a healing (and activating influence) over the third eye, crown, and stellar gateway chakras. Other names for Victory include "Lady Victory" and "Jochara".

The Diamond Ray, which Victory expresses, along with the unicorns and their celestial cousins, the Pegasians, is the highest and most expansive vibration we can attune to and partner with at this time. Until 2015, when the Pegasians, especially, began to anchor the Diamond Ray codes into the vibrational grid systems of Earth, the highest Light humanity could consciously access was the Gold Ray, aka, the

Christ Ray. Equally purposeful, the Christ Ray helps us remember our spiritual nature, while the Diamond frequencies help us exemplify our spirituality; to be the Christ we came here to be.

Archeia Victory assures you that because you're reading this, you have once been a Wisdom Keeper, Sage, Priest, Priestess, and/or Presti. The Diamond Ray can activate the remembrance of these realities and the skills and talents you once had and bring them back online in your current lifetime, thus weaving together the wholeness of your multi-dimensionality with seamless grace. The process couldn't be simpler, for **the awareness of the Diamond Ray is the attunement to it**.

Since 2012, during many of the Angel Healing® courses, Archeia Victory has been preparing students to access the awareness of the ray by activating their "Diamond Heart", whereby she places an etheric diamond into their heart centre, which acts as both a reflection and receiver of the ray. She would like to activate this gift for you if you feel your Diamond Heart has yet to awaken.

In Victory's words:

Dear One, know yourself to be a diamond. And like a diamond, which thrives underground at high pressures and temperatures, when you feel the compression and discomfort of being misaligned in Joy, in coherence, presence, and resonance with Source, open your wings, open your heart. Glow. Grow. Shine. E x p a n d. Breathe into your heart Diamond Fire, and use this might for all forms of alchemy, alignment, and purification. Let life buffet you, for contrast only polishes you more, revealing the brilliance, clarity, and resilience that has always been there.

Receiving Your Diamond Heart

◊ Sit in a place where you won't be disturbed. Ask your guardian angels to be present, and for them to hold the space of this ceremony high. Relax your breathing, and look to Archeia Victory's picture. Gaze into her eyes, and feel your Light blend with hers.

◊ Close your eyes, and sense how Victory places a huge radiant diamond above your head, representing the heart of Source. As it begins to gently spin above you, cascades of pristine Diamond, Rainbow, and Gold Light shower down upon you. Breathe in these heavenly rays . . . then breathe them out into your space. Repeat this sacred breath twice more.

◊ Watch how the diamond shrinks, and as it condenses it moves into your body through the crown of your head. Breathe down the diamond until it rests in your heart. As it starts to spin gently, sense Light reflecting from every facet as your body begins to glow. With Archeia Victory assisting, an awakening is taking place right down at cellular level and the creative void in between your molecules.

◊ The wisdom codes within the memories of you as Angel, as Wisdom Keeper, Sage, Priest, Priestess, and Presti, are being uploaded into your Awareness as your Diamond Heart is (re)born.

Archeia Victory now shares:

*Focus your loving attention and intention
on what lights you up, for you are here to blaze new
trails and co-create the ascent of New Earth.
All you create and empower in this life is
the legacy you'll leave.
Make it great. Make it meaningful.
Empower all through the fire that burns within you.
You are a Diamond.
Stand tall and brilliant.
Radiate all-ways, and in every way.*

◊ Breathe in Victory's message, and become the embodiment of this Truth. Your Heart Diamond starts to dissolve as it melts into, and reinforces, every physical and non-physical aspect of you with the virtue of Triumph. Breathe in Triumph . . . breathe out Triumph. Close this energetic space by asking Archeia Victory to step out of your field, thanking all concerned.

Rise Like an Angel

◊ "Receiving my Diamond Heart felt . . . "

◊ "I am going to fuel the following areas and projects . . . with the energy of Triumph and the Diamond Ray."

Over the days, weeks, and months following this attunement, notice when you see the symbology of diamonds in your dreams and during the waking day. You may feel drawn to meditate within an etheric diamond, invest in a physical diamond to hold, wear, or make diamond-crystal water, or receive the inspiration to paint or place a picture of a diamond in your space. (Since 2012, one has graced my desk and another on my vision board, infusing every book and manifestation with the Diamond Ray. Oh my, such powerful alchemy!)

The more you're aware of the Diamond Ray and use it creatively, the deeper you'll attune to its medicine, thereby refining not only your spiritual gifts from past, parallel, and future timelines and bringing them into your now reality but recognizing *yourself* as a spiritual gift, too! For you have a great purpose to share with the world. If you feel you don't know what that purpose is, or if you feel you've lost your spiritual mojo, keep working with the Diamond codes and invite in Archeia Victory to reveal to you the understanding that's always been there.

Raising Your Energy Benefits All

Archeia Victory guides that when we focus on raising our vibration, the doorway to our consciousness opens. Walking through, two pathways appear. The first propels us forward to fulfil our karma (the earthly lessons we chose before incarnating). The second helps us spiral upward, allowing our consciousness to ascend into pure Awareness. Daily meditation is the key to escort us on these pathways, especially when combined with effective hand mudras.

In her depiction, Archeia Victory asked for her hands to be shown in Prana Shanti mudra, a symbolic hand gesture that boosts the flow of vitality (*prana*) and peace (*shanti*). By meditating with our hands in this position it becomes easy to centre into calm, activate the higher crown chakras, and remember that we're forever aligned with Source, even if our thoughts and feelings are contrary. This wellbeing practice is also an act of service, giving back peace to the world. Similar to how the Universal Code of Communication works, as we feel peace, we naturally send out peace and receive its glory back.

Aligning into Source

◊ Sit in a meditative pose, and begin to slow down your breathing . . . Close your eyes, and take your attention to your heart. Imagine that upon every inhale your heart is opening, rekindling your inner Diamond Fire . . . upon every exhale, the fire grows strong and bright. Keep breathing in this way until you feel your heart is fully open and lit. As your energy raises within and around, invite Archeia Victory to be with you, affirming aloud:

"Loving Archeia Victory, thank you for bringing me into alignment with Source and all that I am. And so it is."

◊ Breathe deeply to merge with Victory. Feel the *prana*, the animism of your breath, naturally cleansing and relaxing you. Stay here, and enjoy a few minutes of angelic breath awareness.

◊ Now bring the little and ring fingers of both hands together, and connect them with the tip of your thumb. Gently stretch out your middle and index fingers, resting your hands on your lap. Breathe deeply, sensing the flow of *prana* moving up and down your chakras.

◊ Inhale slowly as you bring your hands (staying in the mudra) up your body, opening your arms wide at the top of your inhale. Hold your breath for a count of five . . . and intend to open your Awareness behind your eyes. As you exhale slowly, move your hands down the front of your body towards your lap again . . . Repeat this movement for the next few minutes. At every breath hold, experience your Awareness opening your inner vision, hearing, knowing, and sensing.

◊ Inhale and bring your hands up one last time, and when your arms are open wide, focus your Awareness on the top of your head. Hold your breath, and visualize pure Diamond Light moving through your crown and up your higher chakra column. As you exhale, slowly open your hands to release the mudra, and sense the Diamond Light showering down around you as you bring your hands to your lap.

◊ Sit for a moment, and imagine you're beaming out peace . . . Experience how good this feels to give and receive back, wholly aligned into Source as Source. Give thanks to Archeia Victory, and drink some water to ground yourself.

◊ "Before this wellbeing practice, I felt . . . "

◊ "After this wellbeing practice, I feel . . . "

◊ "I'll add this to my toolbox and explore other meditative mudras and their effects, such as a mudra for . . . "

Angelic Feng Shui

Wherever we meditate and enjoy practices like the last one, we raise the vibration of the surrounding space.

As Archeia Victory shares: **"You are not the product of your environment; your environment is a product of You."**

It has taken me 15 years of working with Archeia Victory and 33 house moves later to really get this, and with it, unlearn much of my training in feng shui, which, while still being purposeful, is ripe for evolution. I could fill a book on this subject, but with Victory's help, we've concentrated the process to five steps to making your home sacred. But first, what is feng shui?

Derived from the Chinese words *fēng* meaning "wind", and *shui* meaning "water", this 6,000-year-old astrological artform and philosophical concept defines the harmonization of a space to harness and bring uplifting energy on those occupying the space.

While charting your home's astrology using a *bagua* (a feng shui energy map) and knowing a room's commanding position help navigate the flow of energy, what about consciously changing the quality of that energy? Similarly, New Age traditions tend to favour "smudging" with sage as a means of cleansing a space, but cleansing without any underlying alchemy beforehand is like spraying air freshener in a dirty room and expecting the room to be clean afterwards. The room will smell nice but it's still (energetically) dirty!

What if our belief in classical feng shui, which states only a third of the flow of energy in our home is within our conscious control, could evolve beyond that, stepping outside the notion that the other two-thirds are influenced by astrology and the physical environment? What if it's possible to create abundant bright energy in our home, independent of external factors?

This is where "angelic feng shui" excels. As a holistic system, it combines tried-and-tested ways to successfully clean, release, smooth, bless, seal, and magnetize spaces, and does so without opening portals (another New Age favourite), which often aggravates the Spirits already occupying the space.

Learn how to honour and communicate with your home as a sentient being, including getting to know your home's elemental being; every house has one or many—the nature spirits and land devas that are linked to the space. Learn also how to re-route the Spirit groups that may walk through, above, or below your home. In this way, you'll avoid what's known as "spiritual trespassing" and live in greater alignment with the flow, quality, and harmony of your space.

Making Your Home Sacred

To date, space cleansing and placement practices have focused on how the environment shapes and influences us. Historically this has served us, but now we're living in the era of Awareness. Each moment the collective Light of humanity is raising (ever expedited by the presence of the Archeiai), reshaping once-rigid rules and practices to become more conscious and empowering.

As we flip the perspective and understand that our vibe influences that of our home, we can start to be more intentional about how we'd like the space to look and feel. This process begins within, through purifying our inner temple to ensure we're feeling our highest vibration when performing angelic feng shui.

Archeia Purity helped us see where we're weighing down our energy and offered ways to detox using her violet fire. Now, we can go a step further using Diamond Alchemy (amongst other means) to raise and expand our vibration and allow our Light to ripple out and positively shape our space.

For a moment, close your eyes and imagine that you're standing at the edge of your property, looking at your home and its surrounding land, garden, or yard. See the garage, if there is one, and sense the atmosphere above your space; imagine the foundations of your home, too. Sense how your home feels now and then shift your perspective to how you'd like it to appear and the quality of its energy.

Imagine bowing to your home with respect, then asking the benevolent nature spirits and your home's elemental guide to assist you in cleansing, raising, and blessing your frequency, and as a reflection of you, that of your home. Sense the Spirits join you as you journey around the harmonious land surrounding your home, then up your ideal driveway, path, or staircase, and through the main entrance of your home.

Move around each room in a clockwise direction, feeling that every room has a specific intention and is vibrating the way you wish. The space feels fresh and pure. There's no underlying psychic interference and emotional imprints getting in the way of the flow, quality, and magnetism of the energy. Even if you live with others who have different views and beliefs from yours, there's house harmony. The lines of communication are easy, open, and respectful. You feel a palpable sense of Love, which others feel when they visit your home, your temple. No conflicts, no clutter—just a smooth flow and a consistently high vibration that magnetizes all that you're ready to receive, grow, and give.

Vibrationally, you've just created your temple. It's done! Now to bring it in physically. . .

The following five steps will help you and can be easily adapted, whether you live in an apartment, boat, caravan, or tent. They can be modified to make your office or work space a temple, too.

I recommend going through these five steps every season, especially if you live with Sleeping Beauties, young children, anyone going through puberty or menopause, and if you have lots of people coming in and out of your property on a regular basis or when moving home. If you notice drains blocking in your space, damp and mould patches forming, certain areas feeling thick, gloopy, and cluttered, and if there's an increase in the number of flies in your space, especially if they gather on windows and doors, incorporate all five steps.

For maintenance, pick one step (or more) that's appropriate in the moment. You'll know when your space needs an overall boost if you feel good when you're not at home and then, within a few minutes of being back, you feel heavy, irritated, and generally, out of alignment.

Five Temple Steps of Angelic Feng Shui

Preparation is key. Use the technique from Aligning into Source from earlier, or relax using any other way that centres you. It's best that no one is in the property when you're performing the steps, that you give yourself plenty of time, and that clutter has been cleared up.

From an energetic stance, where there's clutter, there's no energy flow. From a psychological stance, clutter equals subconscious stress, representing things we're putting off and the past we don't want to face. Dust and clean, especially around windows, window sills, doors, and doorways. Keeping the entry and exit points of your space clean and clear of clutter will help you and your space to vibrationally sing!

When you're ready, physically come to the periphery of your space. Mentally bow to your home, your home's elemental guide, the surrounding spirits, the earth elementals, and the overlighting devas of the environment. Ask them for permission to create your home and land to be a temple.

If you receive a no, reassure the spirits that you walk in Divine Innocence and aren't here to spiritually trespass. Show the spirits the ideal haven you've created vibrationally and let them know how they'll benefit from this uplifted space and that you're open to incorporating their positive intentions for change, too. Ask for permission again, and when you receive a yes, give thanks, and invite the benevolent spirits to assist you.

As those willing to help come into your Awareness, invite in your guardian angels to hold the space high, along with the Archeiai and their twin Archangels, positioned in this following configuration:

◊ On your left-hand side, invite Archeia Virtue and Archangel Raphael to bring their Emerald and Pink Fire into you.

◊ Behind you, invite Archeia Faith and Archangel Michael to bring their Sapphire and Gold Fire into you.

◊ On your right-hand side, invite Archeia Hope and Archangel Gabriel to bring their Pearlescent White Fire into you.

◊ In front of you, invite Archeia Grace and Archangel Uriel to bring their Ruby Red Fire into you.

◊ Below you, invite Archeia Patience and Archangel Sandalphon to bring their Rainbow Crystalline Fire into you.

◊ Above you, invite Archeia Constance and Archangel Metatron to bring their Orange and Indigo Fire into you.

◊ Stepping into you, invite Archeia Purity, Archangel Zadkiel, Archeia Victory, and Archangel Raziel to bring their Violet, Magenta, Silver, and Diamond Fire into you.

Now blended with the angels, their alchemical fires, and your own angelic Light, affirm that you're ready to make this space a reflection of your Divinity. Affirm that you're ready for your temple to become a magnet for the best guides and angels to support and inspire you; an oasis of calm where you can rest and renew; a platform where you can dream, create, and manifest; and a haven where you can nurture love, family, friends, and community. Breathe in any extra energetic virtues you'd like to embody—and by extension, your home—such as breathing in Wellbeing, Prosperity, Pleasure, Magic. Become a living template and temple of these virtues as you enter your space and perform step 1.

Step 1—Breaking Up Density

Begin by opening all the doors and windows, letting in the fresh air, and providing an exit to everything that's less than Love. To break up density, emotional imprints, and other vibratory entanglements, use a means of physical sound, such as clapping your hands, beating a drum, or chiming a *tingsha* (Tibetan cymbals). Clap your hands in your aura to break up stagnancy and then shake your body! (This quick vibe-raiser lifts feelings of apathy, depression, and stress.) Then move counter-clockwise around your home, and within each room, using sound to dislodge the energy in your walls, floors, ceilings, furniture (including under your bed), the corners of each room, around all electronic devices, door and window frames, and above all sinks and taps. Imagine the angels (and your other etheric friends) are clapping their hands in these places and then sense them joining together as one Force to clap above, below, and to the sides of your home. These loud, yet harmonious tones are breaking up all dense pockets. Keep breathing deeply throughout this process, noticing how the air begins to thicken as the energy clumps.

Step 2—Lifting and Releasing

To lift and release the energy, this step draws from the elemental forces of air, earth, and fire. Choose your favourite purifying plant, such as white sage or palo santo sticks, to smudge (burn) safely. You may want to create your own smudging sticks combining pine, rosemary, frankincense, or lavender, which all have cleansing and magical properties. (Note: You can also use incense sticks, but most are overly processed and often need to be cleansed before use!)

Before lighting your smudge stick, recognize the spirit of each plant consciousness you are partnering with. Give thanks to the plants for helping you create a sacred space, and ask their smoke to attract and catch all negative thought forms, earthbound spirits that are ready to move on, curses, psychic binds, expired contracts, and replaying memories within you, the space, and land (on all levels of time, space, and dimensions) that are less than Love, and that aren't a match for the vibration you're setting. Using an ash catcher and a blessed smudging feather (if you have one), smudge under your feet, around your aura, and above your head. Then, moving counter-clockwise, smudge your home and each room, paying close attention to the areas you brought sound frequencies into. Also, smudge around mirrors, phones, TVs, fridges, freezers, electronic devices, and the places where you charge the devices.

If you're guided to smudge in a figure-eight motion, creating the sacred geometry of Infinity, especially within the corners of the home and in places that receive no sunlight, flow with this. The angels are moving with you, helping lift, release, and purify on all levels of being. As the smoke is carrying the energy out of your space for transformation, go outside too and begin to smudge (counter-clockwise) the surrounding land, garden, or yard. This will help the energy that comes into your home vibrate in alignment with you. Note: Energy can never be "cleared", but it can be transformed, and this is taking place now. As you come inside, you may begin to feel how s p a c i o u s your home is, like you can breathe again! So take a deep breath in . . . and a full breath out.

Step 3—Smoothing the Space
To smooth and balance the vibration within and around you and your home, use the sacredness of your breath. You can work with Source Breath (as introduced in Chapter 1, page 31) alone or couple this "breath of intention" with a

devotional room spray. Pre-made room sprays are great, but it can be fun to make your own; plus, everything you create will be infused with your vibe, making it more effective in your space. You can create an overall spray to meet the intention of this step, as well as sprays for different rooms and their intentions, such as an energizing spray for your kitchen and a relaxing (or passion-stirring!) spray for your bedroom.

To make your sprays devotional, first align into Source and set a focused intention for what the spray will help facilitate. Ask Archeia Victory to be with you so she can assist in selecting the best oils, plants, crystals, colours, sound frequencies, Source Rays, and alchemical fires to use, and in which composition. The water within the spray will imprint and anchor these frequencies, given that water retains an energetic memory.

To make your own spray for this step, you'll need a diffuser spray bottle labelled with the words "All Is in Divine Balance"; fresh water; soothing plant essences, such as celandine, comfrey, daffodil, nasturtium, nettle, passionflower, or sage; calming crystal elixirs made from amber, amethyst, angelite, aventurine, celestite, fluorite, or shungite; and balancing essential oils, such as cedarwood, geranium, lemongrass, myrrh, sandalwood, or ylang ylang. Research the best stores to buy your essences, elixirs, and oils from, or make your own wherever possible. Combine the ingredients you're guided to use and then bring the spray close to your lips. Open your heart and breathe in deeply Gold and Diamond Fire . . . and then slowly breathe out these celestial codes into your spray, supercharging all the components.

Moving clockwise around your home and in every room, use Source Breath or in combination with your spray. Breathe your angelic Light, and spritz into every nook and cranny of your home and surrounding land. Sense the angels joining you, bathing everything in their alchemical fires and unconditional Love. As this happens, sense a central Diamond grounding column in the centre of your space, and within any rooms or land where you'd like the energy to move more freely. See this column(s) connecting with the heart of Mother Earth and the heart of the Great Central Sun. Sense the column(s) gently spinning, reflecting high-vibrational Light in all directions of your space.

Step 4—Raising the Vibe
This step draws from the sound frequency of your Diamond Heart and the Light of the angels to amplify the vibration of your now-temple.

With your heart open wide, move clockwise, and sing into your space, sensing your house elemental guide joining you, too. Sing your favourite song, mantra, affirmations, or a little ditty that comes through in the moment. The angels also emanate a celestial sound current in order to raise the vibration of your temple and anchor it at the highest and most expansive level of being, seeing, feeling, and magnetization. These sound waves positively influence the other currents of energy that come into your space— including the vibration of the surrounding land (now brought up and aligned with Source), other people, and your water, gas, power, and internet supply. Affirm that everything coming in and leaving your temple is unconditionally loved and blessed. Now sing or say your intention for each room while you are in it. Be deliberate with how this room will feel from this point on, and what it will magnetize; for example, intend your bedroom to be a haven for love and intimacy, attracting your highest beloved, if you're looking for love. Visualize this as already done, and experience the positive outcome with all your senses. Now ask the room what it needs to bring this outcome into the physical plane. What needs to resolve within you first and then in the space? Also, do you need to move objects, bring in different colours, elements, crystals, pictures, or plants? Tune in, and follow through for each area of your temple.

Note: Archeia Victory would like to share an extra tip here: to hang crystal suncatchers in every window of your space to reflect diamond rainbow prisms into the room and onto the walls. Bless your suncatchers first by asking Archeia Victory (and the Unicorns) to charge them with the Diamond Ray, so that when they catch the sunlight, they are bringing in this ray to charge the energy of your space and help everything within to stay Source-aligned.

Step 5—Blessing and Sealing
Blessing and sealing your temple is a crucial step, for it's not a bricks-and-mortar house anymore. The more you treat your space as a sanctuary, the more it will vibrate as one.

Come into what feels for you to be the heart of your temple. Asking the angels to join you, visualize your space (and the surrounding land) overlaid by the Gold and Diamond Rays. Affirm your space to be blessed and sealed in the purest unconditional Love. Include the "muggle overlay" (see below) if it resonates for you and then close the angelic feng shui process by giving thanks to all concerned. Ask the angels (and any guides, ancestors, and spirits that joined you) to step out of your field, then ground yourself by drinking some water and journal your insights.

A further invitation is to ask your guardian angels to outwardly project the appearance of your temple as a "muggle home", so that anything untoward passes it by— "muggle" (thank you, J.K. Rowling!) meaning a Sleeping Beauty unaware of their magic yet. Why is it necessary to add an additional seal to give the appearance of living in a muggle home? While like attracts like in our Universe, many non-physical beings exist outside universal laws such as the Law of Attraction and don't have our best interests at heart. This is nothing to fear; in fact, it's testament to how rapidly we're advancing that more intra- and inter-dimensional beings are trying to engage us.

As empaths, we are most susceptible to being psychically engaged when we're asleep. If you wake up often through the night and feel like something is in your room, or you feel exhausted upon waking and have a sense of working or travelling in your dreams, the likelihood is you're being energetically engaged. To counter this, place a "muggle overlay" over your temple to project to everything in the vicinity that there's nothing important in your space and nothing to gain, as only sleep-walking muggles live here. Imagining the overlay is the creation of it. I've been using this overlay for the past year as I and my kids (who are highly sensitive) had so much Spirit activity coming and going. Thankfully, we all sleep soundly now. Our home is still a temple, and everything within sings in sweet alignment with Source, forever magnetizing all we're ready for. Our angels and guides can easily interact with us, too. The overlay over our space helps us live in greater harmony with each other, the land, and the benevolent Spirits that also occupy the space.

 *Rise Like an Angel*

◊ "From following all five temple steps (including the preparation), I feel . . . and my home feels . . . "

◊ "I am ready for each room in my temple to have a specific vibration, look, and feel. In the entrance to my home, I am ready for it to feel and look like . . . In my kitchen, I am ready for it to feel and look like . . . In my living room, I am ready for it to feel and look like . . . In my bathroom, I am ready for it to feel and look like . . . In my bedroom, I am ready for it to feel and look like . . . "

◊ "The action steps I need to take to make these rooms (and the other rooms in my home, garden and land space) sing are . . . "

◊ "I understand that my personal vibe creates my temple vibe, not the other way around. This gives me a sense of empowerment and . . . "

To merge fully with the magical Presence of Archeia Victory, please enjoy the following attunement. I recommend to first read "How to Prepare for Attunements" in Chapter 2, page 50.

Archeia Victory Attunement

Feeling centred, sense yourself held in a column of sparkling Diamond Light. Breathe this Source Ray in and out. Allow it to fill every part of you, including your aura and wings, and then see it connect through you to the centre of the earth and the centre of the Sun. Feel your guardian angels standing on either side of you, radiating their Love, which further expands your Light. When you're ready to invite in Archeia Victory, affirm aloud:

"Loving Archeia Victory, angel of Universal Ascension, Magic, and Wisdom and master of the Diamond Ray, may you now attune me to your vibration and consciousness, so we are forever One, and allow me to channel your Light for the greatest good of all concerned. Assist me to feel triumphant in my life, so I may consistently stand tall in full loving alignment with Source. Help me uncover the spiritual understanding that can propel me forward and upward, and kindly support me to develop my spiritual gifts to benefit my life and All. Gift me your talent of Angelic Feng Shui so I can resolve my space to be a temple to live, breathe, and serve from. Thank you. And so it is."

Breathe in Triumph . . . and breathe out Triumph, as you merge with this Divine angel. Ask Archeia Victory what the highest and best guidance is for you at this time, and if there's anything you can support her with.

As you continue to attune to Archeia Victory, you can also channel her Light. If there's a part of your body you'd like to empower, bring your hands to that area now, or place one hand on your third eye and the other on your crown (the chakras that Victory influences the most). Sense the sparkling Diamond Fire filling these areas, and switch on your most expansive vision, hearing, knowing, and sensing. Affirm aloud three times:

"Everything I need to know comes to me effortlessly."

Breathe in . . . breathe out, anchoring the Light of this Truth. When you feel the energy beginning to wane, intend the attunement to be complete. Thank your guardian angels and Archeia Victory before opening your eyes and drinking some water to ground yourself.

Rise Like an Angel

◊ "Attuning to the upliftment of Archeia Victory felt like . . . "

◊ "Her guidance for me at this time is . . . "

◊ "I'll continue to invite in Archeia Victory to assist me with . . . "

Daily Affirmation to Connect with Archeia Victory

"I delight in knowing that my invincibility, like my vibrational alignment, is within my control."

Crystal Allies

Angel aura clear quartz, diamond, silver quartz

Plant Allies

Larch, magnolia, star tulip

Invite In Archeia Victory for . . .

Angelic Feng Shui of your inner and outer temple; creating positive revolution; embodying your Magic and Source Awareness held at the third eye and crown chakras; and turning ideas into wisdom to share.

Chapter 7

ARCHEIA GRACE
"I AM ready to flow"

Advancing Angelic Connection

In every chapter's "reveal" section, each Archeia is defined using etymology, because the Divine Feminine angels help us go straight to the source of our fears and limitations. The origin of their name, which is also the core virtue they express and gift humanity with, is also the clearest way to define them.

The Archeiai didn't want to be described through a religious lens, given that much of religion has been misconstrued. Instead, they guided this book to be universally relatable, so that we, as a human family, can connect to them as non-denominational sisters and brothers of Creation. Through this grounded relationship, we can more readily apply their teachings to our day-to-day life and spiritual development.

Our Divine brothers, the Archangels, supported us in the last Piscean Age because their Light and teachings were exactly what we needed. Even though they are still with us, it's our Divine sisters, the Archeiai, who now come forward to address what we're ready to heal and empower on a personal and collective level, namely the suppression of the Divine Feminine inside and outside us.

Illuminating the Subconscious

Where the Archeiai excel is in helping us illuminate our subconscious, or some would call our "shadow" selves. Our subconscious is like a basement storing the root vibration of the limiting beliefs, karma, stories, and traumas that are influencing our conscious reality.

Ultimately, our core shadows boil down to imprints, scars, and wounding around feeling unloved and separate from Source. These can be further defined as the internal wounds associated with the masculine and feminine aspects of Creation; for example, the perceived hurt our soul felt when it originally separated from Source to live a physical experience.

Although we can never be "separate" from Source, if the wounded masculine could be encapsulated into a belief, it would be, "The world is not enough." Likewise, the wounded feminine would believe, "I am not enough." Both beliefs are distorted stories of scarcity that we've carried for eons but can choose to transform at any time.

Such internal beliefs create the hang-ups and blocks we bring into our day-to-day lives. They are the things that rattle us and the essence of why we may think and act in destructive ways. Why do we need to shine a light on such shadows? Why can't we just leave them in our basement?! We could do just that, but we must realize if that's our choice, we'll continue to live our lives from the vibrations of our blocks. We'll manifest from the perception of lack rather than flow; we'll connect in relationships through filters of cynical love rather than unconditional Love; and we'll define ourselves by our shadows, which witter on about our unworthiness rather than the Truth of who we are. Because we've entered a new era of Awareness, our inner being is asking us to stop living as a diluted version of who we are, and instead, be the empowered soul we came to be.

The Alchemy of Heartfulness

All angels help us illuminate our subconscious by attuning us to the virtues they express. Each virtue liberates our being in different ways. Archeia Purity and Archeia Grace both express the virtue of "Divine Alchemy", a powerful process that brings to the surface subconscious blocks from our cellular makeup and then acts to transform their energy back into life-renewing *prana*. By consciously recycling the old for the new, we create space within our body for our Light to flow freely, while increasing the size and integrity of our aura from the boost of *prana* that the alchemy process creates. Manifesting then becomes easier, as there are no underlying blocks getting in the way. We become free to move in sync with the forward focus of our inner being.

While Archeia Purity focuses on alerting us to things in our energy field so that we can be more deliberate in our thinking, choices, and actions, Archeia Grace helps us recycle and redirect stagnant energy into pranic flow. Through this process, we can experience the bliss of being both a sovereign soul (aka, knowing ourselves as a reflection of Source in body) and realizing that we are One with all life (aka, knowing ourselves as Source).

As Archeia Grace guides, all of us carry some degree of inner scarring. Like scratches on a mirror, no matter how much we buff that mirror, the scratches still play out in our vibration, emerging in different ways and from different perspectives throughout the varied course of our lives.

Depending on our soul's path in this lifetime, we may know what these inner stories and wounds are. When they arise, we may choose to feel disempowered by them and go into victimhood or opt to ignore or deny them, because we feel we've already healed them or believe we don't have what it takes to surmount them. All the while, the inner stories become more ingrained until we choose to face them.

While the masculine way to ascend may be to focus on a better-feeling thought to transcend such inner blocks (for example, using practices such as mindfulness), the feminine way—as the Archeiai inspire—is to face blocks heart on! This means feeling and listening to the consciousness of our blocks, so that we can acknowledge their positive learning and end their internal looping. You could say this is the practice of "heartfulness"! Both paths of Ascension are valuable and are always available to us.

The Key to Transformation

No matter the inner blocks, stories, and wounds you feel you're carrying, know that you have the power to transform them! As Archeia Grace guides, **we never experience anything that we're not ready for**. Why? Because there is a Divine timing and order to all. When we understand this, the underlying grace—the positive learning and understanding—of everything is revealed.

To embrace this intrepid path is to embrace our journey of personal and collective Ascension, which we can define as the process of accepting and integrating our shadows as much as our Light, for all is Divine.

The key to alchemy is to understand how our shadows are serving us. Paradoxical as it may sound, our inner wounds give us something; if they didn't, we simply wouldn't carry them. We must unearth what their value is and be willing to exchange this if we want to transform the old into the new. Much like a caterpillar melts within its chrysalis to become a butterfly, so, too, must we soften to step out of our old identities and beliefs.

To put this into context, while writing the initial version of this chapter, I was grieving the passing of my dad. By being real with the grief, underlying anger emerged, and under this a core shadow appeared that's been present throughout my life: abandonment. When I invited in Archeia Grace, she guided me to go within and ask: "What is the belief of being abandoned giving me? Am I willing to exchange this for knowing I'm forever One with Source?" Her guidance assured me of the need to feel the answers and expand upon them, rather than be swept up in stories.

Anger may not be classed as a virtue, but like all emotions, it has value. Feeling into it first, I realized that anger was giving me a creative push to cut through the bullsh*t of feeling like a victim of abandonment, and was also helping me free suppressed feelings around the action and inaction of my dad. As I felt into the anger rather than attaching to it, I witnessed it come up in order to come out of me. Processing emotions like this is the crux of transformation. We can work with alchemical forces like the Violet Flame all we want, but if we're not willing to arrive at the core of emotions by becoming the Awareness behind them, rather than their victim, such forces only act as "energetic Band-aids".

As the energy of anger transformed into *prana*, it was easier to feel into the underlying sensation of abandonment and where it was manifesting in my body, namely in my root, sacral, and solar plexus chakras. I asked how abandonment was serving me, and if I was willing to exchange the sense of "protection" that its "excuse energy" provided via the "comfort" of people-pleasing. It was allowing me to justify not standing in my Power, as opposed to accepting the responsibility of tending to my own vibration. As I handed over these energies in exchange, they transformed. By being honest with myself and acknowledging the victimhood mentality I'd been carrying, I was able to see how this story had been serving me.

After 20 minutes of dialoguing with my subconscious through compassionate listening and the alchemical magic of Archeia Grace, I felt incredible! I exchanged every sense of desertion by affirming my unbreakable connection with Source, for myself and my inner being are always One. As a result, my vibration felt vast and pure. My inherent Innocence returned, for we're never born with such hang-ups. Yes, our soul comes into physical being with a desire to expand upon certain areas, but our choices and beliefs are our own earthly design. **We cannot blame or shame others for how we feel, as we are sovereign beings who can release limitation as quickly as we empower it.**

Divine Alchemy Session

Archeia Grace would like to escort you through a session of Divine Alchemy. For this, you'll need the Energy Drainers list you compiled in Chapter 5. Many of the self-limiting beliefs or behaviours from this list will stem from a core self-limiting belief or shadow. As you read over the list, is there a common thread that unites everything? Elect as your intention that you're ready to transform this thread. In exchange, whatever this commonality has been giving you, ensure you're willing to give up how it's been serving you. If you're not ready for that, pick something else that you're ready to transform, and follow the steps below. Note: I've used "binge-eating" as an example, but please substitute with whatever you're transforming:

◊ Sit up, and close your eyes. Rest your hands (palms facing upwards) on your lap, and come into a meditative state. Ask Archeia Grace to be with you, seeing yourself completely enveloped in her Ruby Ray. Breathe in this alchemical fire . . . and as you exhale, connect to the centre of Mother Earth and to the center of the Sun. Feel yourself merge with your inner being, as you step into your choice to transform the identification, story, root, cords, and webs of binge-eating from all timelines, space, and dimensions now.

◊ Invite the energy of binge-eating to arise in your body. Where is your focus drawn to? Expand the sensation you're feeling (for example, if you feel the root of binge eating in your base chakra, breathe into your base chakra). Bring all your awareness here, then ask aloud, "What is binge-eating giving me?" Listen. Feel. Acknowledge everything. Perhaps what comes up is a sense of eating to self-soothe, suppress feelings, fill boredom, or feel pleasure that you feel isn't present in your life. Whatever arises, ask aloud, "What are these things giving me?" Feel into the reply, as Truth reveals and layers are peeled away. As this happens, keep offering up the sensations and stories into the Ruby Fire.

◊ As you arrive at the root of the issue, which invariably will be connected to a lack of worthiness or a disconnection from Source, ask aloud, "Am I willing to exchange the story and action of binge-eating for fully loving myself?" If yes, move into how this feels as the alchemy continues to transform the energy of binge-eating into new *prana*. If not, ask aloud, "What do I need to permit to allow the alchemy to take place?" Give yourself permission to transform the old and limiting into the new and expanding.

◊ Keep breathing in Ruby Fire, honouring everything you're witnessing. Any physical sensations, such as burping, crying, laughing, nausea, yawning, or a need to shout and vent, are signs that the alchemy is working, so just let your body flow. If anything feels too much, hand over the sensations to Archeia Grace. Focus less on what you're releasing and more on how you want to feel and what you're creating through this process. If you feel nothing, ask aloud, "What am I avoiding?" Be real to heal, as you witness what's coming up to come out in grace. Side-step attaching to stories, and instead, feel the sensations under the story. Keep expanding the sensations to purify them. Breathe into any knots to allow undigested shadows to lighten.

◊ Ask Archeia Grace to release on all timelines, space, and dimensions the root, cords, and webs of binge-eating from your akashic (soul) blueprint and habitual consciousness, and recycle this into *prana* now. As this takes place, feel yourself lighter and vaster, as your wings begin to flutter! Witness the alchemy, and enjoy the bliss that ensues. Ask for the bliss to be increased 10 times, then 100 times, then 1,000 times! Breathe in Grace . . . breathe out Grace, as you close the session. Thank all concerned, and feel the LoveLight sparkling in your eyes as you open them now. Drink some water to ground yourself.

Rise Like an Angel

◊ "This Divine Alchemy session afforded me . . . "

◊ "I'll continue this process of sacred exchange by transforming . . . "

Becoming a Divine Alchemist

The best time to do Divine Alchemy is when the Moon or the Sun is undergoing an eclipse. Three weeks before and three weeks after an eclipse are powerful cosmic windows, when our personal and collective shadows rise to be addressed. I can wholeheartedly say that by taking time to do shadow work during these windows, it makes Ascension much more graceful. Plus, day-to-day life becomes more fulfilling, as self-limitation morphs into unbridled flow.

You may feel tired from doing Angelic Alchemy, but know that your body is just asking to rest. As you would when undergoing an operation, let your body recuperate afterwards, for alchemy creates huge shifts within our emotional, mental, physical, and energetic bodies. Our nervous system, DNA blueprint, and auric field undergo great change. Be gentle and spacious with yourself to honour and allow the integration to take place.

As is the case in nature, Divine Alchemy is cyclical, meaning it may take a few days, weeks, or months to appreciate the full manifestation of your breakthroughs. Nature never rushes her process of transformation; she never wishes to be all seasons at the same time. She simply flows from one season to the next, enjoying the moment she's in. Likewise, as one season unfolds into the next in sacred exchange, keep offering up limiting beliefs and behaviours to Grace, if you find yourself embroiled in their stories again. Let them come out of your habitual consciousness, as you exchange how they've been serving you for renewed *prana* and flow. Remember, **change is the one constant of Creation you can count on!** Welcome change. Lean into it to become it. Trust all is transforming and appearing in your life in the perfect time and order for you.

Archeia Grace Revealed

Archeia Grace, whose name is derived from the Old French word *graciier*, meaning "to thank", serves on the Ruby Ray of Peace, Devotion, and Inspiration with her counterpart, Archangel Uriel. This energetic stream, which contains the Red and Pink Rays, represents the creativity that's born through inspired action. When used, the Ruby Ray helps light our way, while combatting inertia and fear of embracing our soul's calling. Other names for Archeia Grace are "Lady Grace", "Aurora", and "Rainbow Aurora". She has a healing influence over the auric field and solar plexus chakra, symbolizing the softer side of the solar plexus; the calm in the middle of our creative fire!

In her depiction, Grace asked for autumn leaves cascading from her hair to remind us of the cyclical movement of everything, and how to embrace the new we must let go of the old. Like Purity, her essence is akin to a Celtic goddess and just as elusive, for you may never see Grace in a physical-seeming form. When you invite her in, you may sense her presence reflected outdoors, for she is the celestial artist who colours the sunrise and sunset with golden pinks and russet reds and the visionary who blankets autumn landscapes with her magical Midas touch.

Archeia Grace heralds that life moves in a purposeful flow. We can either flow in sync with the stream of wellbeing and feel the bliss that results or against the flow and experience the discord that ensues. By connecting with Grace, it's easier to lean in and surrender to the flow (that is, choose to live as your highest Self). You know when you're in sync with the stream because you'll feel good, and everything in life just seems to come together. Archeia Grace wants you to know that you can create this harmonization any time you want by trusting and following your intuition. This is what is known as the Law of Grace (aka, the Law of Divine Will), where everything appears in your world in the perfect timing and perfect order.

Whenever you're going through periods of change you find uncomfortable, lean on Archeia Grace. She'll help you uncover the root of any uncertainty and will reveal the blessings of your now and future reality. As you move into a state of appreciation, she can help you acclimatize to this new chapter of your life.

As Grace guides:

Your path is constantly in motion. Like the turning of the seasons, and like your soul, it is forever seeking to be in sync with Mother Earth. When you become aware of the cycles of nature, you can better understand who you are, why you are here, and what your unique expression of Creation is—your soul's calling. Let yourself flow like nature, for everything stems from you and is returned to you.

Grace Is Always Flowing

I'm sure you've experienced moments of grace in your life, when someone has entered your reality at the perfect time. I believe these people are sent on behalf of our guardian angels to say something that means the whole world to us or to offer help or the space to heal. These beautiful souls show us, as Archeia Grace does, that there's light at the end of the tunnel for us to come out upon. It's not just physical people or angels that remind us that grace forever flows, but also our loved ones in Spirit. This was my experience around my dad's passing.

His death brought up so much to the surface for healing. I'm going to be honest with you: There were moments when I just didn't want to be here. I didn't want to feel all I was experiencing, because the anger and abandonment felt too big for me to contain. A few days after burying my dad, the relationship with my fiancé (a connection I wanted to work but knew in my heart was toxic) also ended. I felt consumed by it all. Fortunately, angels were ever present, as they always are for us. They inspired me to feel my feelings instead of being consumed by them. As I listened, compassion flowed in and eventually escorted me through the alchemy process we've just explored. The more I leaned into Archeia Grace; the more grace manifested in my life!

My dad loved wild cats. Not just because they are the animal on our clan's badge (MacGillivray) but because he respected their nature. Following his passing, I kept seeing images of wild cats, accompanied by the sense that my dad was saying, "Hi!"

One day, my mum said she had one of his belongings to give to me, and before she told me what it was, I saw an image of a wild cat statue, which it turned out to be. On the same day, my American friend, Katherine, texted me a picture she was guided to send. It was of a bobcat, which looks just like a Scottish wildcat.

The signs didn't end there.

I began receiving visitations from my dad in meditations and in my dreams. He asked if he could become a member of my spirit team, to offer the love and support I felt were missing from him in my physical life. He also guided me against reconciling with my ex, as I'd done so many times before. He saw himself in him, and he didn't want me to go through more heartache. Now was the time to walk away and begin anew.

Through his signs and support of healing inner and outer blocks, my dad reminded me of how grace moves through all life experiences. If we move forward in union with this stream of wellbeing, instead of against it, we begin to see the blessings in everything. Moreover, Grace helps us see that we're never alone. Even when a loved one graduates into non-physical existence, they aren't alone. As a virtue, Grace carries us and illuminates our path all-ways and in every way, inspiring us to find our inner Light when we feel it's been extinguished.

Notice How Grace Manifests

Before enjoying the following meditation with Archeia Grace, feel into how grace is showing up in your world right now. Just realizing its presence will amplify its peaceful momentum.

As we witness how grace moves in our world, we become available to new fulfilling experiences as inner wounds and tendencies towards stagnation naturally transform. In the process, we can better articulate the vision we want for our life and how to flow in this direction. Our higher vision then drives our thoughts, words, actions, and behaviours to line up with Source's vision, and we experience sustained moments when everything just comes together in our life. We then witness miracles in flow as the embodiment of the flow!

Grace Begins with Me

The following meditation, inspired by my Kundalini Yoga training, will help you see that every moment of life can be a miracle to savour and enjoy!

◊ Sit in a place where you won't be disturbed. Keep your spine tall, so your energy can move freely, then close your eyes and relax your breathing. Invite Archeia Grace to be with you, feeling her autumnal Ruby Ray surrounding you. Breathe in her ray . . . and breathe it out.

◊ You're going to recite the mantra "Grace begins with me" in the following ways: As you say the word "Grace", bring your index finger to touch your thumb; as you say "begins", bring your middle finger to touch your thumb; as you say "with", bring your ring finger to touch your thumb; and as you say "me", bring your little finger to touch your thumb.

◊ For either, three, 11, or 22 minutes, slowly repeat the mantra "Grace . . . begins . . . with . . . me", as you touch each finger in turn. Experience the calming resonance of the words and their intention to soften any need to do anything else. Breathe deeply and in-joy.

◊ After your last repetition, bring your hands together in a prayer position at your heart centre. Notice how different you feel in your mind, body, and mood. Thank Archeia Grace, and drink some water to ground yourself.

To fully merge with Archeia Grace's teachings, please read "How to Prepare for Attunements" in Chapter 2 (page 50), then follow with her beautiful attunement below.

Archeia Grace Attunement

Feeling centred, sense yourself held in a column of rich Ruby Light. Breathe this Source Ray in and out. Allow it to fill every part of you, including your aura and wings, and then see it connect through you to the centre of the Earth and the centre of the Sun. Feel your guardian angels standing on either side of you, radiating their Love, which further expands your Light.

When you're ready to invite in Archeia Grace, affirm aloud:

"Loving Archeia Grace, angel of Peace, Devotion, and Inspiration, and master of the Ruby Ray, may you now attune me to your vibration and consciousness, so that I am forever linked with you and may channel your energy. Open my heart, ears, eyes, and senses to know you as your Light awakens Source into every part of me and in every area of my life now. Assist me to flow as Creation, as I sync with the current that breathes worlds into existence. Help me manifest with your ease and elegance, and support me to colour my life with the same joy as you do. Thank you. And so it is."

Breathe in Grace . . . and breathe out Grace, as you merge with this Divine angel. Ask Archeia Grace what the highest and best guidance is for you at this time, and if there's anything you can support her with.

As you continue to attune to Archeia Grace, you can also channel her healing Light. If there's a part of your body you'd like to heal, bring your hands to that area now, or rest your hands on your solar plexus (the chakra that Grace influences the most). Sense the Ruby Ray that expresses itself as Golden Red, Purple, and Pink flames moving into your solar plexus and then fills your body and aura. Breathe in these flames . . . and breathe out their vibrancy into your space. Sense everything around you awash in colour. Beam this renewed inspiration to anyone or anything that comes to mind, then sense all of Creation enhanced by the beauty of Grace.

When you feel the energy beginning to wane, intend the attunement to be complete. Thank your guardian angels and Archeia Grace before opening your eyes and drinking some water to ground yourself.

 *Rise Like an Angel*

◊ "Attuning to the elegance of Archeia Grace felt like . . . "

◊ "Her guidance for me at this time is . . . "

◊ "I'll continue to invite in Archeia Grace to co-create . . . "

Daily Affirmation to Connect with Archeia Grace
"Every moment of my life is a miracle to savour and enjoy."

Crystal Allies
Fire opal, mookaite, clear topaz

Plant Allies
Ginger, hound's tongue, red poppy

Invite In Archeia Grace for . . .
Renewal, reassurance, intuitive and intellectual guidance, inspiration, devotion, determination, elegance, ease, creativity, and accepting and moving through change.

Chapter 8

ARCHEIA CHARITY
"I AM ready to love"

Softening into Love

The more we connect with the Archeiai, the more we reclaim our Divinity. Our heart opens and aligns with our spiritual calling, and in the process, any shadows that have been in the way dissolve. We can accelerate this journey of Ascension by learning to soften, for the limitations we carry often represent the equivalent of scar tissue from our past experiences. If we soften this scar tissue, it heals and reveals all that we are and all that we've always been: *Love.*

There are so many aspects to Love: awareness, care, compassion, empowerment, expression, joy, and integrity, to name just a few. Like a diamond, our capacity to accept who we are is faceted, with some sides lit for the world to see and others shadowed in darkness, waiting to be lit. As Archeia Grace shared, we don't need to stay in the story of our shadowed facets, for identifying with them keeps us in their loop of limitation. What's important to remember is that our thoughts, feelings, and actions hinge upon the degree of Love we're allowing in and expressing out in each given moment.

Revisiting the metaphor of the caterpillar transforming into the butterfly, the caterpillar may not understand the process that's taking place, but it knows how to surrender. **It trusts that miracles happen outside of limitations**. By softening and surrendering into Love, we, too, dissolve the barriers of self-created rigidity. And so, whatever you may be holding onto or feel another has inflicted on you, or you them, *let it go*. Open your heart and express your true Self to the world. Not the self you feel that others want to see, but purely and simply You!

Listening to Love

One of the greatest lessons I've learnt in life so far is that when I love myself, I love the world, and in turn, the world loves me right back. I unapologetically accept from life and feel deserving of its many blessings. It's been a long road to arrive here, and some days are still challenging, yet these are the most powerful days—when I'm asked to come out of my comfort zone to break free in order to break through into the wholeness of who I am. And the beauty is, we are all Love at our core.

As Archeia Charity guides, as she comes forward now:

> You are Love and Love is you, and nothing can ever separate you from who and what you are. It is time to open your heart, for you are the Love you have been seeking. Be fearless. Be bold. Accept yourself, for all of Creation adores you.

For many years, I set myself apart from Love. In my late teens and twenties, I experienced sexual abuse that emotionally and mentally scarred me. I didn't want to share what had happened, and as a result of feeling ashamed, I became withdrawn. There was a comfort in turning away from Love, as my ego feared that past experiences would repeat themselves. Through connecting with the angels in later life, I realized that **amidst our greatest challenges, our greatest strength appears**. In each moment, we have the choice to either feel like a victim or a victor; to perceive a lack of love or affirm its eternal presence.

Listening to your heart now, do you feel you're embodying Love in your life or turning away from it? Is it easy for you to accept Love and share it unconditionally? If not, what would it take to restore the balance? Honour the honesty of your heart as it shares now.

Another empowering question, especially in challenging life moments, is to ask yourself, *How can I bring more Love to this situation?* Because Love is the universal conditioner, it detangles all! By giving, receiving, or being a lighthouse of Love, you can lay to rest any resistance that shows up in life. For instance, if there's something troubling you right now that you feel you can't resolve or let go of, ask yourself, *Do I need to give, receive, or be Love in this situation?* Your heart will know. Having these regular "heart-to-heart" chats is a way to transform potential fears, so that Love can flow freely to, through, and from you.

Rise Like an Angel

Please pause and look at Archeia Charity's image. Gaze into her all-knowing eyes. Breathe her powerful presence into you and your space . . . then feel into the following questions, journaling your answers:

◊ "Do I need to give Love, receive Love, or be Love to enjoy greater flow with myself, my partner, my family, my friends, my home, my communities, and my relationship to Source?"

◊ "What actions (if any) do I need to take to enable loving shifts in these relationships?"

Archeia Charity Revealed

Archeia Charity, whose name is derived from the Old English word *deore*, meaning "beloved", serves on the Pink, Red, and Ruby Rays of Divine Love and Devotion with her counterpart, Archangel Chamuel. She also expresses on the Ruby and Red Rays and has healing influence over our higher heart, heart, and causal chakras. Other names for Archeia Charity include "Lady Charity" and "Seraphina".

When I was channelling Charity's imagery, she manifested as emerging from the temple of Divine Love. This crystalline temple existed physically in Golden Atlantis, and it still exists in ethereal form. From this sacred place, Charity taught many of her initiates, including Ascended Masters, such as Lady Nada and Paul the Venetian, who herald the essence of Love throughout Creation, and Heros and his counterpart, Amora, who together are the Elohim of Love.

Charity's temple takes the form of a pink pyramid, but in her illustration, Marie-Joe made the pyramid a "spotlight", as self-love is the very act of illuminating ourselves. In her depiction, Archeia Charity wears a ruby heart pendant that connects her with Chamuel. She was also inspired to give Archeia Charity big breasts, for, in her words,

"Love is curvaceous, bold, and delicious!" Big boobs, big heart!

Archeia Charity and Archangel Chamuel are powerful emissaries of Light and are among the most intense of the angels in their expression of Love. Together, they merge the Universal Mother/Divine Feminine and the Universal Father/Sacred Masculine within our being to help us live in balanced integrity.

Both aspects of this loving angel form the symbol of a heart. Looking at this shape, it has two halves, reminding us that to embody Love, we must bring all the parts of our being together. (Interestingly, seeing the shape of a heart reflected in the environment is a sign that angels are with you, just like seeing a pair of wings or a feather, which also have two halves.) By embracing wholeness, Love can flow freely from our hearts, with no judgement or conditions placed upon it. And if we can be dear with ourselves, we can love others unconditionally, too.

Archeia Charity heralds that Love isn't something we create but is the infinite flow of Source energy that we are. When we open and merge with this flow, we accept ourselves and all around us as unique, holy beings. By seeing Source in all, it's easier to love everyone equally, especially those that poke and provoke us the most (aka, our greatest teachers, who are often angels in disguise). As we raise our self-worth, we in turn raise the vibration of all our relationships. Cycles of self-sabotaging thoughts and masks dissolve as we recognize and express our value. By becoming our own beloved "soulmate", we can attract the fulfilling, romantic relationship we've always wanted. An infinite number of compatible loves are waiting in the wings, literally, for us to love ourselves enough to accept them.

Loving Yourself

Love is not just about how we show up in our relationships; it's a way of life. Living life truly is living Love, but to know the experience of this, we must first learn to love ourselves. In the following ritual, Archeia Charity provides the first step on this fearless path. This ritual is best enjoyed while having a bath, but if you don't have a bath or don't like bathing, you can enjoy this while lying down somewhere comfortable. Schedule this sacred "me-time" on your calendar to enjoy monthly. If it's scheduled, it won't be forgotten or buried under other priorities. **The first rule in self-love is to prioritize You!**

Love Yourself Ritual

◊   Create a sacred space in your bathroom by dimming the lights and lighting candles. Smudge the room, and bless the space by singing or playing binaural beats set at 528 Hz, which is the frequency of Love (YouTube has many free binaural beat tracks to choose from). Add your favourite essential oils and potions to your bath, and adorn your space with anything else that lights you up.

◊   Place your hands over the bathwater and say aloud:

*" Loving Archeia Charity, may you now channel
your pink uplifting Light through me and into this water,
so I may bathe in the frequency of Love. Thank you
for assisting me to soften into fully loving myself and
transforming all opposing beliefs now.
Thank you. And so it is."*

◊   Lie down in your bath, and place your left hand on your higher heart chakra (3 inches above the centre of your chest) and your right hand on your heart chakra. Connect to these energy centres as they open along with your wings. As you inhale, say to yourself, *Love*, and as you exhale, say to yourself, *Gratitude*. Breathe in Love . . . and breathe out Gratitude, sensing yourself, the bathwater, and everything in your space filling with the loving presence of Charity and her Pink Ray.

◊   Raise your left hand and cradle the back of your skull, while allowing your right hand to hover about 3–4 inches above your head. This position connects you to your causal chakra, which brings Source energy into your body while linking you to your past lives. Breathe Love into your causal chakra as Charity begins to vacuum out all past life vows, memories, cords, contracts, and attachments that are in opposition to you fully loving and appreciating yourself. Consciously cancel these other life agreements and reclaim your Power back from them as you affirm aloud:

"On all levels of time, space, being, and dimension, I now withdraw my consciousness from feeling and believing that I'm unloved and unworthy. I let these pass into Source for transmutation, as I decree,
'I am loved, lovable, worthy, and wonderful.
I am loved, lovable, worthy, and wonderful.
I AM loved, lovable, worthy, and wonderful.'
And so it is."

◊   Breathe into this decree as you seal it with your breath.

◊   Rest your hands on your heart and then wrap your wings around you. Enjoy the warming embrace of pure Source Love and feel it moving through, to, and from you. Breathe in, and feel how good it is to be alive! Breathe out, and send gratitude to all concerned. When you're ready to get out of the bath, intend your bath-water to be purified and blessed as it circulates back into the world.

Rise Like an Angel

◊ "This nurturing, self-love journey felt . . . "

◊ "I realize that loving myself is a form of sacred work, which I now commit to, not just for myself but for those who are waiting for me to love myself fully. To the beautiful souls who are ready to give me Love, to receive my Love, and together to shower blessings of Love upon our planet, I open my heart for you, for me, for us."

Acts of Self-Care

Before I could teach Angel Healing® from a truly open-hearted space, I had to soften the limiting beliefs I was carrying, such as thinking self-care is a frivolous waste of time, which of course it's not! Under the tutelage of Archeia Charity, I realized that self-care is central to how I chose to live life, and that it's mandatory for becoming a teacher who walks her talk. I recognized that acts of self-care could be going to the bathroom when I needed to, instead of feeling "too busy", paying my bills instead of ignoring them, and ending the relationships that weren't serving me.

As I learnt to love myself, I gleaned more gems along the way. These are compiled in the Self-Care Manifesto below, where you can discover 23 ways of dissolving limiting beliefs and building a diamond-like foundation of self-care to vibrate from. Please add to this manifesto, and attach it somewhere you can read it daily, then witness the magic! Your nearest-and-dearest will begin to respond differently to you, for they'll reflect your transformation. And you may find that your bank balance, home, and work life equally reshape, as you hold yourself high in, and as, Love.

Self-Care Manifesto

1   Say No to anyone or anything you don't want to associate with.

2   Say Yes to what lights you up!

3   Honour your gut instinct—Acknowledge that you have this super-power! Trust and follow your inner guidance, for this is your heart speaking (aka, the Love of who you are).

4   Be kind to everyone, especially those who are unkind to you! Love them fiercely, beautiful soul, for they represent an unloved part of you.

5   Believe in yourself, as your inner being and angels do. Write a list of your greatest accomplishments, and read the list in moments of self-doubt.

6   Unplug from drama, whether social or political, familial or environmental. Even if others want you to weigh in, if it doesn't feel right to you, don't flow in this direction. Be an activist for change by alchemizing your shadows, rather than attaching to the unloved shadows of others.

7   Untech—Schedule one day (or more) per month when you ignore all technology—internet, television, phone, computer, and so on. Devote the day to connecting with people face to face, rather than through a screen.

8   Be devotional in your self-talk. Instead of berating yourself, build yourself up. If you can be compassionate towards others, you can spotlight yourself in the same way. Say to yourself out loud every morning, "Hello Beautiful! Let's seize this day!" and before going to sleep at night, list your Magic Nine, an appreciation exercise described in the next chapter.

9   Clear clutter, especially in your bedroom. If you have piles of clothes strewn over your space, realize you're "dumping" on yourself, too! Tidy up, and use your newly acquired Angelic Feng Shui skills to purify the space. Having a bright vibration will support Love to move freely.

10   Water your plants—Similar to no. 9, if your house plants look drier than the Sahara Desert, water them! Remember, your outer space reflects your inner one. If your plants are being neglected, recognize that you're neglecting yourself.

11   In-joy pleasure—One day a month, set hourly alarms to sound on your phone to signal you to stop what you're doing and in-joy a "pleasure moment". Whatever turns your senses on—be they physical, emotional, mental, spiritual, or auditory pleasures—bring your full being into the moment. Let your day be one rolling orgasm!

12   Rest—As well as "pleasure moments", include pauses of rest throughout your day. Quieting your mind allows you to sense your angels and resets your nervous system to the vibration of Source.

13   Reframe the things you dislike or put off doing. In the past, I disliked the admin side of my job and would delay answering messages until the angels guided me to reframe this perspective. I now call admin "Communication that Matters" in order to bring in Love instead of apathy.

14   Delegate the things you can outsource in your home or work life. For example, if you're a busy parent and have the means, hire a cleaner or babysitter, or join a parents' group and take turns to look after one another's children to give yourself some well-deserved "me-time".

15   Get active in order to get out of your mind and into your body. Enjoy the activities that make you feel good, whether dancing, lifting weights, making love, or yoga. Fall in love with the brilliance of your physicality!

16   Fuel yourself with nutritious food. Before reaching for overly processed junk food, ask yourself, *Would I give this to my child? Would this help them to grow?* If you wouldn't give young children processed junk, then why feed it to yourself? Rethink. Redo. Re-vibe your diet.

17 Play—Before smart phones and games consoles, you might have been told to "go out and play" as a child, but do you bring "play" into your adulthood? Whatever outdoor activities you loved as a child, in-joy them. Jump in the mud, twirl in a circle, lean back as you speed through the air on a swing—who cares who is watching . . . life is for living!

18 Meditate with your angels to remember that you are angelic, too! Side-step the humdrum and the busy to come into the peaceful purity of You.

19 Go to bed earlier, and invest in sumptuous pillows and sheets. Make where you spend one-third of your life a sacred haven by adorning it with aromatherapy candles, halite (salt) lamps, and sleep-promoting crystals, such as amethyst, selenite, and celestite.

20 Write yourself love letters. Be encouraging in your words and affirmations. Display them (and hide some to find later!) in your home, car, and workspace.

21 Learn something new, for expanding the mind expands the heart.

22 Join supportive, high-vibe communities that share your passions, especially in-person groups where you can meet kindred souls.

23 Lastly, reclaim the courage to lead your life—perhaps the greatest act of self-love!

To further your self-loving journey, please enjoy attuning to Archeia Charity. You might want to first read "How to Prepare for Attunements" in Chapter 2, page 50.

Archeia Charity Attunement

Feeling centred, sense yourself held in a column of sparking Pink Light. Breathe this Source Ray in and out. Allow the Light to fill every part of you, including your aura and wings, and then see it connect through you to the centre of the Earth and the centre of the Sun. Feel your guardian angels standing on either side of you, radiating their Love, which expands your Light more.

When you're ready to invite in Archeia Charity, affirm aloud:

"Loving Archeia Charity, angel of Divine Love and Devotion, and master of the Pink, Ruby, and Red Rays, may you now attune me to your vibration and consciousness, so that I am forever linked with you and may channel your energy. Assist me in all matters of the heart, inspiring greater compassion, communication, and Love to flow freely through, from, and to me. Help me stay in the state of appreciation all-ways and in every way. Thank you. And so it is."

Breathe in the beloved energy of Charity . . . and breathe out her energy as you merge as One. Ask Archeia Charity what the highest and best guidance is for you at this time and if there's anything you can support her with.

As you continue to attune to Archeia Charity, you can also channel her healing Light. If there's a part of your body you'd like to heal, bring your hands to that area now, or rest your hands on your heart (the chakra that Charity influences the most). Sense ruby, pink, and golden Light moving into your heart and filling the rest of your being.

As you enjoy the healing, take yourself to the moment of your birth. Imagine the first breath you took, and now breathe Love into this inhale and breathe out Gratitude for being born. Keep inhaling Love and exhaling Gratitude, as you step onto a new timeline of worthiness and kindness.

Affirm aloud (three times):

"I am bountiful. I am beautiful. I am Love. Love in flow is the essence of me."

Now, contemplate all the babies who are being born in this very moment. Sense them taking their very first breath and then open your heart to them. Tell them how loved they are, and invite them into the bright, loving New Earth you're co-creating together.

When you feel the energy beginning to wane, intend the attunement to be complete. Thank your guardian angels and Archeia Charity before opening your eyes and drinking some water to ground yourself.

◊ "Attuning to the generosity of Archeia Charity felt like . . . "

◊ "Her guidance for me at this time is . . . "

◊ "I'll continue to invite in Archeia Charity for support in . . . "

Daily Affirmation to Connect with Archeia Charity
"I am loved, lovable, worthy, and wonderful."

Crystal Allies
"Heart of God Within" pink andara, rose quartz, ruby

Plant Allies
Buttercup, harebell, mariposa lily

Invite In Archeia Charity for . . .

Tolerance; strengthening romantic relationships; reclaiming Love; prioritizing self-love and self-care practices; expanding the heart; compassion; and drawing in the ideal lovers, partnerships, and friendships.

Chapter 9

ARCHEIA CLARITY
"I AM ready to free my mind"

Empowering the Sacred Masculine

As we learn to open our hearts and begin loving ourselves fully, what's in opposition to this rises to the surface for us to acknowledge, heal, and transform. Such inner wounds emerge to empower the feminine and masculine aspects of our being.

In our Universe, the Sun represents the heart of the Sacred Masculine, whereas Mother Earth represents the heart of the Divine Feminine. While the feminine gives us a perception and experience of our instinctual senses, the masculine gives the drive and wherewithal to take this knowing and use it as fuel to put action towards living our dreams.

As I was writing this chapter, I was reminded how important it is to connect with the Sun and Earth each day by simply going outside and consciously breathing in sunlight. By doing this, we begin to empower our yin and yang facets, allowing them to marry within us. For it's not just the Divine Feminine that's rising, but the masculine, too.

In our current age, the ascent of the feminine often appears at the expense of the masculine. Given the misogynistic leanings of so much in our society, feminism has taken to vilifying not just the misogynist but the masculine in general.

Before connecting with the Archeiai to understand the greater Truth underlying this misguided wave, I was swept up in the tide of its bias. But then, I had my two sons—my two Suns! Both taught me (as they still do) to appreciate the masculine in a new light, and to love, as Archeia Clarity would say, my Christ Self. Again, this teaching reiterates that to enjoy a happy life, we must honour the sacredness of both the male and female energies within and without us, and to embody balance, we only need to lean into the other's medicine.

Embrace Your Divinity

In this chapter, Archeia Clarity helps us specifically reveal and reconcile the masculine wounds we're carrying, which exist mainly within our belief systems and mental perceptions. In her words:

> Your personal power is not derived from an outside source. If you believe your power belongs to someone else, then they will hold dominion over you. Know the kingdom of Heaven lives within you. Not externally, but now, within your very breath. You are both Goddess and God in form. Reclaim all that you are by illuminating all that you are. Begin by embracing your Divinity, and be the Christed Self you came here to be. This is your calling card. Trust your instincts. Trust your Light.

Note: The root meaning of the Greek word for "Christ", *christos*, taken out of a religious context, comes from the word "crystal". As we embody all that we are, our vibrational being transforms from a carbon, third-dimensional (3D) state to a crystalline, fifth-dimensional (5D) diamond state. We literally become a human diamond! In the process, we can feel more sensitive to the energies of others and see beyond any illusionary facades they may wear.

Trust Your Instincts

Despite Mother Earth becoming a fourth-dimensional (4D) planet in 2012 (as part of her ascent into New Earth), there are many souls living on her that are still attached to the material 3D world. Within the 3D matrix, much of the misuse and abuse of masculine energy still resides. Connected with this are control agendas and fear-based, illusory remnants leftover from the Piscean Age.

Although the patriarchal mind control tactics are falling away as we transition into the feminine flow of the Aquarian Age, they are still playing out in our governments, the pharmaceutical and food industries, politics, and in the media. For example, many TV programmes are purposely created to promote a certain way of thinking.

Coupled with this is the global increase in technology. Our nervous systems and auric fields are bombarded with more electromagnetic stress in just one day than our ancestors experienced in a year, and before that, a lifetime. If we haven't learned to hone our sensitivity, we can feel off-kilter because of these frequencies and allow them to influence our thinking, and, if left unresolved, to unconsciously direct our beliefs and behaviours. Archeia Clarity is here to open our eyes, while giving us practical ways to manage the times we're living in.

My ex-fiancé often talked about the control agendas and conspiracy theories within the 3D world. Ever the empath, I felt the density of these things, too, but while I wasn't ignorant or fearful, I simply didn't want to empower them through lengthy discussions. As our relationship became more toxic, I saw the presence of a lower-level entity looking through his eyes. This being wasn't him; it had only attached to him. Although all beings in Creation serve a purpose, as we've touched on earlier, **what we choose to focus on becomes part of our vibration**. This includes the TV programmes and movies we watch, what we listen to, and who we communicate with. Whatever the vibe, we can absorb it if we're not in alignment.

As much as I loved my ex and respected what he was interested in, the more he focused his gaze within the 3D matrix, the more the separation between us grew. Like Archeia Clarity, I'm all for illuminating Truth, but this was a lesson for me to stay centred, for the more I joined in with the conspiracy conversations, the more my energy plummeted. While we're all Christed beings, we're equally human, and therefore susceptible to limiting patriarchal influences that would otherwise prefer us hypnotized by fear, hype, and drama.

Keep Lit in Appreciation

One of the best ways to keep your energy field free of unwanted attachments, while honouring the Christ within you and others, is to practice appreciation. Even amidst difficult times in life, there's always something to be thankful for. As we acknowledge our blessings, problems soon ease into solutions and our path clears.

Below is an adaptation of Magic Nine for Sleep Divine from my book *Unicorn Rising*. Archeia Clarity nudged me to include this, as it creates an impenetrable barrier of Light that bounces off 3D nonsense! When enjoyed as a daily practice, it'll positively transform the relationship you have with the world, with your significant other, and with yourself. Plus, you'll have the best night's sleep ever!

Part I releases the events, energies, and interactions of your day and can be enhanced by using the Mirror Technique detailed in Chapter 16 (page 281). Part II focuses on appreciating your blessings in order to draw more of them to you.

Magic Nine for Sleep Divine

Part I

It's important to wind down before sleep by detaching from everything that has filled your day. This removes the weight of the world from you and takes unwanted attachments out of your auric field, preventing concerns from trickling into your slumber.

The best way of preparing for this is to immerse your feet in cold water! Feet are often overlooked in self-care, despite being the part of us that experiences the most pressure. They contain over 7,000 nerve endings, which, when stimulated with cold water, can help our body to flush out the toxins and energetic frequencies accumulated during the day. This practice is especially cleansing if you're feeling mentally or emotionally disorientated, and is a must during puberty, menstruation, and menopause. Immerse your feet or hold them under the cold tap for 15 seconds while affirming:

"I surrender all beings, events, energies, and interactions of my day, giving everything to Source now [exhale deeply to release all energetic attachments and imprints]. Thank you. And so it is."

Part II

Feeling fresh from the inside out, get into bed and enjoy the cherry on the top, the Magic Nine! This life-altering form of appreciation will wrap you in pure Source Love. It's divided into three sections:

◊   First, list aloud three general things you appreciated about your day.

◊   Second, list aloud three things you appreciate about another person. This could be your significant other, or a family member, friend, pet, your angels, or guides. If your beloved is physically with you, look at them when you say, "I appreciate . . . " Tell them what you love and value about them, or what they did or didn't do during the day that you appreciated. As everyone is a reflection of you, by expressing unconditional love to another, unconditional love will shine back to you.

◊   Lastly, list aloud three things you appreciate about yourself. This may be the hardest of all, for often our biggest mental hurdle is believing we are worthy. While this is illusionary, feeling unworthy can be real to many. By illuminating what you appreciate about yourself (for example, consciously acknowledging your qualities and feeling good about all you've accomplished in your day), you'll bolster your self-worth and enjoy crystal clarity.

Rise Like an Angel

◊   "My Magic Nine for today is . . . "

I ask my young sons, Rowan and Eden, to tell me their Magic Three every night. This condensed form of appreciation consists of asking them before bed what are three things that made them smile during the day. Since we began this evening ritual, both boys have gone to sleep smiling, hearts wide open, and eager for an "even better and more magical tomorrow!" If you have children in your life, share with them the Magic Three, and watch how they—and everyone around them—glows!

Brighten Your Self-Talk

While the Magic Nine promotes mental clarity in the evening and as you sleep, you can brighten your self-talk during your day by deciding to make appreciation your default setting, for **as you empower your mind, you empower your life**.

The following phrases are a selection of those I found myself saying while writing this chapter. As I'm sure you'll experience after attuning to Archeia Clarity, her sunny Light can't help but positively uplift your mind and mood! Please adapt these phrases so they feel perfect for you, while creating new ones. Say them either in the moment you're feeling them, or write, paint, or consciously imprint them into your space.

Sunnier Self-Talk

Anything is possible.

Everything always works out for me.

Everyone is doing their best.

I appreciate feeling so good.

I am so blessed. I am proud of myself.

I can change anything in my world.

I can do this! I deserve this.

I have time for this. I love my life.

Rise Like an Angel

◊ "I choose to change my inner dialogue by acknowledging and saying to myself what feels . . . "

Notice Recurring Thoughts

Give yourself a week of bringing the last two practices into your day-to-day life. If, after this time you still feel yourself snagged in loops of negative thinking—whether you feel these thoughts are coming from you or projected by another—employ mindfulness by noticing the thoughts that are replaying.

Scientists have now found that just eight weeks of a regular mindfulness practice not only changes the way we think for the better but transforms our stress response, too, helping us be more proactive about prioritizing our mental health.

In general, everyone has around five thoughts, concerns, or judgements that repeatedly swirl around in their mind. While it can be frustrating to hear these habitually sticky and all-consuming mental opinions, we can break the cycle of rumination by noticing when we're lost in them. This takes practice, but mindfulness meditation can help. Plus, this means of meditation supports us to partner with the clarity of the Sacred Masculine to dissolve limiting beliefs—which often stem from patriarchal inner wounds—and regain our power. In practice, this means we intentionally bring our mind back to the present moment each time we feel ourselves hooked on a thought, and in this way, strengthen our focus and will.

Use the following Mindfulness Meditation, and afterwards, as you go about your day, notice when one of your familiar thoughts begins to play. Catch it before you move into its story, for this is when it's at its weakest. Rejoice that you've noticed the thought, and just laugh while saying to yourself, *There's that thought again!* Breathe in deeply and breathe out deeply, as you bring your Awareness back into the moment.

As you notice your thoughts, instead of being lost in them, your mind will open and you'll naturally sync with the loving, truthful, higher mind of your inner being. Remember: Your inner being has no interest in any narrow sets of fear-based worries, judgements, fantasies, or concerns, which tend to make up the lyrics that mentally loop. Your inner being lives solely in the moment, facing the forward direction of your future, dreams, possibilities, and potential.

Mindfulness Meditation

◊ Sitting upright in a comfortable, quiet space, rest your hands on your lap, and close your eyes. Focus on the inward and outward flow of your breath. Do nothing else, just stay with your breath as it moves in . . . and flows out. Invite Archeia Clarity to be with you, sensing her envelop you in bright golden Light as she steps in.

◊ After a few minutes of relaxed breathing, notice where your mind is. Is it swept up in a story of the past, future-tripping in a concern, or judging something happening in your environment right now? Just notice, without adding any extra commentary.

◊ The tendency to attach to thoughts is a habit you can release. As each thought appears, observe it, and then let it pass by as you return to the breath. Breathe in Clarity . . . breathe out Clarity. Repeat this for the next few minutes. Keep drawing yourself out of mental loops by witnessing what's emerging and then choosing to gently focus back on your breath. Close the meditation by thanking Archeia Clarity and journal your insights.

Rise Like an Angel

◊ "The five thoughts, concerns, or judgements that often loop in my mind are . . . "

◊ "When these begin to play, I'll notice them and release them with my breath. Being deliberate in my thinking helps me be deliberate in my vibration. As I enlighten my self-talk, I empower myself."

Archeia Clarity Revealed

Archeia Clarity, whose name is derived from the Latin word *claritas*, meaning "brightness", serves on the Yellow and Gold Rays of Illumination, Beauty, and Wisdom with her counterpart, Archangel Jophiel. Together, they represent the angel of the Sun (and Great Central Sun), and as such, they bring forth the qualities of the Sacred Masculine to Earth.

In recent years, angel books and oracle card decks have portrayed Archangel Jophiel as feminine in form. Interestingly, Archangel Haniel, who, together with his twin, Archeia Radiant, represents the angel of the Moon and brings the qualities of the Divine Feminine to Earth, has also been portrayed as feminine in form.

I believe there is a grace to this, for unlike other Archeiai, Clarity and Radiant carry a gravitas more akin to the masculine vibration of the Archangels. Their energy acts as a robust base for the lissome flexibility of Jophiel and Haniel to move from.

This perceived manifestation of vibrational "gender fluidity" parallels the shifts taking place on our planet as many reshape the way they see and identify with gender. As prefaced in Chapter 2, many awakened souls have a knowing of being a Priest, Priestess, or Presti in other lifetimes. I believe that those who no longer wish to assign to a specific gender have either been a Presti or are reshaping their consciousness to embody this path.

Essentially, angels are genderless beings, yet they recognize there are many paths of Ascension available to us. As such, angels can manifest as female, male, or a unified blend of both expressions so that they can relate to everyone.

Archeia Clarity, whose other names include "Lady Clarity", "Christine", "Christophina", and "Lucida", has healing influence over the crown chakra. This is symbolized in her depiction, with the double lotus emerging from her crown. The central lotus of bright yellow denotes Clarity's Light, while the electric-blue threads that form the second lotus represent the lithe presence of Jophiel. When I was channeling Clarity to receive her imagery, she also manifested with an eagle around her crown. Any time that we connect with eagles (or birds of prey, in general), we're also connecting with Clarity's presence, for they are intimately linked.

Archeia Clarity helps us remember who we are beyond our physical perspective and belief systems. She helps us access the higher mind of Source to unveil Truth underlying political, societal, familial, and cosmic agendas, and gifts us with ways to regain our personal power. Clarity is the best angel to work with for increasing determination, concentration, and mental acuity.

To merge with the percipience of Archeia Clarity, please enjoy attuning to her after first reading "How to Prepare for Attunements" in Chapter 2, page 50.

Archeia Clarity Attunement

Feeling centred, sense yourself held in a column of glowing, golden yellow Light. Breathe this Source Ray in and out. Allow the Light to fill every part of you, including your aura and wings, and then see it connect through you to the centre of the Earth and the centre of the Sun. Feel your guardian angels standing on either side of you, radiating their Love, which further expands your Light. When you're ready to invite in Archeia Clarity, affirm aloud:

"Loving Archeia Clarity, angel of Illumination, Beauty, and Wisdom, and master of the Yellow and Gold Rays, may you now attune me to your vibration and consciousness, so that I am forever linked with you and may channel your energy. Help me see myself in the highest of Light. Connect my mental body to Source to enjoy greater mental clarity and access Creator's higher mind. For I realize that I'm not apart from God, nor a part of God; I am God. He is me, and I am him. She is me, and I am her. I am All. Thank you. And so it is."

Breathe in the radiance of Clarity . . . and beam it out on your exhale. Feel yourself merge and become as One now. Ask Clarity what the highest and best guidance is for you at this time, and if there's anything you can support her with.

As you continue to attune to Archeia Clarity, you can also channel her healing Light. If there's a part of your body you'd like to heal, bring your hands to that area now or rest your hands on your crown (the chakra that Clarity influences most). Sense golden yellow Light soaking into your skull and brain and fortifying the rest of your spine and nervous system. Know this intelligent ray is resetting your neural pathways to sync with your highest vision for how you want to look, be, and do your life. Breathe in Clarity . . . breathe out Clarity . . . to integrate the healing frequencies.

Archeia Clarity guides you to trust your instincts in the situations that are unfolding in your life. She shares to notice the signs, symbols, and synchronicities that are indicating the best direction to take. Your path (and purpose) is never fixed, they evolve as you evolve. Trust your hunches, trust your choices; you are the Path!

As the energy begins to wane, intend the attunement to be complete. Thank your guardian angels and Archeia Clarity, before opening your eyes and drinking some water to ground yourself.

Rise Like an Angel

◊ "Attuning to the wisdom of Archeia Clarity felt like . . . "

◊ "The highest vision for how I am ready to think, feel, move, and do looks like . . . "

◊ "The steps I'll take with Archeia Clarity to bring this into being are . . . "

Daily Affirmation to Connect with Archeia Clarity
"Resting is my new doing."

Crystal Allies
Natural citrine, solaris andara, yellow phenakite

Plant Allies
Ash, fig flower, lemon flower

Invite In Archeia Clarity for . . .
Shamanic practices; sacred masculine healing; reclaiming personal power; mental concentration, focus, and memory; detaching from political, societal, and familial agendas; determination; and amplifying inner knowing.

Chapter 10

ARCHEIA MERCY
"I AM ready to free my body"

Honour Your Sacredness

As we empower our mind with practices that align us with Source perspective, so too can we empower our body and revel in its Divine perfection. As Archeia Mercy guides as we enter her realm:

Everything in the Universe is a manifestation of Love, including you, Dear One. Cherish and honour your sacredness.

While the masculine way to ascend is to use practices such as mindfulness to observe feelings in the moment, the feminine way is to go into feelings and unearth their root through practices such as alchemy, art, dance, movement, and sound. In this chapter, Archeia Mercy, angel of Soul Ascension, invites you to merge both ways to begin a balanced love affair with your physical body.

Loving Your Body

Despite working intimately with the Archeiai for 15 years, some days I still struggle to love my body. Despite appreciating its physicality, I can look in a mirror and wish it looked differently. After navigating bulimia, chronic dis-ease, self-harm, and sexual abuse, my body has certainly experienced a lot in life! Yet, no matter what my body has or hasn't done for me, it is uniquely beautiful and worthy of my adoration.

Through partnering with Archeia Mercy, I've realized that our bodies aren't cages for our consciousness; rather, they are the means for experiencing the fullness of all we are. Often, we blame or shame our bodies and ignore how they speak to us through our feelings. By taking the time to listen to our emotions in the moment, and being willing to move into them, we can gracefully flow from disliking to liking, and eventually, to loving ourselves. To assist with this process, Archeia Mercy has gifted the Love Your Body ritual, outlined a little farther down, on page 176.

From my experience, if you allow yourself to lean into rather than against any resistance this sensory journey may bring up, you'll feel as if Source is stroking your skin, for, of course, Source is doing just that! Although this ritual takes up most of this chapter, it's worth your time to enjoy it. On days when I'm not feeling so great about my body (or in need of comfort or grounding), I'll begin the steps in the shower and then continue to self-appreciate afterwards, as I apply moisturizer, imagining as I do that rose-gold Light is sinking into my skin. Oh, beautiful soul, try this. It's heavenly!

Mirror Alchemy Session

To create a loving foundation for you to gain the most from the ritual, let's do more angel alchemy! You'll need your journal for this, as well as access to a full-length mirror.

◊　Before looking in the mirror, feel into the parts of your body you admire the most and the parts you criticize the most. How you feel about the you that's reflected to the world is rooted in your beliefs. These may parallel any actual opinions of others or what you think they believe about you. Nevertheless, it's only what you choose to empower that shapes the personal relationship you have with your body.

◊　Face yourself naked in the mirror. As you look at your reflection, what messages play in your mind? Don't try to change them or be enticed by their stories; just observe and listen. Do these thoughts, feelings, and/ or beliefs feel approving or disapproving or do they feel neutral?

◊ In your journal, list the parts of your body you love the most and the aspects you dislike the most. Beside each, note how these parts positively serve you now or have served you in the past. Take time to appreciate and be as loving as you can about your body, then repeat this exercise after the Love Your Body ritual and compare your notes. You may be surprised by the results!

As I look at my body, transformed by three rounds of pregnancy, delivery, and breastfeeding, I admire it as a work of living art. It has moved and grooved in every which way to grow the miracles it cradled and now is adorned with coloured stripes, a sign of a job well done! I invite you to look at your body as if looking at art. Appreciate the colours, curves, patterns, and textures that comprise you! Loving yourself as living art blasts the heart wide open and paves the way for accepting yourself as the miracle you are.

More Tips for Success

As you perform the ritual, aim to keep your hands on your body, allowing them to gently caress each part of you as guided. If you feel uncomfortable at any time, consciously embrace the feelings and sensations that arise. Lean into them, and ask them to share their underlying Truth in order to purposely uproot their core.

Invariably, their core will stem from a limiting belief, so try on that belief. Does it still fit you, or is it worn out and ready for recycling? Often, the limiting beliefs (and their emotional charge) we adopt from those we love the most are the stickiest to strip away because we value and trust their opinions, but if their views no longer match our own, then it's time to reclaim our power by realigning with the perspective of our inner being. So unplug from the cords, roots, and webs of beliefs that are old and limiting. Let them come up in order to come out of you to be recycled.

It's best to do the ritual while bathing (as a second option, while showering), as being in the water element will help you engage your physicality, while at the same time softening any sharp emotional edges. Lastly, create a sacred space around yourself, as you did for the Love Yourself ritual, and dedicate at least 30 minutes for enjoying the bliss…

Love Your Body Ritual

Take a few minutes to relax and come into the present moment. Place your hands over the bathwater (or shower head) and say aloud:

"Loving Archeia Mercy, may you now channel your rose-gold Love through me and into this water, so I may come into my inherent frequency of Divine Sacredness. Thank you for helping me love and honour my body and transforming any harsh words, feelings, or acts I've directed towards myself. I step into appreciating and accepting myself fully. Thank you. And so it is." Breathe in rose-gold Love . . . and breathe it out. Let any discomfort ease into Mercy's kind embrace.

◊   Begin to touch your body, imagining Source is stroking and adoring you. Bring your hands to rest on your feet. Appreciate your toes and the soles of your feet, which help you stay rooted to Mother Earth and help you journey through life. Feel into the many adventures your feet may have taken you on, then bring up your hands to your ankles. Your ankles provide balance, flexibility, and the foundation to stand tall in your world. Energetically, ankles can bear the weight of guilt, so breathe in Love

. . . and breathe out guilt. Pour Love into your feet and ankles.

◊ Move your hands up to your calves. Appreciate the tissues, muscles and cells that support your lower legs. Your calves help you walk, run, jump, and move through life. They support you to move forward with confidence. Without them, many of the physical activities you enjoy wouldn't be possible. Pour Love into your calves . . . and then move upward to your knees, which support you to forever ebb and flow in rhythm with Creation. Energetically, knees can bear the weight of ego, fear, pride, and stress, so breathe in Love . . . and breathe out stress. Pour Love into your knees.

◊ Draw your hands over your beautiful thighs. Adore their shape, strength, and endurance. No matter how you'd like your thighs to look or feel, appreciate them as part of your sacred Self. Often, the energy of self-punishment can be stored in our legs, so breathe in Love . . . and breathe out criticism. Thank your legs, and pour Love into them.

◊ Caress your pelvis, hips, and bum, and appreciate how these parts help you rest, maintain balance, and move in joyful expression of all you are. Pour Love into these areas . . . and then stroke your genitals, thanking your reproductive organs for gifting life, pleasure, and sacred sexuality. If you have children, thank your body for in part forming these wee masters and then rejoice in the bliss of being a creative, sensual being. Often, the energy of repression and shame can be stored in the female vagina and womb (or male penis and testes), so breathe in Love . . . and breathe out disgrace. Thank your genitals, and pour Love into them.

◊ Gently stroke your stomach, allowing it to rest naturally. Appreciate the shape and feel of your stomach and all that it processes and assimilates on your behalf, then pour Love into your tummy. Feel into your organs. Love your liver for detoxifying the old for the new, love your kidneys for filtering anger and resentment, love your intestines for absorbing all that supports you, and love your colon for letting go of past energies. Pour Love into these organs . . . and then into all your tissues, systems, glands, and cells. Thank them for maintaining your health and providing a network for your Awareness to experience physical life. Appreciate and pour Love into your blood, bones, and DNA, for holding your ancestral wisdom and constantly helping you rebirth your reality.

◊ Rest your hands on your heart, and feel into all your heart provides, both physically and energetically. Since the moment of your birth, your heart has never stopped beating in rhythmic union with Mother Earth. Revel in its genius, and appreciate its capacity for helping you experience giving and receiving Love, and for guiding you to know and live your Truth. Pour Love into your heart . . . and then into your ribcage and lungs. Thank your lungs for pumping your breath and circulating it on your behalf. Love your lungs and thymus gland for supporting your immunity and helping you experience Source's Love.

◊ Gently cup your neck, and feel into your throat and voice. Appreciate the gift of expressing your Truth, your songs, and saying "I love you" to those you hold most dear. Pour Love into your throat and neck . . . then focus on your fingertips, touching each finger with your thumb. These polar tips of your body, so rich in nerve endings, gift the sense of touch. Appreciate all the things you

love to touch and the sensations they bring to you
. . . then rejoice in your hands for all you've created
with them. Pour Love into your hands for helping you
craft, write, pray, heal, and feel.

◊ Begin to stroke up and down your arms, admiring and
adoring their shape and texture. Contemplate every
person you've hugged and who has hugged you . . .
thank your arms for helping you reach, dance, climb,
and build. Pour Love into your arms, shoulders, and
back . . . then, thank your spine and your inherent
Kundalini energy, which connects you to Source and
gives you the experience of your Infinity. From your
back, caress your face . . . your unique, beautiful face.
Adore your face as Source does. Touch your lips, and
appreciate them for the ability to speak and kiss. Pour
Love into them, as well as into your teeth, tongue,
and nose. Thank these parts of you for their gifts of
expression, taste, and smell, reliving the favourite
sensations you've experienced so far in your life.

◊ Still caressing your face, pour Love into your smile for
its ability to communicate without speaking and then
rejoice in your laugh for the joy it brings. Place your
hands over your eyes, giving Love to the windows of
your soul, which help you witness so much beauty in
life. . . and then recount all your favourite sights. Then,
recount all your favourite sounds, as you draw your
hands over your ears. Whether you love the sound of
the wind through trees, the laughter of loved ones, or
hearing "I love you" from your beloved, appreciate your
ears, and pour Love into them.

◊ Lastly, bring your hands to rest on your head, feeling
into the skull, brain, and glands for maintaining a
Source connection. Pour Love into your beautiful mind

for its ability to think, imagine, envision, and dream, appreciating how, along with your heart, it brings everything that's important to you into being . . . then pour Love into your intellect, wisdom, and knowing.

◊ Now move your hands over your entire body, feeling your curves and textures—be like Love stroking a body of Love. Open to the sheer magnificence that is your physical Self, for you are a miracle of Creation. Although you are One with all life, you are wholly unique, a gift to be celebrated not chastised.

◊ Breathe in the rose-gold Love once more . . . and then breathe it out. Smile as your whole body smiles, too. Sense all your cells rebirthed with renewed vitality, and appreciate that the more you love your body, the sooner it heals and returns to its natural state of wellbeing. If there's a part of you ready to be soothed, rest your hands on that area and let Love flow in. Let yourself receive until the energy begins to wane. Thank Archeia Mercy, then gently exit the bath (or shower), and as the water circulates back into the world, affirm that it's purified and blessed.

Rise Like an Angel

◊ "This sensory landscape helped me feel better about my body and . . . "

◊ "I'll continue honouring and loving my body daily by . . . "

Archeia Mercy Revealed

Archeia Mercy, whose name is derived from the Old French word *mercit*, meaning "kindness", serves on the Copper and Magenta Rays of Acceptance, Rebirth, and Soul Ascension with her counterpart, Archangel Azrael. The Copper Ray can manifest from deep metallic brown to a light peach in colour and helps bring the un-manifest into physical being. The Magenta Ray acts in a similar way, but specifically helps us know what our soul's calling is, and how to express it with ease in our lifetime. When both rays blend, they form a goddess-like hue of rose-gold.

As Archeia Mercy guides, **we all possess varying depths of the Source Rays within our DNA and akashic blueprint, and we express the rays that are a match to our soul's calling**.

For example, if your consciousness is intrinsically connected with the Magenta Ray, you'll have a passionate leaning towards helping others discover their soul's path and purpose. You may also be drawn to Celtic- and Elemental-based spirituality, remembering lifetimes in Avalon (now Glastonbury) with Merlin, the Knights Templar, and Mary Magdalene, and having a connection with the star systems of Pleiades and Arcturus. However, as we advance our Awareness as one collective tribe, we can attune to more rays within Source's rainbow buffet and anchor these frequencies into Earth.

Archeia Mercy has a healing influence over the soul star, throat, heart, and base chakras. Other names for Archeia Mercy include "Lady Mercy" and "Magdalena".

In her depiction, Mercy steps out of the womb-like Black Ray, where all of life births from. She is illuminated with a golden MerKaBa above her head. This symbol reminds us to adore our soul and Spirit as much as our body, for we are multi-dimensional, multi-talented beings. In Hebrew, MerKaBa translates to light (Mer), spirit (Ka), and body (Ba). This star tetrahedron represents the sacred geometric shape of the field of light that exists around our body, aka our "light body".

Roses adorn Mercy's dress, to symbolize the deep connection she shares with Mary Magdalene, the Ascended Master who epitomizes the essence of Divine Feminine consciousness. In her physical life, Archeia Mercy was an ethereal guide to Mary of Bethany (aka, Mary Magdalene). She helped her stand up for her beliefs and encourage her soulmate, Jesus, to share his wisdom and follow his calling of empowering humanity. Mary of Bethany was given the name "Magdalene" once she ascended, because this word relates to the feminine form of "mar", meaning "master" in Aramaic. As such, Mercy helps empower our inner Magdalene, or as she has referred to it in recent years, adapting the vibration of the word towards the feminine, our "Magdalena Self".

Interestingly, Mary Magdalene wasn't a prostitute, as has been suggested in texts, yet this story represents the collective story of persecution and suppression of feminine power over the last 2,000-plus years. Mary and Mercy are among a host of heavenly beings that are currently helping rebirth humanity by supporting us to rebirth ourselves first.

Archeia Mercy inspires us to champion our inner Magdalene to reveal all her glory and then unify with our Christed Self. She understands the importance of balancing all we are if we are to rebirth ourselves and our life in alignment with our soul's calling. Mercy teaches that through change we grow, and as such, change cannot be resisted. Her quality of humanity helps us live in greater ease and union with the forward momentum of our soul. Mercy specializes in helping us heal karmic wrongdoings we've inflicted on ourselves and that we feel we have projected onto others, so we can keep evolving. She also helps us reframe inner wounds relating to feminine suppression and self-sabotage, for her essence is compassion in action.

In her own words, Archeia Mercy shares:

What is it in life you feel you cannot accomplish? What have others said that you cannot become? Are you ready to prove them wrong? Let go of all feelings and attachments of suppression in your personal and collective story. Believe in your ability to reshape your world, for nothing can shackle you when you choose to live in Love.

To feel the fullest expression of Archeia Mercy, please enjoy attuning to her after first reading "How to Prepare for Attunements" in Chapter 2, page 50.

Archeia Mercy Attunement

Feeling centred, sense yourself held in a column of sparkling rose-gold Light. Breathe this Source Ray in and out. Allow it to fill every part of you, including your aura and wings, and then see it connect through you to the centre of the Earth and the centre of the Sun. Feel your guardian angels standing on either side of you, radiating their Love, which further expands your Light. When you're ready to invite in Archeia Mercy, affirm aloud:

"Loving Archeia Mercy, angel of Acceptance, Rebirth, and Soul Ascension, and master of the Copper and Magenta Rays, may you now attune me to your vibration and consciousness, so that I am forever linked with you and can channel your energy for the benefit of all concerned. Thank you for filling me with your limitless compassion and kindness. As I integrate my soul and Spirit gifts into my everyday reality and service, I recognize you're right there beside me. Thank you. And so it is."

Breathe in Mercy . . . and breathe out Mercy . . . as you allow your sister angel to blend her Light with yours. Ask Archeia Mercy what the highest and best guidance is for you at this time, and if there's anything you can support her with.

As you continue to attune to Archeia Mercy, you can also channel her healing Light. Instead of laying your hands on a part of your body to heal, invite Archeia Mercy to dance with you! Experience the joy of getting into your body and moving any way that inspires you in the moment. Sense yourself ablaze in Mercy's Rose-Gold Fire as its positive vibes bless the space you're in. Breathe in Joy . . . breathe out Joy. Envision everyone on Earth dancing with you as they fall back in Love with their bodies, and so it is.

As the energy begins to wane, stop dancing, and intend the attunement to be complete. Thank your guardian angels and Archeia Mercy, before opening your eyes. Drink some water to ground yourself.

Rise Like an Angel

- ◊ "Attuning to the Bliss of Archeia Mercy and dancing with her felt like . . . "
- ◊ "I'll continue to invite in Archeia Mercy to support me with . . . "

Daily Affirmation to Connect with Archeia Mercy

"Body, you are a living, thriving genius, a work of art and a temple to adore. Thank you for everything you do. I love you. I honour you."

Crystal Allies

Cuprite, garnet, magenta Vesuvianite

Plant Allies

Freesia, hawthorn, rose

Invite In Archeia Mercy for . . .

Self-acceptance, selfless service, rebirthing, kindness, integrating your soul's gifts and wisdom into your everyday reality, grief, counselling and accepting (and loving) all aspects of yourself.

Chapter 11

ARCHEIA FREEDOM
"I AM ready to free my sexuality"

Empowering the Divine Feminine

We don't have to martyr ourselves to ascend. Living in conscious union with all we are can be easeful and graceful if we're willing to embrace the process of letting go of all that isn't serving our joy.

So far, we've explored many ways to do just this, but as Archeia Freedom steps forward, we're being asked to release the unhealed aspects of our inner Goddess.

We all possess this feminine power no matter which gender we identify with. In general, our inner Goddess has six facets: *girl, mother, grandmother, Magdalena, priestess,* and *warrior*. As we acknowledge these internal archetypes, we can feel into whether they are in an empowered state or in a wounded state (that is, vibrating from Source's perspective of wholeness or entrenched in a limiting story of scarcity).

For example, if our *girl* aspect is vibrating from a wounded state, our outlook is based upon fear and shame, versus feeling naturally carefree and curious. We only need to look at how we relate to ourselves, others, and the world at large to understand how the wounded feminine is manifesting in our life. Although Archeia Freedom is one of the best angelic allies to lean on to liberate all aspects of our worthy, wild goddess, she has chosen for this chapter to focus on our inner Magdalena with the aim of empowering our sexuality and sensuality, so we may live in greater pleasure, play, and innocence.

Archeia Freedom Revealed

Archeia Freedom, whose name is derived from the Old Norse word *freyja*, meaning "to love", serves on the Orange Ray of Acceptance, Compassion, and Understanding with her counterpart, Archangel Jeremiel. She also works with the alchemical fire of the Electric Blue Ray. Despite being the lesser-known angel of compassion and forgiveness, Freedom and Jeremiel's healing qualities are integral to the Ascension of humanity and Mother Earth. Other names for Archeia Freedom include "Lady Freedom" and "Annacea".

Archeia Freedom is less "embodied" in her depiction (compared to the other Archeiai) in order to remind us that freedom can't be encapsulated; it must remain open. This sense of being is mirrored in her image, along with Divine Light emanating from her throat and hands. When you consciously connect with Freedom, don't be surprised if you *feel* her more than see her. When we first met in 2007, I remember leaning my head into her ethereal presence, as if she was gently drawing me towards what would be her heart. Beautiful soul, I could have easily slept in her embrace for hours! Freedom's energy may be subtle, but oh, is it comforting!

Archeia Freedom is the caretaker of the heart. She shines Love on what we may feel is dirty or dark within us. Working together as one angel, both Freedom and Jeremiel help us acknowledge the positive lessons in painful experiences, so we can alight from the heavy 3D perception of duality (for example, judging things as "good/bad" or "light/dark").

If you've ever called upon Jeremiel for emotional healing, know that Freedom first liberates any knotted pain before handing it over to Jeremiel for transmuting back into Love. Freedom also helps us voice our feelings, so that we can contour them with ease. No matter if we're feeling stuck, lost, hurt, or in fear, Freedom can guide us to acknowledge our feelings in the moment. Then, as we choose how we want to feel instead, she pairs with Jeremiel to help us landscape our life accordingly. As ever, this reflects how the yin and yang aspects of an angel work in unison, as each aspect blends into the other's medicine to facilitate balance.

Adopt Archeia Freedom's comforting yet empowering Light by looking for the underlying blessings in situations and choosing to not settle for discomfort or bondage in any area of your life, especially when flow and freedom are your birth right.

In Freedom's words:

> Freedom does not exist outside you. Freedom will not be yours once you've achieved something external, like increasing your bank balance or finding your soulmate, for freedom is always yours! You will experience the exhilaration of this when you realize that you are enough. You do not need to add or subtract anything to yourself to be free. Simply recognize and express your worth to integrate this Truth.

Archeia Freedom and the Navel Chakra

Archeia Freedom has a healing influence over our throat, heart, navel, and sacral chakras. However, it's her focus on helping our 5D navel centre (situated within and slightly under our belly button) that's most fundamental.

At the start of 2020, we, as a collective tribe, embarked on a new seven-year Ascension cycle, in which the central theme is integration (that is, coming together in Divine tantra with all we are). By actively stimulating and working with our navel centre, we can transform the subconscious stories of separation and repression we've stored there since the fall of Golden Atlantis and help balance our inner feminine and masculine energy. At the height of the Golden Age of Atlantis, our navel chakra was fully open and glowed a deep orange. To this day, our navel contains within it the akashic blueprints of all earthly Golden Ages, and as such, holds the seeds for growing New Earth.

If you've consciously connected with this chakra before, you'll be aware that it pulses to the warming rhythm of Oneness—Love—that weaves us all together. Although Archeiai Hope and Strength (along with their counterparts, Archangels Gabriel and Ariel, respectively) are inspiring us to become aware of our 5D (and beyond) navel center, it's Freedom and Jeremiel who are assisting its vibration to fully anchor within us.

When the navel is fully activated, we can enjoy—as we have experienced in other Golden Ages—joyful symbiosis with all life. From the stars to the land to one another, we see Source in all and vibrate Love through our hearts, minds, and beings without conditioned resistance getting in the way. Moreover, as this centre switches on, our greatest potential is realized, creating light ripples through time and space for those Sleeping Beauties who are ready to arise from.

Liberate Your Habits

Be prepared that when you connect with Archeia Freedom, she'll challenge you to look at your life and acknowledge where you're actively numbing your potential, for one of her roles is to support us to end cycles of habitual anesthetization. This will be different for everyone, and the list may include over-consumption of alcohol, drugs, debt, entertainment, food, shopping, social media and work, to name but a few of the addictive behaviours that dull our vibe and distract us from living our potential.

Although we may reach for these things because we feel they make us happy, or because they provide "instant relief", when we experience discomfort we must ask ourselves, *Do these things actually make me happy? If so, for how long? If not, do they come at the price of me suffering long-term?* The fleeting pleasure we may experience through the ways we numb ourselves is deceiving. For example, we may reach for a cookie as a "sweet fix", but end up eating the whole packet and, consequently, feel sick for hours later. This act may also go against a deeper desire to shed excess weight.

And so, we must become aware of our habitual patterns and the underlying impulses, triggers, and urges that fire when we're feeling uncomfortable, because they inevitably stimulate us to act in limiting or numbing ways. Through Awareness, we can release these tendencies and, instead, make better choices that serve our deeper happiness and wellbeing.

To put this into context, Freedom often nudges me to unplug from binge-watching Netflix because she knows that I "comfort-watch" when I'm feeling overwhelmed. Her affectionate prodding reminds me that my vibration festers when I choose to lie on the sofa all day, reiterating the teaching, "What we watch, we become." For example, if I'm bingeing on a drama series, I must be prepared for my life to get dramatic!

Archeia Freedom also inspires us to look at our closest relationships, for often our loved ones reflect the more subtle, habitual patterns that are equally restricting our potential. For example, my mum is retired. She could be enjoying a relaxing life, but instead, she feels the need to "keep herself (overly) busy" as a measure of her worth. This pattern was echoed in my gran, who within the first minute of being in her company would proclaim all the things she'd done that day. Often, I find myself doing the same now that I'm a "busy" mum of three. It's bullsh*t, beautiful soul! It's simply conditioned, societal nonsense that steals our joy and keeps us entrenched in a loop of guilt and shame.

I love author Brené Brown's definition of shame:

> Shame is the intensely painful feeling or experience of believing that we are flawed and, therefore, unworthy of love and belonging—something we've experienced, done, or failed to do makes us unworthy of connection . . . Shame says, "I am bad," whereas guilt says, "I did something bad."

From an angelic perspective, **the vibration of shame is the opposite of knowing how inherently free and loved we are, and guilt is acting from that space**. As ever, what liberates us from these dense loops is going to their core to feel and transform them. As we heal ourselves, we heal each generation (past and present) that follows, for wounding is passed through ancestral lines until someone is ready to feel it, heal it, and let it go.

 *Rise Like an Angel*

◊ "My go-to comforts are . . . "

◊ "Do I reach for these as a quick "joy" fix, or are these serving my overall wellbeing?"

◊ "Do these things come at the price of me suffering long-term by sabotaging a bigger desire for change? If so, am I ready to release these limiting ways?"

191

Consciously Release

Archeia Freedom is all for grounding our spirituality, so we can be all we are in our everyday lives. She inspires us to be deliberate in releasing our limiting habits through using the outward flow of our physical body. For example, during the time when I was healing the trauma of sexual abuse, I had a tooth removed. Instinctively, I found myself packing into that redundant tooth everything I was ready to surrender, from shame and guilt to fear and pain. As the tooth was extracted, I felt the cords, roots, and webs of the trauma I'd been carrying for years lift out of me, especially from my navel and sacral chakras. It was a profound experience!

But you don't have to go to the extremes of having teeth removed to consciously release! You can simply release on your exhale, or when you pee or poo. Just affirm what you are energetically liberating as you physically expel it from your body, kindly asking Mother Earth to transmute these energies back into life-renewing *prana*. If you menstruate, you can work with your outward flow, too.

As I was writing this chapter, my soul sis'star and fellow spiritual teacher Kahreela shared with me that if we bleed on or around the full moon, we're inherently healing inner masculine wounds and releasing them to support the Sacred Masculine to collectively rise. Conversely, if we bleed on or around the new moon, we're healing and empowering the Divine Feminine within and without. Between these moon phases, we bleed to bring balance to ourselves and to the collective.

Shame Be Gone

Archeia Freedom would now like to lead you through a ceremony to liberate the energy of shame from your consciousness. Why? Because carrying shame is one of the main reasons we subconsciously distract and numb ourselves from feeling the fullness of our potential and sexual Truth.

This healing space will liberate any toxic vibes in your intimate relationships, thereby supporting you to receive deeper levels of pleasure in your life. The ceremony will also help activate your 5D (and beyond) navel chakra, which is where we can hold onto the energies of shame and self-sabotage.

Although your inner being and angels never judge who you allow into your heart or into your bed, if you're experiencing any type of toxicity, you're within your sovereign right to walk away. In the past, I've continued to stay with abusive partners because I believed we shared a soul contract together, and while energetic contracts are valid and have their place in our spiritual growth, if we're suffering, we can withdraw ourselves from them.

Remember: Your inner being never wants you to suffer or be a rescue centre for wounded souls. It's not your job to change, fix, or parent your romantic partner, no matter what the ego believes and buys into. From my experience, I've learnt that when we enable another person, it only disables their own empowerment. We can support and we can inspire, but we can't do their shadow work for them.

The following ceremony will give you an experience of your true sexual power, so don't be surprised if you feel turned on! Embrace your sexiness. Give yourself permission to feel sexy in your own skin—not for anyone else's pleasure . . . just yours! Likewise, if you want to climax, just let yourself flow into orgasm as you embody your magnetic Magdalena Light.

Part of collapsing old patriarchal energies is letting go of believing that sex and self-pleasure is shameful, wrong, dirty, or should be censored in "polite" conversation. Ever the rebel, I say f*ck that!

Enjoying our body as a sacred, sensual temple, and more so, by being fully present with ourselves and our pleasure is a gift of physical life! Moreover, Archeia Freedom guides us to masturbate whenever we feel like it, and to do so without low-vibe porn for stimulus or external aids, unless our intuition guides otherwise.

Touching ourselves skin on skin, as we connect our heart and mind with our genitals and then breathing ourselves into orgasm, can heal, empower, and free our being on all levels. This is also a method of "Divine alchemy" and "Divine manifesting" that we enjoyed in previous Golden Ages in Atlantis and ancient Egypt.

To best prepare for the ceremony, first ask yourself: *Where is shame showing up in my life, beliefs, and habits? Where do I feel trapped? Where is shame rooted in my body? How am I distracting or numbing myself from receiving real multi-dimensional pleasure?* Listen. Don't go into any stories. Just bring all to your Awareness. Get ready to hand over all to Archeia Freedom to transmute into her alchemical fires.

Empower Your Sexuality

◊ Create a comfortable space where you can lie naked. Light candles, bring in orange, ylang ylang, and other essential oils that awaken your lower chakras; have yellow roses nearby; play tantric music; sip cacao; or do whatever else turns you on, as you come into sacred ceremony with yourself. Lay your hands on your heart, and affirm yourself as One with Source. Breathe in Love . . . and breathe out Love. Start to stroke your skin as you connect your heart, mind, and body with your soul, Spirit, and Light. Activate and align every part of you with Source.

◊ Lay your hands on your pelvis, and breathe into your inherent sexual energy. Sense it as a swirling ball of Light that's becoming blended with Diamond, Silver, and Gold Fire. With every in-breath, increase the intensity. Then, bring your empowered sexual Light into your earth star chakra, below your feet. Affirm yourself as One with the heart of Mother Earth, breathing up her energy, and allowing her Love to move into your body on your exhale.

◊ From your earth star chakra, now bring up your sexual Light into your root chakra, sensing it swirling and pulsating here. Breathe into this feeling, and stroke your root chakra (physically for women, this chakra corresponds to the cervix, and for men, the perineum).

◊ Bring up your sexual Light into your sacral chakra, again sensing it swirl and pulse as you stroke this part of yourself (for women, this corresponds to the clitoris, and for men, just above the penis).

◊ Bring up your sexual Light into your navel chakra, as you stroke this part of yourself. Breathe into this area and feel the pulsating swirl of energy (for women, imagine your womb fully illuminated, and for men, envision all women are aligned in their sexual power).

◊ Continue to bring up your sexual Light through each of your chakras, from your navel into your solar plexus and then heart, higher heart, throat, third eye, crown, and into the chakras above your head: the causal, soul star (6 inches above your head), and stellar gateway (18 inches above your head). Keep stroking your body throughout, letting your hands flow over, in, and around you.

◊ As you bring your sexual Light into your stellar gateway, imagine that it pours out of this sacred bridge towards Source and then showers its radiance around your body, brightening your aura, before flowing back down into your earth star chakra, below your feet, then up again. Breathe in, and allow your sexual Light to move up through each of your chakras and then see it shower and recirculate on your exhale. Breathe in Bliss, travelling up . . . and breathe out Bliss, travelling down and recirculating.

◊ Softly focus on your navel. Know yourself as a sexual sovereign being. Invite in your guardian angels to be with you, and Archeia Freedom, breathing in and out her Orange Ray and Electric Blue Fire. Sense these alchemical flames infusing the sexual energy in your navel.

◊ Feeling Archeia Freedom with you, decree aloud:

"I now release the vibrations, people, and circumstances of abuse and toxicity from my field, and call back my Power from them and all my sexual and romantic relationships [breathe in . . . breathe out]. I now release the attachments,

cords, roots, and webs concerning unworthiness, repression, shame, guilt, disconnection, and cruelty on all levels of being, time, space, and dimensions [breathe in . . . breathe out]. I now cancel all vows, contracts, and binds that have kept me numb and distracted from allowing the fullness of my sexual brilliance to be realized, expressed, and enjoyed [breathe in . . . breathe out]. As these energies dissolve into Source for transmutation now, I affirm: 'I am the Light within the dark. I am the solution to every problem. I choose to live life through a new lens, for I am free, I am Freedom.' [breathe in . . . breathe out]"

Stay in sacred ceremony with yourself for as long as you wish. If you'd like to orgasm, flow with this. This form of release and integration of your sexual energy will help seal the decree you've made. When you're ready to close the space, thank all concerned, and gently ground yourself by drinking some water.

Rise Like an Angel

◊ "This ceremony was significant for me because . . . "

◊ "I'll open to receiving more pleasure in my life by . . . and recite Archeia Freedom's mantra often: I am free—free to be me."

Please enjoy merging fully with Archeia Freedom to continue the transformation, after first reading "How to Prepare for Attunements" in Chapter 2, page 50.

Archeia Freedom Attunement

Feeling centred, sense yourself held in a column of swirling orange and electric-blue Light. Breathe in this Source Ray . . . in and out. Let it fill every part of you, including your aura and wings, and then see it connect through you to the centre of the Earth and the centre of the Sun. Feel your guardian angels standing on either side of you, radiating their Love, which further expands your Light. When you're ready to invite in Archeia Freedom, affirm aloud:

"Loving Archeia Freedom, angel of Acceptance, Compassion, and Understanding, and master of the Orange Ray, may you now attune me to your vibration and consciousness, so that I am forever linked with you and may channel your energy. Help me release any destructive emotional patterns and behaviours that have been holding me back from embodying the beauty and bliss of all that I AM. Thank you for inspiring me to adopt a compassionate, merciful attitude in all my relationships, especially the one I have with myself. Thank you. And so it is."

Breathe in Freedom . . . and breathe out Freedom, as you merge with this angel. Ask Archeia Freedom what the highest and best guidance is for you at this time, and if there's anything you can support her with.

As you continue to attune to Archeia Freedom, you can also channel her healing Light. If there's a part of your body you'd like to heal, bring your hands to that area now, or rest your hands on your navel (the chakra that Freedom influences the most). Sense deep orange Light flow into you and come into your heart to use the Universal Code of Communication. Affirm aloud, "Universal Code of Communication, I now send Liberty to all of humanity." Breathe in and feel the essence of Liberty (to love openly) fill you, and as you exhale, beam it out through your heart. Envision everyone on Earth smiling. Create a world where suppression and shame no longer exist. See everyone being themselves and living wholeheartedly in joy, and so it is.

As the energy begins to wane, intend the attunement to be complete. Thank your guardian angels and Archeia Freedom before opening your eyes and drinking some water to ground yourself.

Rise Like an Angel

◊ "Attuning to the vastness of Archeia Freedom felt like . . . "

◊ "Her guidance for me at this time is . . . "

◊ "I'll continue to invite in Archeia Freedom to co-create . . . "

Daily Affirmation to Connect with Archeia Freedom
"I am free—free to be me."

Crystal Allies
Carnelian, Lemurian amber andara, tangerine aura quartz

Plant Allies
Easter lily, hibiscus, walnut

Invite In Archeia Freedom for . . .
Shame, respect, repression, reconnecting sexually and sensually, pleasure, life review, joy, forgiveness, and healing inner feminine wounds and stories.

Chapter 12

ARCHEIA HARMONY
"I AM ready to balance"

Staying Centred

Partnering with Archeia Harmony has been life-changing for me! As a single mama of highly sensitive children, catering to their needs while attending to my own and those of my students, I'm often asked how I maintain work–life balance. My reply—with music and lots of chocolate! Because, let's face it, balance is an unpredictable journey, not a destination—one we shape in the moment, whether amid the plain-sailing waters of life or in storms of challenges, changes, and emotional triggers. To escort us through all weathers and provide everyday tools we can use in the moment comes Archeia Harmony.

Archeia Harmony Revealed

Archeia Harmony, whose name is derived from the Latin word *harmonia*, meaning "joining", serves on the Pale Blue Ray of Co-Operation and Unity with her counterpart, Archangel Raguel. Raguel tends to express himself more in relationship to the earth element and manifests as a pale blue Light, while Harmony, being linked to the qualities of air and sound, manifests more as sparkling pearlescent Light. Her presence can be likened to a soft breeze, and her joy in harmonizing relationships with such playfulness is reminiscent of the romance faeries. Other names for Archeia Harmony include "Lady Harmony" and "Laceiatta".

With her healing influence over our heart and throat, Archeia Harmony is the best angel to work with when we feel disconnected or blocked from speaking our heart's Truth. In this instance, she'll often guide to breathe in her Light as we visualize our heart and throat connected and in communication with each another.

As one supreme angel, Harmony and Raguel help rebalance frayed relationships, making them more conscious and intentional. For example, while Raguel is practical in his approach, such as bringing a couple into the same space after an argument has taken place, Harmony is more subtle, such as delivering sweet whispers of compromise and compassion into the Awareness of the arguing pair.

Both teach us that the ego always wants to be "right" and the other person to be "wrong". By coming into our heart, we can choose kindness over righteousness and relate to all with respect and integrity. If we feel we can't do this, Harmony especially guides us to accept the situation and wait for the fires to subside before making relationship decisions. Once centred, it's easier to know whether there's value in the growth that's been offered to rebirth the connection or if it's the end of this relationship and to gracefully walk away.

In her depiction, Archeia Harmony's white diaphanous wings are barely there, for her vibration is so light. She holds a sacred violin and plays with her eyes closed, for she is wholly merged with the sound current of our Multiverse, adjusting the harmonics of our world, and our neighbouring universes.

Harmony shares:

Sound has a purity to soothe, uplift, and inspire, facilitating meaningful expression and connection. Listen to music when you feel out of sorts, for sound joins your energy back together. She also shares that angels hear our vibration—our being literally sings to them! This is how angels know when we're feeling "off" and disconnected from Source.

Invite in Archeia Harmony to help you tune in to the rhythm and frequency of your inner being and bring balance to your significant relationships. If you're experiencing relationship conflict, you can ask Archeia Harmony to play her angelic music over you both to soften emotional edges and create a common ground to build upon. The best relationship we can have with others is one where we maintain our centre without losing our sense of freedom, our sense of Self.

Using Sound to Contour Emotion

Everything is energy vibrating at different frequencies. Like a musical scale, emotions exist on a sliding scale. All emotions are valid and worth our attention, but dense feelings, such as anger, lower our vibration, while lighter emotions, such as appreciation, raise our vibration.

When we feel anger (at one end of the scale) we can come to accept how we're feeling and use many of the techniques already explored in the book to bring up our vibration to the other end of the scale, and with it, enjoy the exhilaration of feeling better.

One of the quickest, and often most enjoyable, ways to bring ourselves back into balance is to use sound. You'll know what I mean when, for example, you're feeling annoyed, hear your favourite song, and by the end of the track—whether just listening to, singing along, or grooving to the music—you're back to You! Not only are you feeling better as you've spiralled up the emotional scale but that thing that annoyed you has, no doubt, faded from view.

There are many ways to work with the unseen magic of music. In the following meditation, Archeia Harmony invites you to explore sound in the form of the Solfeggio Frequencies. These frequencies are musical tones (expressed in hertz) that penetrate the conscious and subconscious mind to stimulate deep change.

Although these tones date back to ancient history, chanted by Gregorian Monks and featuring in Indian Sanskrit mantras, there is recent research supporting the positive effects of these frequencies on the human body. A 2019 research paper aiming to demonstrate how music therapy can heal the mind, body, and spirit concluded that the Solfeggio Frequencies are effective in healing physical, generational, and emotional trauma in our DNA.

The Solfeggio Frequencies

The Solfeggio Frequencies include, but are not limited to, six main tones. These comprise:

◊ 396 Hz (hertz)—Sound at this frequency inspires a sense of upliftment and security. It's also helpful for removing subconscious fears and worries, dissolving feelings of guilt, and

203

disrupting the limiting beliefs that are otherwise preventing personal success.

◊ 432 Hz—Before the mid-20th century, many musical instruments were made for 432 Hz tuning. Interestingly, this calming frequency resonates with the sound of Earth's heartbeat (known as the Schumann Resonance) and has been seen to slow down human heart rate and promote restful sleep and feelings of peace.

◊ 528 Hz—A 2018 Japanese study found that listening to just five minutes of music set at 528 Hz significantly reduced stress in the endocrine (hormone) system and autonomic nervous system. Also known as the "love frequency", this miracle tone has been seen to repair DNA, increase cell life, and bring people into their heart to experience the Love they are.

◊ 639 Hz—If Archeia Harmony's overall vibration could be set at a singular frequency it would be at 639 Hz, for this sound current helps balance emotions and inspire greater communication, positivity, and understanding within relationships.

◊ 741 Hz—Similarly, if Archeia Purity could relate to a singular Solfeggio tone it would be 741 Hz, for this music helps us to physically and spiritually detox. This musical sound is also helpful when struggling to simplify life and adopt a healthier lifestyle.

◊ 852 Hz—Music set to this frequency promotes the awakening and development of our intuitive and instinctual senses. It's said to help replace negative thoughts and associated loops of rumination with inspired ways to live our fullest potential.

While we can listen to the uplifting effects of the Solfeggio sounds at any time, we can be more intentional and devotional with the music by bringing them into meditation with our angels. For example, by inviting in Archeia Harmony, the positive effect of the music will be enhanced. Harmony can also help us contour our inner emotional landscape and its outward effect on our relationships.

Tuning In to Harmony

To prepare for this meditation, select one of the following miracle tones that calls to you, choosing from:

174 Hz—Pain relief
285 Hz—Tissue repair
396 Hz—Liberation from fear and guilt
417 Hz—New beginnings
432 Hz—Sleep
528 Hz—Healing (especially DNA repair) and Love
639 Hz—Relationship harmony
741 Hz—Physical and spiritual detox
852 Hz—Awakening intuition
963 Hz—Connection with Spirit

Although you can purchase recordings of each frequency, for this journey, you may wish to type in your chosen tone to the Search feature on YouTube, then pick a recording of the tone you like best and settle in for this balancing meditation.

◊   Sitting in a comfortable place where you won't be disturbed, press "play" on your chosen frequency. Look to Archeia Harmony's picture. Open your heart to her and to the loving consciousness of the music that's playing. Close your eyes and sense Harmony's sparkling Blue Ray enveloping you. Breathe in this renewing sky-blue light deeply . . . and breathe it out. Allow yourself to fully relax as you imagine floating up to sit on a cloud near Harmony. The cushioning embrace of this cloud fits you perfectly.

◊   Physically lay your hands over your heart, or over another area you're guided to. Invite Archeia Harmony to channel her healing energy through you and into you for the next 20 minutes. Relax and enjoy how her Light and the Light of the sound current naturally restores balance in your body now. Any time your mind wanders, recite the following affirmations or others your inner being shares:

"I am in sync with the natural rhythm of the Universe."

"I am allowed to create balance in my life."

*"It is safe for me to feel peaceful
and create peaceful emotions."*

*"It is easy for me to tune in to Source and feel the
sweetness of alignment."*

*"No matter what happens on the outside,
my inside world is at peace."*

"I am at One with Creation, and all is well."

Before ending the meditation, ask aloud:

*"Loving Archeia Harmony, how can I create and maintain
more balance in my life? What in-the-moment ways and
tools can you suggest?"*

Chat with Harmony for as long as you wish and then give her thanks as you float back down into your body. Sense Harmony step out of your energy field and drink some water to ground yourself.

Rise Like an Angel

◊ "After listening to the Solfeggio Frequency . . . I feel . . . "

◊ "Archeia Harmony suggested . . . to bring more balance into my life. I will adopt these tools and ways as well as . . ."

Just as it can be joyful to sample new foods, you may wish to sample new sounds other than these frequencies to bring more uplifting vibes into your life, such as devotional mantra music, binaural beats, bilateral music, and ASMR sounds. ASMR stands for Autonomic Sensory Meridian Response and is a tingling sensation that many experience when exposed to a form of auditory (and visual) stimuli, like gentle whispering or the sound of wind blowing through trees. Throughout writing this chapter, I repeatedly played one of my favorite ASMR sounds: a crackling campfire! The cosy, comfort afforded by this sound is the perfect partner for all that Harmony is sharing with us. And so, try on some new beats and discover what can escort you up the emotional scale.

Breaking Ancestral Codes

As music is made up of notes and nuances, so too are we made up of the musical melodies of our foremothers and -fathers. Their vibrational beat lives within us, influencing how we speak, act, and do, especially within our relationships. As we become more intentional about the music we listen to, we can become more deliberate about resolving inherited conditioning.

For the last few years, as a collective Light, the Archeiai have been helping me and those who attend my events to heal our ancestral patterns, with the aim of liberating our generational timelines and providing a better now and future reality for all to enjoy. The angels often say it is up to us to break generational trauma.

This path is by no means for the fainthearted, but essentially, **we came here to be the "the odd one out in our family"— the rebel**

change-maker and New Earth pioneer with the inner tools to code-break the root hurts in our line! If you feel truth-bumps in reading that statement, know that before incarnating you decided what you were going to resolve within your family's DNA to bring freedom into your past, parallel, and future genealogy. You may be the only one in your family who feels spiritually awake, but take heart in knowing that never have there been so many angels helping to rouse the "Sleeping Beauties" who are ready to awaken!

Global awakening is happening, but it takes time. We can further the process by unbecoming the emerging conditioned programming and karmic stories within our close family, and within humanity's collective consciousness, for we are all connected. Unbecoming everything that's less than Love while staying compassionate in all our relationships is the key.

Angelic Breathwork

Along with Archangel Raphael, Archeia Harmony excels at helping us breathe better! Breathwork practice is as ancient as working with sound and has undergone a revival in recent years and ongoing research is showing the health benefits of breathing consciously.

Being a Kundalini yoga teacher, I'm no stranger to the effectiveness of breathwork (known as *pranayama* in Sanskrit), but there's always more to discover. Recently, I've been attending breathwork classes held by my Australian sis'star and qualified practitioner Siobhan. I love the way Siobhan holds space, and the music she picks to accompany each class is gold!

Every time we gather, Siobhan guides us to split our inhale in two. We first inhale (through our nose) into our belly (as our belly expands outwards), and then inhale into our chest. This is swiftly followed by a deep exhale through our mouth as our tummy draws back towards our spine. We continue breathing in this way for 45 minutes, during which time everyone has their own experience of release, healing, expansion, or wherever their breath leads.

While writing this chapter, and immersed in the energy of Archeia Harmony, the breathwork form began to change for me. Instead of dividing my inhale into two parts, I stretched it over three specific segments: first breathing through my nose and down into my solar plexus, then up into my heart, and then my throat—the three chakras Harmony influences the most—followed by a deep sigh out through my mouth. These subtle differences elevated the breathwork to a whole new level! Breathing intentionally into these chakras created a sense of space within me that I'd never experienced practising other forms of *pranayama*.

I've since coupled this form of angelic breathwork with music set to 639 hertz and focused (along with my angels) on healing the limiting ancestral patterns that are adversely affecting me and my relationships. The results have been so extraordinary that I'd like to invite you to try this, too. You can easily adapt this technique just by changing your initial focus and welcoming in the best angels (and music) that are a match to this intention.

Ancestral Breathwork Healing

For this breathwork session, you'll be connecting with three generations of your family: 14 ancestors—your parents, grandparents, and great-grandparents. (If you were connecting with 33 generations, you'd be linking with 7 billion ancestors, illustrating how profound the ripples of change can be when you intentionally empower your timeline!) For this practice, Archeiai Patience and Virtue will join in alongside Harmony and Archangel Metatron to reveal the patterns, behaviours, and hand-me-down beliefs that are ready to be transformed, creating greater space and balance within your life.

◊   Play your favourite recording of music set to 639 hertz. Follow The Four Essential Steps (see page 75), and in the fourth step, invite in your guardian angels— Archeiai Patience, Virtue, and Harmony—to be with you, alongside Archangel Metatron. Ask the angels to hold the space of this session high and to bring about the greatest resolve for your family line.

◊   Knowing yourself to be enclosed in a bubble of angelic Light now, imagine your parents are standing to the side of you. Which side do they stand on? How do you feel in their company? Ask your grandparents to come and stand behind your parents. How does the dynamic change as they step in? Experience what you're feeling. Now invite your great-grandparents to come and stand behind your grandparents, noticing again how you feel in their company. Thank all 14 of your ancestors for being here. Honour them and the lives they led or are leading.

◊   Imagine scales in front of you. Are the scales tipping to your mother's side or your father's side, or are they balanced? What healing needs to take place to balance the scales? Observe what's coming to you intuitively and instinctively. Bring all of this into the next part of the session where you're going to be breathing intentionally for your family. Know as you do this that the angels will be transmuting everything that's released, including any burdens you're carrying for your family, plus any root cords, webs, and attachments that relate to feeling out of balance within yourself.

◊   Begin the angelic breathwork now. Split your inhale into three equal parts: First breathe through your nose as you focus your attention into your solar plexus, then into your heart, and lastly into your throat. Sigh out through your mouth to release the breath. Continue breathing in this way for 20 minutes (or for as long as you're guided to do so). Flow at the pace and depth that feels right for you, keeping your face soft and your body relaxed. Imagine your ancestors are breathing in the same way, helping to bring the scales into balance.

◊ As you continue the breathwork, invite in all of your ancestors, both earthly and cosmic. Welcome in your angelic ancestors, your star nation families and councils of Light, and all the facets of your Multi-Dimensional Self. Breathe for all and with all, as the releasing, resolving, and restoring of codes, patterns, and frequencies take place within your family tree.

◊ As you come to the end of the session, sense a blanket of green unconditional Love comforting and drawing everyone close. Its warmth, like liquid Light, melts into you, cleansing and liberating the cellular and vibrational DNA of all your connections. Give thanks to your ancestors and angels as you reverse the Four Essential Steps, and drink some water to ground yourself.

Rise Like an Angel

◊ "To breathe for my ancestors and offer up all relationships for the highest healing and resolve felt like . . . "

◊ "The limiting patterns that tend to repeat in my intimate relationships are . . . "

◊ "In terms of my ancestors, these patterns also belong to or are linked with . . . "

◊ "Am I ready to unbecome the identity of these patterns, surrendering them up for the highest resolve and believing that I can enjoy balanced, happy relationships without the influences of the past getting in the way? If not, what would it take for me to believe that this is possible?"

◊ "To help me in this process, I'll add angelic breathwork to my bag of tricks, along with . . ."

To fully attune to the musical genius of Archeia Harmony, first read "How to Prepare for Attunements" in Chapter 2 (page 50), and enjoy the following attunement:

Archeia Harmony Attunement

Feeling centred, sense yourself held in a column of sparkling white and pale blue Light. Breathe this Source Ray in and out. Allow it to fill every part of you, including your aura and wings, and then see it connect through you to the centre of the Earth and the centre of the Sun. Feel your guardian angels standing on either side of you, radiating their Love, which further expands your Light. When you're ready to invite in Archeia Harmony, affirm aloud:

"Loving Archeia Harmony, angel of Co-Operation and Unity and master of the Pale Blue Ray, may you now attune me to your vibration and consciousness, so that I am forever linked with you and may channel your energy. Thank you for showing me that I can move beyond emotional and mental triggers to more deeply love myself and others. Support my heart to speak through my voice so my words and music are filled only with Truth. Thank you for lifting me above judgement into the harmonic bliss of angelic perspective. I love you, dear sister, and appreciate how attuning to you is expanding my vibration more. And so it is."

Breathe in Harmony . . . and breathe out Harmony . . . as you merge with her, and then ask what the highest and best guidance is for you at this time, and if there's anything you can support this angel with.

As you continue to attune to Archeia Harmony, you can also channel her healing Light. If there's a part of your body you'd like to heal, bring your hands to that area now, or rest your hands on your solar plexus, heart, or throat—the chakras that Harmony influences the most. Sense her fresh sparkling Light flowing through your hands and into you, breathing deeply throughout.

Imagine yourself sitting on a white, fluffy cloud that fits you perfectly. Beside you is Archeia Harmony, playing her holy violin. Watch how the notes she plays morph into bubbles of coloured light, before moving through you, popping, and dissolving everything that is less than divine Love. This may tickle, so let yourself laugh! As her music gathers pace, stand up, and begin to dance in sweet harmonic convergence with the music. Dance freely—moving, releasing, expanding in all directions beyond time and space. Breathe in . . . breathe out.

As the energy begins to wane, bring yourself back into your body, and thank your guardian angels and Archeia Harmony. Experience the positive changes that have taken place as you open your eyes and drink some water to ground yourself.

Rise Like an Angel

◊ "Attuning to the music of Archeia Harmony felt like . . . "

◊ "Her guidance for me at this time is . . . "

◊ "I'll imagine Harmony's music as effervescent bubbles within me any time I'm feeling discord and continue to partner with this beautiful angel for . . ."

Daily Affirmation to Connect with Archeia Harmony

_"I am living in joyous co-creation with life,
honouring its diversity and contrast,
while staying centred and balanced."_

Crystal Allies

Brucite, blue lace agate, celestite

Plant Allies

Grapefruit flower, lungwort, vervain

Invite In Archeia Harmony for . . .

Coming into Source Resonance, easing hostility, feeling emotions without being ruled by them, lessening emotional triggers and reactions, mastering the air element, meditation, stress-relief, understanding the restorative nature of music and sound.

Chapter 13

ARCHEIA PATIENCE
"I AM ready to prosper"

The Nature of Manifestation

To consciously bring something into our physical reality, we must realize that "reality" is the spiralling dance of two worlds: *manifested reality*, the world we walk upon, and *vibrational reality*, the world that's always in a state of becoming.

In other words, what we see around us now is the physical result of what we've allowed for in our life and crafted through our desires, yet it isn't the totality of our life.

From the vantage point of Source, our material world is yesterday's news, for our inner being always focuses on the vibrational reality we're creating. The more we understand this, the more we naturally sync with our vibrational reality, making it easier to be deliberate about manifesting what's important to us.

As Archeia Grace prefaced earlier, everything in Creation manifests in Divine flow and order, meaning that everything we ask to come into our life will appear, which has been the case from the moment of our conception. Even your reading of this book is the physical manifestation of a prior non-physical request you made to know these teachings.

Creation never judges what we ask for, but if we feel in receipt of what we've asked for, rather than feeling its lack in our life, everything will emerge with ease in our physical world. Likewise, our degree of trust in our power to manifest is proportional to the speed with which our manifestations move from our vibrational to our physical reality. As we embody this, we see the material evidence accrue, and with it, we develop greater trust that we're the creator of our reality.

The key, whether manifesting small gifts or large dreams, is to have no attachment to how or when things appear, only trust their inevitable emergence.

As we enter her magical domain, Archeia Patience shares:

You are a living sacredness who can be, do, or have anything you desire. Relax, and trust that all that is for you will not go by you. At the start of each day, open your front door, raise your arms to the sky, and intend your heart to be open at the front and back. Then, affirm aloud, "I am the heart of Creation and One with Creator. I possess the potential for ALL life to emerge from me." Now, visualize your needs met and your desires already manifest in your world. Allow your dreams, ideas, and intentions to birth, rather than feeling their absence. Remember, everything blooms in perfect timing.

Aligning to Prosperity

Prosperity truly is everywhere. It is the ability to find, organize, and use the resources we need to fulfil our highest destiny. From an angelic perspective, prosperity ("pro-spirit", as angels call it) has nothing to do with wealth or scarcity and everything to do with knowing and living our Truth. To be prosperous is to stay graceful amid distractions and diversions of life, trusting the underlying Divine order and timing to everything; in other words, accepting we'll receive what we're meant to receive in accordance with our calling.

Most people want to feel prosperous but think that they need to attain something in order to gain it. As with all virtues, we don't need to gain prosperity; we already are prosperous. We simply need to summon its vibration from within, **for prosperity projects from the inside out, rather than being something external or measurable that we need to reach for**.

There are many books about manifesting what we desire by using universal laws, such as the Law of Attraction and the Law of Creation; however, Patience reminds us that our thoughts don't necessarily influence what we receive, as many of these texts proclaim; the Truth is, we receive what we are a match for vibrationally.

There's a section in every Angel Healing® class when we go around the group and everyone shares what they'd like to see show up in their world. If a student says they want to be financially rich, no degree of "thinking rich" or affirming "I am rich" will work until they truly *feel* rich from the inside out. Source (aka, our inner being) can only give us what we wholeheartedly believe and feel we deserve. This is why the Archeiai are so emphatic about us unearthing unworthiness, so that we can transform our feelings and beliefs about money, for example, and align our vibe with our heart's desires.

As I cleared my limiting beliefs about money, which we'll dive into shortly, it became easier for me to embody the teaching that prosperity is an inner state of consciousness. Now, no matter what's physically in the bank, I always feel rich. That's because I'm constantly recognizing and appreciating how richness shows up in my life—from being rich in family, friends, food, and breath to forever saying thank you, which naturally creates the feeling and belief of more prosperity! And the more I feel rich, the more my vibration radiates richness, and in turn, my inner reality creates the physical equivalent in my outer world, as money manifests, opportunities arise, and blessings appear. I'm not attached to the presence or absence of prosperity, nor am I forcing or controlling what comes into my world. Simply, I am just allowing in what I am vibrating. This is the key, beautiful soul, for where allowing flows, magic grows!

Rise Like an Angel

◊ ". . . is the one thing I'd like to see show up in my life."

◊ "What would it take for me to shift my vibration from perceiving the lack of this thing to feeling and believing its presence in my life?"

◊ "What action steps do I need to take?"

Manifesting Money

A big part of embodying prosperity is to give yourself the permission to receive. You may be carrying, as I was, conditioned ideas and beliefs about money. The stickiest one I transformed was "'I want' doesn't get'", which was something my mum said to my sister and me throughout our childhood. Even now, she repeats this to her grandkids, not that they take any notice! What we hear around us growing up, and what is impressed upon us as adults, can easily become the beliefs we empower.

As Archeia Patience inspires, we never need to deny ourselves anything, especially money. True, money doesn't give us value, for we are priceless beings, but the energy of money is linked with self-esteem.

Our relationship with money is really our relationship with our inner being, and it can indicate whether we're allowing the fullness of who we are to blossom or repressing it. Because money is such a conflicting, contradictory area within our consciousness, when we investigate our relationship with it, we can see what blocks or triggers we need to resolve in order to move from "struggling with money" to "befriending money", and how these relate to other areas of our life.

Uprooting Financial Beliefs

To align with an overflow of financial prosperity, please journal the completion of the following statements. Note: Don't give too much thought to the statements. Let yourself be in a state of open-hearted curiosity, and bring any feelings that emerge into the Money Alchemy Session that follows this section.

◊ My relationship with money can be summed up in one word as . . .

◊ As a child, my parents and peers said money was . . .

◊ Growing up, I believed money was . . .

◊ My current beliefs concerning money are . . .

◊ Out of 10 (0 = feeling disconnected from money and 10 = feeling aligned with money), my current relationship with money is . . .

◊ Being wholly aligned to financial overflow would make me feel . . . and would enable . . .

◊ I am deserving of financial prosperity—yes or no?

◊ I am ready to release beliefs, stories, and vibrations around unworthiness, rejection, lack, and abandonment—yes or no?

◊ I am ready to understand that my needs are (and will always be) met—yes or no?

◊ I am ready to feel supported and allow Source to sync with my intention and attention of being financially prosperous—yes or no?

◊ I am willing to make friends with money for the rest of my life—yes or no?

◊ I am ready to awaken, activate, and align to the vibration of prosperity in myself and my life—yes or no?

Money Alchemy Session

This alchemy session will transform any beliefs you've just uprooted, while dissolving any past, parallel, or future life patterns of poverty you may also be carrying. When you're ready, let's begin:

◊ Sit with your palms facing up on your lap. Close your eyes, and come into a meditative state. Invite Archeia Patience to be with you, seeing yourself completely enveloped in her Rainbow Ray. Breathe in the prism of alchemical fires within this ray . . . and as you exhale, connect their LoveLight through you to the centre of Mother Earth and to the centre of the Sun. Feel yourself merge with your inner being, as you step into your sovereign choice to transform the identification, story, root, cords, and webs of financial lack from all timelines, space, and dimensions now.

◊ Invite the energy of poverty to arise in your body. Where is your focus drawn to? Expand the sensation you're feeling (for example, if you feel the energy of poverty rooted in your base chakra, breathe into your base chakra).

◊ Ask aloud, "What is the energy of poverty giving me?" Listen. Feel. Acknowledge everything. Perhaps what arises is the comfort of having an excuse to not shine fully in your life because you feel don't have the resources to do so. Or maybe you like the drama or attention of reiterating lack. Whatever emerges, try not to judge; just feel into the reply, offering up the sensations and stories into the Rainbow Ray.

◊ As you arrive at the root of the issue, which invariably will be connected to a lack of worthiness or disconnection from Source, ask aloud, "Am I willing to exchange the belief and story of prosperity shortage?" If yes, move into how this feels, as the alchemy continues to transform the energy of poverty into new *prana* you can use. If not, ask aloud, "What do I need to permit to allow the alchemy to take place?" Give yourself permission to transform the old and limiting for the new and expanding.

◊ Keep breathing into the Rainbow Ray . . . Be real to heal, as you witness what's coming up. Side-step attaching to stories, and instead feel the sensations under the story. Keep expanding the sensations to purify them. Breathe into any knotted feelings, as you allow undigested shadows to lighten.

◊ Feeling Archeia Patience with you, decree aloud:

*"I fully release the attachments, cords, roots,
and webs concerning financial poverty and scarcity
on all levels of time, space, dimension, and being now
[breathe in . . . breathe out].
I cancel all vows, contracts, and binds concerning
keeping myself poor or in shortage, and release the
memories and trauma of hardship, starvation,
and war from all levels of my being now
[breathe in . . . breathe out].
I fully release any need to compare my blessings
to others or be envious of what I perceive they have, for
now I know there's enough for me.
In fact, there's an overflow
[breathe in . . . breathe out].
I affirm, 'It's easy for me to give and receive without
thought of what I'll gain nor lose, for I am the essence
of unconditional prosperity
[breathe in . . . breathe out].'"*

◊ Witness the alchemy, and enjoy the bliss that ensues. Ask for the bliss to be increased 10 times, then 100 times, then 1,000 times! Breathe in Prosperity . . . breathe out Prosperity. As you close the session, thank all concerned and feel the LoveLight sparkling in your eyes as you open them. Drink some water to ground yourself.

Rise Like an Angel

◊ "The biggest takeaway from this alchemy session is . . ."

◊ "Although my inner being is eternally prosperous even when I don't feel this in my physical life, I need only remember that prosperity is a vibration that can be easily switched on and programmed into my consciousness. To consistently vibrate wealth, I'll pin the following mantra on my bathroom wall and recite the words mentally while brushing my teeth: "I awaken, activate, and align to the vibration of prosperity within me and in my life.""

Archeia Patience Revealed

Archeia Patience, whose name is derived from the Latin word *patientia*, meaning "endurance", serves on the Rainbow Ray of Music, Manifestation, and Integration with her counterpart, Archangel Sandalphon. This ray is a more earthly, grounded aspect of the Diamond Ray. It projects a crystalline iridescence, akin to the vibration of unicorns. Other names for Archeia Patience include "Lady Patience" and "Shekinah". Archeia Patience has a healing influence over the auric field, base, and earth star chakras.

In her depiction, Archeia Patience, who acts as a vessel for all earthly Creation to emerge from, is represented as Mother Earth, for both she and Mother Earth are forever pregnant with life, filled with Infinite possibilities and potential! Patience is also adorned with flowers. She has one hand pouring blessings into the world and the other holding a daisy, reminding us to keep our intentions pure and in a state of Innocence as we define what we want to show up in our world. Patience's eyes are closed, as she has unwavering trust that everything manifests in Divine flow. She knows anything can grow in any terrain when we allow the process to enfold in faith.

As I was talking with Archeia Patience in order to write her chapter, she told me that her essence—patience—is "faith in action". That patience is a process of trust, of knowing wholeheartedly that everything comes together in the perfect flow, order, time, space, and composition, just as everything in nature comes together so seamlessly. And as with nature, **patience cannot be achieved through effort only through allowing, for it involves the workings of the heart not the mind**. To be patient, therefore, is to be open without restriction, so that everything that's coming to you will also move through you and continue to bless others. As Archeia Patience shares, *"Manifest from Love, not need, for what you give, you always will receive."*

Therefore, when we feel impatient or annoyed that our manifestations haven't showed up in our life, all we need do is open ourselves—to hold our head and wings high and exude the fullest of all we are, no matter who we are with, where we are, or what we are doing. As we give to life, so too does life give back to us.

As you invite Archeia Patience into your life, don't be surprised if you find yourself (literally) opening your arms wide and coming into greater awe with the world. In this way, Patience is helping you lift your heart energy, and through this state of Awareness to recognize yourself in every wonder you're appreciating, to know yourself as part of an Infinite cycle. This is the dynamic Law of Patience, which this angel inspires us to know, express, and embody.

The Dynamic Law of Patience

Read this spiritual law anytime you're feeling frustrated but are ready to reconnect with the stream of abundance and creativity you inherently are:

"Patience is an open doorway, the balance of giving trust and receiving flow. Nature is always in patience; she never wishes to be summer and winter all at once. Seasons flow in a cycle of trust, blooming in their perfect order and timing. Nature teaches us about patience. Growing plants teaches us about patience. Allowing our children to grow can also teach us about patience. Accepting yourself and your creative potential is the ultimate test of patience."

"To be patient is to love yourself wholly, openly, freely, and abundantly. Knowing that everything you ask for is always given. Everything you feel is always felt. Everything you say is always heard. Trust [flow in] . . . receive [flow out], just like breath; unconditionally effortless. Everything that is important to you is coming to you, for everything is You, beloved One."

Observe the Signs

As you embody the teachings of Archeia Patience, decide on what you're ready to bring into your life and then send your intentions out on your breath. During the minutes, hours, days, and weeks that follow engaging with this form of conscious manifesting, watch for signs that what you asked for is materializing.

Common signs to recognize are repetitive thoughts and feelings to make a certain change or take a course of action. You may also notice reoccurring number patterns, dreams, symbols, books falling off a shelf or opening at particular pages, or songs playing in your reality that carry a meaningful message for you.

For example, in 2011, when I set the intention of teaching Angel Healing® internationally, I kept seeing references to go to Maine in the United States. After a few weeks of seeing and hearing the word "Maine" everywhere, from the internet to conversations with strangers, I asked the angels for one more confirmation. At the time of requesting this, I was sitting on a bus and heard the angels say, Look up, and as I did so, I saw the word "Maine" written on the jacket of the gentleman in front of me! Faithful signs like these, which indicate we're in flow with the emergence of our manifestations, are always present if we allow ourselves to remain open.

Remember, your manifestations will physically come to you when you're ready for them, and not before, so don't worry! Remain patient and in vibration with your thoughts, words, and actions—whatever the match is to your intentions.

For example, reciting a morning affirmation associated with what you want to see show up in your world won't work if you're countering it all day with negative self-talk! So be mindful (and heartful) of your inner and outer conversations, remembering that you're the creator of your reality—there's no outside force orchestrating your life. If you believe there is, you deny your Divinity and accept yourself as separate from Source. This ultimately divides you from your dreams, instead of allowing them to birth with ease as the master manifestor you are!

To fully merge with the earthly wisdom of Archeia Patience, please enjoy attuning to her after first reading "How to Prepare for Attunements" in Chapter 2, page 50.

Archeia Patience Attunement

Feeling centred, sense yourself held in a column of sparkling Rainbow Light. Breathe this Source Ray in and out. Allow it to fill every part of you, including your aura and wings, and then see it connect through you to the centre of the Earth and the centre of the Sun. Feel your guardian angels standing on either side of you, radiating their Love, which further expands your Light. When you're ready to invite in Archeia Patience, affirm aloud:

"Loving Archeia Patience, angel of Music, Manifestation, and Integration and master of the Rainbow Ray, may you now attune me to your vibration and consciousness, so that I am forever linked with you and may channel your energy. Thank you for supporting me to thrive on my path, surrounded always with an aura of gentleness, kindness, and integrity. I trust I am always aligned with Source and have everything needed on an emotional, mental, physical, and spiritual level to joyfully express my highest Truth in this lifetime. Thank you. And so it is."

Breathe in Patience . . . and breathe out Patience . . . as you merge with this Divine angel. Ask Archeia Patience what the highest and best guidance is for you at this time, and if there's anything you can support her with.

As you continue to attune to Archeia Patience, you can also channel her healing Light. If there's a part of your body you'd like to heal, bring your hands to that area now or rest your hands on your base chakra (the area that Patience influences the most). Sense the Rainbow Ray swirling in this chakra and then expanding outward to fill your body and aura with each breath you take. Come into your heart to use the Universal Code of Communication. Affirm aloud, "Universal Code of Communication, I now send prosperity to all of humanity." Breathe in, and allow prosperity to fill you . . . then beam it out on your exhale, seeing everyone on Earth showered with good fortune. Envision everyone fed, sheltered, happy, and wholly connected to their inherent worth. See everyone with their arms open to receive and their hearts open to give. All is smiling. All is blessed. And so it is.

When you feel the energy beginning to wane, intend the attunement to be complete. Thank your guardian angels and Archeia Patience, and drink some water to ground.

Rise Like an Angel

◊ "Attuning to the beauty of Archeia Patience felt like . . ."

◊ "Her guidance for me at this time is . . . "

◊ "I'll continue to invite in Archeia Patience to co-create . . ."

Daily Affirmation to Connect with Archeia Patience
"Within my world there's an overflow of abundant prosperity for all to enjoy."

Crystal Allies
Cinnabar, raspberry garnet, tsavorite

Plant Allies
Baby blue eyes, trillium, white daisy

Invite In Archeia Patience for . . .
Connecting with the magic and manifesting power of Mother Earth, development of the base chakra and auric field, faithfulness, gentleness, prosperity, reassurance, and trusting that you are worthy to receive.

Chapter 14

ARCHEIA SERENITY
"I AM ready to conquer"

Bursting the Fear Bubble

The Roman philosopher Seneca once said, "We suffer more often in imagination that in reality." The stories we can conjure up in our heads often lead us to become paralyzed, as we empower our fears more than our Truth. Help is at hand, in the form of Archeia Serenity, who together with her counterpart, Archangel Cassiel, helps illuminate fear by inspiring us to move through it.

When I became spiritually aware, I believed there was something to fear in the world of Spirit. As my first mentor said, "Where there is Light, there is darkness." Because I trusted this, my belief triggered a need to invite in many forms of protection during hands-on healing, thinking that this was guarding me against something dark. But in my heart, this practice didn't feel right, and I thought: *What am I protecting myself from? The energies I'm channelling aren't dark or to be feared. By embodying their Love and staying heart-centred, surely no protection is needed?*

At this stage of my life, I'd just started meditating with angels. I asked for an angel to come forward to help me better understand "spiritual protection". I expected Archangel Michael to appear, but a lesser-known angel, Archangel Cassiel, came forward. Cassiel shared that he and his twin, Archeia Serenity, acting as one supreme angel, are tasked to help humanity to understand and transcend fear.

When I asked if there was anything to fear in spiritual healing (and in general), their reply was, *Fear itself.* Archeia Serenity then showed me the fears I was carrying: the fear of putting my head underwater, of spiders, and being in the dark. Serenity said: *If you conquer these, you will never feel the need to protect yourself again.* I knew in my heart what she meant, but my mind still questioned it. I asked for more help.

Throughout the month that followed, I felt called to take up swimming lessons and gradually, shed the dread of being in water. I also studied to become a shamanic practitioner and discovered that the fear of putting my head underwater, as well as being in the dark, stemmed from an apprehension of embodying myself fully.

I realized that holding onto these fears was giving me the excuse to not to believe in (and express) my gifts and Light in the world. Similar fears are stored within the collective human subconscious, which drive many people to sabotage their dreams or prevent them from fully loving themselves. Such fears derive from previous Golden Age memories, when our Light was misused and abused. Archeia Serenity guides that the past will not repeat itself as long as we align with our inner being, which is inherently fearless.

Three initiation ceremonies were needed in order for me to become a shamanic practitioner. During each initiation, spiders crawled up my legs or appeared around me. Although this was terrifying the first time around, after the second ceremony, I was guided to learn about spiders and appreciate their medicine in the hope that this would dissolve my anxiousness.

Fears soon began to fade, as I realized how fascinating spiders are, weaving their webs with such elegance and intricacy, happily following their purpose, and living their joy. I also learned that spiders represent fear, in general, and as such, are closely linked with Cassiel and Serenity. In fact, every time a spider appears in our space, it's doing so to prompt us to break free of a fearful thought we're running in that moment or a deeper apprehension we're carrying.

Archeia Serenity guides us to acknowledge our spider friends, and if we're called (when we find them in our space), to place them outside and to do so consciously by affirming the fear we're releasing at the same time as releasing the spider back into nature.

While I was sharing the link between spiders and Serenity during an Angel Healing® course a few years ago, a student (who was sitting opposite me) began to get very anxious. She said that she was petrified of spiders and just hearing about them was making her feel uneasy. In that moment, a spider crawled out from under her feet! Everyone in the group watched in astonishment as this spider nonchalantly walked from her toes over to mine. It was Serenity manifesting herself! We knew it, and we could all feel her. And bless this student, she was less than pleased (!), but it served as a Divine lesson for her, which later, she was very grateful for.

Rise Like an Angel

Please pause and look at Archeia Serenity's picture. Connect with her bright, golden eyes, and invite her to show you the fears you're carrying. Then journal:

◊ "The fears I'm currently carrying are . . . feeling into them, they are giving me . . . "

◊ "Do I avoid enjoying particular experiences, events, people, and places out of fear of something? If so, what am I most afraid of . . . ? What is the worst that can happen . . . ?"

◊ "I choose to learn about these fears to disrupt their attachment within and around me. I now surrender to Archeia Serenity whatever they have been giving me (for example, an excuse not to follow my dreams) in exchange for feeling . . . Thank you, and so it is."

Understanding Fear

When we give light to fear, it no longer seems dark or scary. It loses its grip upon us because we've broken it down through curiosity and understanding. As I lightened the fears I was carrying, the sense of having to protect myself lifted because I realized that there's nothing in the spirit world to be fearful of, only what we can conjure up and then buy into.

During my stint as a medium on the show *Ghost Hunter: Psychic Investigations*, I came face to face with many beings that others feared, yet in every case, these beings just wanted acknowledgement and/or a release of the aspect of them that was attached to the physical plane. Even in the case of the man who had haunted my gran's house as a child, I came to understand his sadness and, together with the angels, we were able to move his energy on.

The key to unlocking fear is understanding that there's no lack of Source in darkness.

Within Source, both light and dark exist. To live in harmony with our inner Source being, we must acknowledge this. True, there are those in Spirit who did horrendous things to themselves and others during their earthly existence, and true, there are those living physically now doing similar things, but we must understand that these souls have lost faith in their Divinity, and so attempt to take it from others.

After undergoing experiences of rape in my past, I came to realize that those who sexually assaulted me were attempting to take my Light. At the time, neither they nor I knew this consciously, but from healing the trauma, I've been able to bring in compassion and to better understand this paradoxical desire. While I'm not condoning crimes or abusive behaviour whatsoever, if we are to ascend past our traumas and fears, we must lean into a perspective of understanding in order to relate to one another with more compassion, more heart, and ultimately, more humanity.

To fully understand fear therefore, we must realize how we relate to what we class as "light" and "dark", and then, with eyes wide open, alchemize the beliefs, conditionings, and judgements—essentially, our fears—accrued through our lifetimes. And as we resolve and transcend our fears, we stop projecting them into the world.

Mastering Fear

While writing this chapter, I saw a paraphrased quote by the writer Mark Twain: "Courage is not the absence of fear, but the mastery of fear." This resonates so deeply with me because no matter how many fears I've transformed, there are always more to burst!

Appreciating that I'm not alone in this, I asked Archeia Serenity to share her guidance for us all. She said:

If you have a desire to take your life beyond what has been before, then fear can still emerge. How you choose to respond to fear, however, is what will dictate your experience. See fear as a blessing, as it manifests only to show you where you have created, or still are creating, limitations for yourself. If you appreciate fear as an indicator of where you are restricting your flow, then fear can be a tool that serves you.

This made sense. We can flow with fear by continuing to break through old beliefs and expand our Awareness, or we can entangle ourselves in fear and drift in an ocean of limitation.

I Am Fearless

Archeia Serenity guides you to pause here and write an "I Am Fearless" list, acknowledging all the instances where you faced fear and came out the other side.

As a forever student of these teachings, I paused here, too, in order to tally my own experiences, and realized that writing this book wouldn't have been possible for me had I not surmounted the personal doubts I was carrying. It's another reminder that when we dare to go beyond self-created limitations, we thrive and, in the process, learn so much about ourselves—plus, being out of our comfort zone is exactly where all the fun and wisdom abides!

And so, beautiful soul, please create your "I Am Fearless" list, reflecting afterwards on all the incredible things you've experienced and built from conquering your fears. Then, dream a little, imagining your life a year from now, as you've continued to master fear by flowing with it.

What has changed mentally, emotionally, physically, and spiritually for you? Remember, who you think you are now is nothing compared with all you can become if you get out of your own way; out of fear, judgement, and limitation. As the poet Maya Angelou astutely said, "We delight in the beauty of the butterfly, but rarely admit the changes it's gone through to achieve that beauty." For as we empower ourselves, we grow.

Rise Like an Angel

◊ "Drawing from my 'I am Fearless' list", the times of victory that are most impactful for me to remember are . . . "

◊ "Seeing fear from a fresh perspective, I am going to enjoy the following activities, experiences, and passions, which I've been avoiding because of fear. These include . . . "

◊ "Imagining my life a year from now, as I've continued to master fear and live life to the *fullest*, what has changed mentally, emotionally, physically, and spiritually for me . . . ? What people have come into my life . . . ? Which places have I visited . . . ? What adventures have tickled me . . . and are yet to come . . . ?"

Unleashing Your Inner Warrior

While any of the alchemical practices already explored will support you to conquer fear, Archeia Serenity inspired me to include a ceremony taken from *The Female Archangels Oracle* deck. For this you will need single sheets of paper, a pen, a white candle, and safe access to a fire.

You may sense a shift in energy as Archangel Cassiel steps in, bringing his masculine balance to soften, transform, and reframe fear as the means to reclaim our personal power.

Unleash Your Inner Warrior

◊   Come standing in a meditative pose. Follow the Four
    Essential Steps (see page 75), and at the fourth step,
    invite in your guardian angels, Archangel Cassiel,
    Archeia Serenity, and the Black Ray, to be with you.
    Breathe in their collective Presence . . . and breathe out
    any concerns.

◊   Imagine below your feet is a huge angelic sword. This is
    your Sword of Power. Begin to slowly pull the sword up
    from the earth until you're holding it above your head.
    Feel its lofty grandeur and how, just holding it, you're
    merging with its strength.

◊   Breathe into your sword, sensing it illuminate . . . as you
    exhale, let out your warrior cry! Be as LOUD as you like,
    for your voice is unleashing your inner confidence and
    ability to surrender all that feels binding.

◊   It is time to release yourself from anyone who has ever
    hurt you, severing traumas, ghosts of the past, and
    anyone you feel has, or is, currently diminishing your
    Light. With your eyes still closed, move your sword
    intentionally around your aura, cutting as you go . . . Go
    with your heart here. Vent. Feel. Scream. Call people out
    for their actions or inaction. Empty yourself fully without
    judging yourself. This means of reclaiming your power
    is also strengthening your boundaries and proclaiming
    to the world what you will and will not accept moving
    forward.

◊   Once this part of the ceremony is finished, place the
    etheric sword back into the earth as you found it,
    knowing that you can use it again any time you feel the
    need to connect with its strength.

◊ Write on the paper everything you've disconnected from and anything else that comes to you in the moment . . . Place this paper into the fire to burn. The past doesn't need to define you, defeat you, destroy you, or deter you any longer. Let what you do with the pain be the gift, as you take your experiences and use them as power to propel you forward.

◊ Rising like the warrior you are, light the candle from the fire to symbolize your rebirth. As you do this, affirm aloud three times, "I have nothing to fear, for I and Source, Source and I, are One." Reverse the Four Essential Steps, thank the angels and ground yourself to close the ceremony.

Rise Like an Angel

◊ "The ceremony helped me know that I can face fear while remaining centred. It also supported me to raise my standards and realize . . . "

Archeia Serenity Revealed

Archeia Serenity, whose name is derived from the Latin word *serenitatem*, meaning "clearness", serves on the Black Ray of Transcendence and Potential with her counterpart, Archangel Cassiel. While Cassiel tends to express the darker hues of the Black Ray, Serenity expresses a softer Light, often manifesting as a pearlescent silver. Other names for Archeia Serenity include "Lady Serenity" and "Kassibella". Archeia Serenity has a healing influence on the crown, solar plexus, and base chakras.

In her depiction, Serenity wanted to reflect how she helps maintain the balance of the Universe. From the hard/soft feel of her dress to the juxtaposition of the black water and white bubbles, to the yin and yang symbol she holds, Serenity epitomizes balance. Although her yin and yang symbol heralds that to grow we need contrast, it's been designed (based on her instruction) with many coloured fractals within, reflecting how nothing is ever just "black and white"; all is simply Source.

Serenity's unwavering peace helps us stay present amid life challenges. She guides us to soften the energies of struggle, resistance, pain, judgement, and hate, which can often arise through calamities, in order to see all sides of situations. If we can keep our heart soft amid the hardest times of our lives—what Serenity terms as "contrast"—we'll transcend seeing life as either "good" or "bad" and live in greater harmony.

All it takes is choosing to release victimhood and the need for drama—to exchange telling the world what's "wrong" with life for appreciating the blessings of everything, because contrast is a gift that highlights the undigested worries, wounds, shadows, and fantasies we're carrying; those we project into the world and play out as subconsciousness beliefs, behaviours, and patterns.

As Serenity shares:

Many look to the sky and see only clouds, yet the Sun forever shines. Some see challenges as opportunities to rise, others that dis-ease is a wake-up call for allowing renewal of health. Creation does not control or direct your perception; that power is yours. To enjoy a more harmonious life, express not what you feel are your limitations; instead, proclaim your capabilities! Tell the world what is working in your life. Voice your blessings to grow more.

Archeia Serenity helps us see beyond self-created limitations and illusions, so that we can come into absolute balance with ourselves and those around us. She does this by highlighting the destructive patterns in our mental and emotional body.

I've seen Angel Healing® students either loving Serenity's empowered influence or deliberately choosing not to work with her or Cassiel! This is because they act like a mirror, reflecting the more uncomfortable

Truths, like our fears and suppressed emotions. Similarly, because Serenity is linked with the water element, unheard emotions easily surface for us to see and bring into Wholeness through her presence. Archeia Serenity also assists Mother Earth in balancing her mental and emotional body by purifying the oceans of fear-based energy. She works closely with Cassiel and the dolphin and dragon realms for this.

Please enjoy attuning fully to the peace of Archeia Serenity, after first reading "How to Prepare for Attunements" in Chapter 2, page 50.

Archeia Serenity Attunement

Feeling centred, sense yourself held in a column of pearlescent silver Light. Breathe this Source Ray in and out. Allow it to fill every part of you, including your aura and wings, and then see it connect through you to the centre of the Earth and the centre of the Sun. Feel your guardian angels standing on either side of you, radiating their Love, which further expands your Light. When you're ready to invite in Archeia Serenity, affirm aloud:

"Loving Archeia Serenity, angel of Transcendence and Potential and master of the Black Ray, may you now attune me to your vibration and consciousness, so that I am forever linked with you and may channel your energy. Help me to embrace all that I AM through staying centred as the calm within all storms, seeing and sensing all through Source perspective. Thank you. And so it is."

Breathe in Serenity . . . and breathe out Serenity . . . as you merge with this Divine angel. Ask Archeia Serenity what the highest and best guidance is for you at this time, and if there's anything you can support her with.

As you continue to attune to Archeia Serenity, you can also channel her healing Light. If there's a part of your body you'd like to heal, bring your hands to that area now, or rest your hands on your base chakra (an area that Serenity influences). Sense pearlescent silver Light flowing through your hands and into your base chakra and then into your pelvis. Experience inner calm as the Light infuses your entire skeletal system, bringing to the surface any underlying anger and fear. As this happens, think about any fearful circumstances you may still be holding onto. Are you ready to let go of these? Are you ready to reclaim your power? If so, Archeia Serenity (along with Archangel Cassiel) now gathers below your feet their Divine spider's web, which they use to catch and transform all forms of density.

Breathe in deeply as the etheric web moves up your body aura now, catching these frequencies, known and unknown. Repeat this process two more times, allowing the web to move intelligently in any direction needed to collect everything you're ready to release . . . Watch now as Serenity takes the web into her hand and blows it away, showering you afterward in effervescent bubbles that "pop" and dissolve anything residual in your aura.

Feeling fresh from the inside out, breathe in Peace . . . and breathe out Peace . . . as the attunement draws to a close. Give thanks to your guardian angels, Archeia Serenity and Archangel Cassiel, before opening your eyes and drinking some water to ground yourself.

Rise Like an Angel

◊ "Attuning to Archeia Serenity felt like . . . Her guidance for me at this time is . . . "

◊ "I'll continue to use Serenity's Divine spider's web to catch and release density on the go, and partner with her for . . . "

Daily Affirmation to Connect with Archeia Serenity

"Thank you, fear, for showing me where I need to let the Light in. As I relax, all softens, for I am Serenity."

Crystal Allies

Cosmic ice andara, larimar, shungite

Plant Allies

Chamomile, Star of Bethlehem, violet

Invite In Archeia Serenity for . . .

Understanding all perspectives; resolving victimhood and dualistic beliefs; overcoming illusion, fantasy, fear, drama, and doubt; and instilling peace and balance to the auric field.

Chapter 15

ARCHEIA STRENGTH
"I AM ready to advance"

Stepping Boldly

In the last chapter, Archeia Serenity illustrated that fear begins and ends in our mind. As we step into the lion's den with Archeia Strength, she'll show us how we can use fear as an energy to build us up rather than tear us down. Get set to grow your resilience, unleash your magic, and blaze new trails as you advance!

Archeia Strength Revealed

Archeia Strength, whose name is derived from the Old English word *strengþu*, meaning "strong", serves on the Orange and Green Ray of Nature, Fortitude, and Acceptance with her counterpart, Archangel Ariel. Often manifesting as a lime green and bright orange energy, this lioness of Heaven has a healing influence over our earth star chakra, as well as our navel and solar plexus centres. Other names for Archeia Strength are "Lady Strength" and "Cloveria".

When channelling Archeia Strength's artwork, a vision came to me of Maid Marian, the fabled heroine of Robin Hood and the Green Lady of the woods. Like Marian, Archeia Strength's energy is strong, bold, kind, and giving, with an ineffable air of magic and alchemy that fully reveals itself when you take the time to get to know this angel.

Much like working with the nature spirits (who Archeia Strength oversees, along with Ariel) there's an invitation to just be your authentic self in her company. For she and the nature spirits don't see your physical exterior but your essence within, knowing your truest intentions as reflected through your vibration. If you've ever left a gift for the nature spirits, such as a token of appreciation for the faeries who bring colour to the land, know the faeries received the vibration of the gift, with its physical aspect offered up to the surrounding wildlife. Knowing this, we can be extra thoughtful to pour our love into something we make for the faeries—for they love homemade gifts especially!—also realizing that this gift may be consumed by wildlife. Gifting with such consideration helps us walk in greater harmony with the land and elementals. Similarly, when out in nature, we can receive gifts, such as feathers along our path. Know your angels have poured their loving vibration into these feathers; they are not just there by physical happenstance!

When I asked Archeia Strength why feathers are such a common "angel sign", she said it's because feathers are both strong and soft, yet wholly aligned. They have a central spine, known in feather anatomy as the rachis, akin to our backbone, energetically representing our connection with Source. Along with two vanes (symbolic of masculine and feminine consciousness) that comprise numerous soft branches, these unite to make a feather—a seemingly simple teaching to never underestimate the reflective wisdom of nature.

As her name suggests, Archeia Strength is solid in her faith that we can all thrive when we realize we have the wherewithal to do so! She helps us spark our inner capabilities and magic, reminding us **that magic is not what we do, it is who we are**. In her midst, we gain the courage to let go of feelings of inadequacy and develop a sense of personal agency.

Strength guides:

You were born from Magic, unique from anything else in Creation. Use your Magic to invent, express, and birth gifts into the world, for you can turn density into diamonds and failures into triumphs. Say with conviction, "I can, I can, I can . . . I will, and I AM!"

Lean into Archeia Strength to dissolve all spells that have kept you asleep to your own Magic, including any cords of competition and comparison energy. Believe in yourself, for you, eternally, have *got this!*

Prioritize What You Put Off

Archeia Strength and her twin, Archangel Ariel, both help us transform any sense that we can't be who we wish to be. They remind us to
apply commitment and discipline to our daily lives, to do the things
we've been putting off, and attend to what we may otherwise deem as
"inconvenient". In their wisdom, they know that by putting off everyday things, we put off our self-care, our dreams, and ultimately, defer
the extraordinary life that's available to us right on the other side of
"inconvenience".

While writing this chapter—and staying aware of doing the dishes
each night, thank you, Archeia Strength!—I was shown an image of
a tree, illustrating that at any given time we are "rooted" in a buffet
of Source-given skills and all we wish to see show up in our world is
already there; we're already connected to our manifestations.

The joy, the money, the health, the romance—everything we've
asked for is already vibrationally manifest and part of our being. We
need only adjust our perception to allow these beauties to appear physically. Similar to Archeia Patience's teaching, Strength guides us to daily
open our arms wide, like the branches of a tree, to catch, harness, and
realize the universal flow of abundance that we're never apart from, for
inner abundance creates outer abundance. Being an angel of Earth and
Fire, however, Archeia Strength understands that not everything we
want, need, or are ready for will just fall into our lap; we need to act.

A Little Light on Procrastination

The Archeiai are all for helping us go straight to the heart of the matter
to target the root of dis-ease and enable a return of personal freedom
and agency. While it's true that the limits of our mind represent the
limits of our reality, we must be prepared to change our actions as well
as our thoughts, for no amount of reciting affirmations will actualize
our dreams if we don't get our butts off the sofa to act upon them!

Psychologists call this "mental contrasting". Inspired by Archeia
Strength, I call this, "practical positivity", the same strategy as looking
under the bonnet of our manifestations to enquire, for example, what's
getting in the way of this thing I desire, this habit I want to change, or
this dis-ease I am ready to heal?

While positive thinking helps us identify what we want in life, practical positivity brings everything to life! by being curious enough to ask, "What is preventing me from acting on this goal?", and "What would it take to make this goal a reality?", which identifies the underlying dynamic at play. Armed with this knowing, we can better overcome the obstacle and arrive at the best action to take to cultivate a better now and future reality.

Before unpacking this further, let's share a little light on procrastination. You may be besties with this energy, too! I find she comes knocking when I have a big event to prepare for or a book deadline. Suddenly, it becomes top priority to sort through my bra drawer, or as in the case of this book, to clean the bottom tray of my toaster. Yup, anything but sitting at my desk to write!

Why do we do this? As human beings, we are creatures of habit, favouring activities that feel familiar and non-threatening to the ego, which doesn't like change, period. However, as spirit beings we thrive on exploration, on taking sacred action to blaze new trails and experiencing the unknown and expanding in all directions that take our fancy, and in so doing, using any residual fear and procrastination as fuel to power our jets. To help our humanity to blend seamlessly into our intrepid Spirit, Archeia Strength guides us to grow our power of resiliency.

Resiliency Is a Superpower

Resiliency is a habit-building skill. An adaption and advancement of life rather than a retreat; the ability to bounce back from adversity and be unmovable when needed, flexible and creative when required.

As the saying goes, "I've yet to meet a strong person with a straightforward past." I believe we forge resilience through the fire of our experiences. While angels help us tap into all that we are (for we are a heavenly storehouse of virtues, just as they are), there's something to be said for the strength that's built from facing life head on.

Like you, I've faced adversity in my life; I've had moments, days, weeks of not wanting to be here, because the heaviness of what was being experienced felt too much to bear. I bought into the belief that my problems were pervasive, all the while separating myself from the vibrational vicinity of solutions, support, and hope that this shall pass.

I was born into this life through a relationship that was filled with physical violence and drug abuse. I became the odd-one-out in my family, was bullied at school, and my first sexual experience was not consensual. Sexual trauma continued in later life, and spurred self-harm, bulimia, and a series of toxic relationships. These experiences in my younger life, and those that have followed, contributed to building grit and diamond-like muscles of resiliency that support me now to say, amid what feels challenging, "I've faced harder. I've got this!"

We are all war veterans with badges representing past battles faced. Some wear their badges as trophies, aptly providing an excuse to not live their greatest life; others wear them as fateful reminders of the past, inciting them to relive conflict over and over again in the battlefield of their mind.

But we don't have to be defined by our experiences, nor use past or inherited wounding as an excuse to not thrive. As the following Four Pillars of Building Resilience convey, when we shift our perspective, we realize that we don't have to be the result of what has happened to us; we can be the result of what we *choose* to be. Just as a bone breaks, it grows back stronger, and so can we. This is the wisdom within all wounds.

Four Pillars of Building Resilience

1. **Adjust your perspective.** Are you a victor or victim of circumstance? By allowing yourself to shift your gaze, what once was seen as an obstacle can be viewed as an opportunity, a way to grow and be grown. Amid the fire, ask yourself, *What is the learning here? What do I need to see and shift to make this an opportunity that works for me rather than against?* Witness any inner negativity, blame, or learned helplessness that may then surface (the opposing energies of resilience). Know this form of energy is manifesting only to come up and out of you as you shift gears from being problem-oriented to solution-driven.

2. **Respond consciously.** Be aware of any tendency to panic and react in the moment and then project this as inner and outer blame. Take a B R E A T H E R . . . and remove yourself physically from the situation, if possible. As alluded to earlier by Archeia Harmony, only make decisions when you're feeling centred, not when you're in "trigger-mode". The best step forward when you're emotionally triggered is to move into curiosity and recognize what the root of the trigger is, thereby helping yourself to spiral up the emotional scale. Now clarity can flood in and wash away the tendency to project blame. With clarity comes calmness and then Awareness, as you naturally find yourself in the vicinity of the best solution/action to take. When we react, the outcome changes, thereby creating the sense of more problems to face.

3. **Find greater meaning.** See the underlying blessing and purpose of what initially shocked and shook you, for fear can be a teacher and bestow blessings when we shift our mindset, as Archeia Serenity shared in the last chapter. Each time you bounce back from adversity, witness how your confidence grows as you acknowledge your capacity to surmount anything. Use your past experiences for good, instead of feeling hemmed in by them. For example, I've found great peace in using my past trauma to help others resolve similar experiences.

4. **Keep going.** No matter the circumstance, keep going. When you feel that you've lost someone or something, keep going. When you feel that you've let yourself down or someone else has, keep going. When you don't know what you're doing, keep going. When money is low in the bank, keep going. No matter what

feels overwhelming, keep going. One choice, one action, one moment can change your life forever! An affirmation my inner being gave me years ago that still sees me through tricky times is: "The choices I make determine my future. What I decide now will be my reality tomorrow." Add it to your repertoire, especially for cutting through addictive tendencies. It'll help wake you up before acting in a way that'll later cause you suffering. Care enough for yourself to advance towards your health, goals, and dreams by moving through resistance, instead of moving away from it. Give yourself the life you've always imagined, as resiliency becomes your superpower and storehouse of calm and confidence within.

Rise Like an Angel

◊ Please pause and look at Archeia Strength's image. Breathe in her powerful presence, and wrap yourself in her Light of loving acceptance. Invite Strength to be with you now, affirming aloud:

"Loving Archeia Strength, thank you for helping me dissolve all spells that have kept me asleep to my magic, my confidence, my capabilities, and my worthiness. I surrender these spells into your Orange and Green fires and take from the flames the courage to move forward with my life and upward on my path of Ascension. Thank you. And so it is."

◊ Close your eyes and visualize this alchemy taking place. Make a commitment to yourself to embrace your inner lioness/lion energy. Breathe in Courage . . . breathe out Courage. Ask Archeia Strength to write through you the answers to the following questions using the template writing guide shared in Chapter 4:

◊ "Which pillar would I benefit the most from applying . . . ?"

◊ "Archeia Strength, what would it take for me to reinforce my resilience and bring more practical positivity into my life. . . ?"

Befriend Discomfort

We don't have to go through major trauma to build inner strength. For example, caring enough to prioritize that meaningful conversation, applying for that job, starting your own business, going an extra five minutes in your workout, trusting your gut over external influences, practising listening instead of interrupting others, leaving toxic relationships, or taking a chance on love again—all of these build stellar resilience while helping us stay present. Every time we face and move through discomfort we grow; therefore, it can be purposeful to befriend discomfort and face fear in manageable bite-size ways.

During my Kundalini Yoga training in 2012, my teacher guided to take daily cold showers before sunrise to cleanse both body and Spirit. Despite living in the cold climes of Scotland, I'm not a fan of the cold, so this was a daily battle, meeting fear where it begins and ends: in the mind. With every shower, however, I got used to the cold, and now, if I miss a day, the difference in my mindset and ability to manage stress is noticeable.

Ishnaan, or as it's more commonly known today, Cold Water Therapy, is an ancient form of purification that pushes us to do something out of our comfort zone, thereby building fortitude and will. This practice stimulates circulation, strengthens the nervous system, supports healthy weight management, and boosts immunity. One

Dutch study found that those who turned the water cold for the last 30 seconds of their shower cut their sick days by 30 percent! Cold-water swimming and ice baths or plunges are all excellent ways to push yourself beyond your limits, making friends with adversity, and in the process, resilience.

During a recent stay at a health retreat, I was given a complimentary cryotherapy session. Not knowing anything about the treatment but loving a freebie, I said yes! When the therapist came to collect me for the session, I asked him at what temperature the chamber was set at. When he said -111°C, I burst out laughing—both at the thought of standing in only my swimsuit in this temperature and at the number "111", which in angel numerology represents growth!

As Archeia Strength and your inner being inspire ways to reinforce your resilience, notice the subtle persuasion of your mind in the moment to not do that thing you know ultimately supports you. For example, notice when your mind begins negotiating, bartering, and/or telling you that you have nothing to prove. This emerges the most for me when I'm on an extended fast or holding my arms in a static yoga pose. When this arises for you, remain present and aware. Let yourself sit in the discomfort and move through the sensations rather than away from them, for this is where you'll meet your Self, thereby fostering an inner grit and a fire that burns brighter than anything the mind can conjure.

Choices ⟶ Chances ⟶ Changes

While angels help us juice reality to the fullest, they cannot live our life. This gift is ours. Archeia Strength guides us to own our reality, to fearlessly take charge of its direction and witness the magic and miracles in each moment by staying grounded and caring enough for the precious fragility of life. We never know when our last day on Earth will be. Our being is eternal, yes, but we only get one chance to savour this lifetime.

Whatever you want to see show up in the world, whatever you feel is missing, or whatever you want to create and leave as your legacy, know this begins with you.

In our digital age, many people content-consume "how-to" videos to help them reshape their life, but few of them act upon the wisdom shared. Theory without practice remains just content. Likewise, sitting on the couch for hours or lying in bed, hoping for positive change without taking action, is futile.

As these words flow through me there's no judgement, as for years, this was my experience around shedding excess weight. I watched countless weight loss videos on YouTube, signed up for courses that promised results, bought books on nutrition, and imagined a future reality as my ideal shape. None of this helped me shift the weight, because I wasn't putting anything into practice in the ever-present, nor caring enough to heal the underlying dynamic of why I was holding onto extra pounds; namely, not feeling safe to be beautiful for fear of what would happen next.

Putting the Divine alchemy techniques shared throughout this book into practice, applying practical positivity, and getting into my body daily helped me to, at last, dissolve the padded protection I was wearing. Discomfort and fear were still present, but I no longer bought into what my mind was saying. Reframing "exercise", from being a chore and something I have to do to an "activity" I *get* to do, shifted my mindset and helped me appreciate my genius body and all it can do. Intentionally pushing through sticky mental moments not only toned my body but toned my inner resolve, too!

Shi Heng Yi, a Shaolin monk, said, "Make a choice to take the chance or your life will never change." I wholeheartedly agree, for nothing changes if nothing changes. True, there's a consequence to every choice we make, but when we deliberately choose what we know will expand us, we start to see new opportunities and chances showing up in our world. Those around us start to see something different in us, and through keeping consistent in moving forward, we change.

As technology continues to encroach on our everyday life, it can be easy to make ill choices, miss out on those chances, and stagnate. For instance, we can choose to sit all day long in front of a screen, order food that comes to our door, self-sooth ourselves with programmes that distract us from living a real life, and buy into the misleading facade of social media—all contributing to less physical activity, increased disease, and overall weakness across the physical and non-physical bodies that comprise our being. Furthermore, checking in with our phone first thing in the morning and going straight into busyness doesn't provide the courage, compassion, or skills to surmount unexpected challenges of the day that a cold shower or morning meditation does. Resiliency muscles grow when we stay present in the face of our choices, applying the virtues mastered through the fire of our experiences and incorporating the teachings of our angels and inner being. Then fear becomes a tool to build us up and a mirror to reflect the innate Strength we have, and are.

Rise Like an Angel

◊ Please pause and feel Archeia Strength within you. Envision the life you've always imagined for yourself. Breathe in, and realize that, if you can imagine this, you *can* experience this and live this reality. Breathe through any resistance that begins to emerge. Let it come up to come *out* of you.

◊ Next write a list of everything you want to do in your life that you haven't already done. What are your goals and dreams? What feels missing in your life and/or in the world that you want to see, bring in, and leave as your legacy?

◊ Now write down a description of your ideal morning and evening. Add as much detail as you like, including activities, how you'd feel, the foods and drink you'd enjoy.

◊ Lastly, and in relation to every question above, what action do you need to take to make these manifestations a reality? *Check in with your action list monthly* in order to stay on course and invite Archeia Strength to support—and celebrate with you—each step of the way. And as those around you see you and your world shift, invite them to do this angel practice, too.

Please enjoy merging fully with Archeia Strength to continue to advance your life, contribution, and legacy, first reading "How to Prepare for Attunements" in Chapter 2, page 50.

Archeia Strength Attunement

Feeling centred, sense yourself held in a column of bright orange and lime green Light. Breathe this blended Source Ray in and out . . . become it as it fills every part of you, including your aura and wings. See the Light connect through you to the centre of the Earth and the centre of the Sun. Feel your guardian angels standing on either side of you, radiating their Love, which further expands your Light. When you're ready to invite in Archeia Strength, affirm aloud:

"Loving Archeia Strength, angel of Nature, Fortitude, and Acceptance and master of the Orange and Green Ray, may you now attune me to your vibration and consciousness, so we are forever One, and allow me to channel your Light for the greatest good of all concerned. Thank you for showing me that I can be strong and soft, bold and kind, connected and grounded, and in every way, Magical. Thank you. And so it is."

Breathe in Strength . . . breathe out Strength . . . as you merge with this Divine angel. Ask Archeia Strength what the highest and best guidance is for you at this time, and if there's anything you can support her with.

As you continue to attune to Archeia Strength, you can also channel her healing Light. If there's a part of your body you'd like to empower, bring your hands to that area, or rest your hands on your solar plexus or base chakra (the areas Strength influences most). Sense your body ablaze with the Orange and Green Ray. Breathe into these flames as they fill you with the energy of sacred action . . . and breathe out the sacred fire to gift this energy into your space.

Affirm aloud three times: "I am strong, confident, worthy, and free. Everything I am manifesting comes effortlessly to me." Breathe deeply, anchoring in the Truth of this affirmation and sending out your appreciation to the angels, guides, elementals, land spirits, and wildlife in your vicinity.

When you feel the energy beginning to wane, intend the attunement to be complete, and thank your guardian angels and Archeia Strength. Open your eyes, and enjoy some water to ground yourself.

Rise Like an Angel

◊ "Attuning to the fiery Light of Archeia Strength felt like . . . "

◊ "Her guidance for me at this time is . . ."

◊ "I'll continue to invite in Archeia Strength to assist me in . . . "

Daily Affirmation to Connect with Archeia Strength

"I am magical, and I use my Magic to conjure spells of worthiness, strength, determination, and love. I embrace sacred action and the positive change that's unfolding."

Crystal Allies

Amazonite, fluorapatite, orange calcite

Plant Allies

Borage, dandelion, star thistle

Invite In Archeia Strength for . . .

Being true to yourself, breaking unhealthy habits, clearing conflict and apathy towards action, courage, focus, expansion of the base and solar plexus chakras, letting in abundance, releasing competition and comparison energy, resilience, and taking personal responsibility.

Chapter 16

ARCHEIA CONSTANCE
"I AM ready to rise"

Journey of Ascension

All of us are ascending, because we have an inbuilt drive to move ourselves forward. We can't help it—at our core we *are* Creation! Yet through the process of descension, as we moved from Source to delineate into partial form as human beings, we forgot our sovereignty, and with it became susceptible to believing we are apart from Creation.

This limiting belief has kept us cycling in an incarnational hamster wheel, all the while accruing both personal and collective density that sets us apart from the Love we are. Now it's time to shake ourselves free of illusionary veils and rise in unity with All That Is. This is the gift and process of Ascension we're now experiencing.

For a moment, visualize yourself fully aware and consistently tuned in to Source, grounded in your roots, and with high, open branches. See yourself unashamedly shining, radiating your Love in all directions of time, space, and being. What dreams are now your reality? How different do you feel, knowing you are the Universe? How do you think, look, and act?

The beauty of who we are is that we're all different while in physical form, thus there is no one-size-fits-all when it comes to our journey of Ascension. As Archeia Constance guides, as she comes forward now:

You are already enlightened! Relax, and remember that the gift of your Divinity is already yours. Whatever you feel currently blocks your path, give it to me, for I am the "I AM" within you.

Step into your authority by imagining your Highest Self and then merge with this glory. Remember, you are both Creation and Creator. Know thyself, and use your experiences to help others rise. Embrace the constancy of your spiritual growth, and know that everything you create from Love showers blessings upon all.

Understanding Ascension

Many spiritual books complicate our journey of rising from Love forgot to Love embodied, but Constance, being the angel of organization, is all for keeping things simple! While in human form (and in our current age) our consciousness explores, but isn't limited to, three main adventures:

◊ **Awakening**—living a 3D, human-driven life and, when our soul chooses, moving past a material-only perspective. Here our attention rests mainly on personal desires.

◊ **Discovery**—living a 4D life, in which we remember our being and explore different forms of spirituality, allowing our path, power, and purpose to emerge. Here, our focus begins to move from *me* to *we*, for co-creative service.

◊ **Embodiment**—living a 5D life, in which we're refining our vibration as a unified human being, enjoying and expressing all we are. Here, our attention rests on how best we can contribute to the Creative expansion of all life.

On any given day, we may feel ourselves moving through these states (and the myriad of shades in between them) depending on the thoughts and emotions we're empowering.

But when we make the conscious choice to raise and expand our vibration, our being—at a cellular, glandular, and energetic level— starts to anchor greater quotients of Light. The greater and finer the frequency of Light we can consistently hold in our body, the more we naturally "in-lighten", adjusting our overall frequency and recognition of experiencing a stable soul state.

As our Light increases, our perspective widens, and the desire to categorize life falls away. From an anchored, 5D state, dimensions become irrelevant, for we no longer judge what's *better* or *less* than Creation; we recognize Source in all. Likewise, as we ascend, the old way of controlling life through the mind alone falls away. Amid this process, it's easy to feel as though we're losing our grip on reality, for in truth, we are. We're choosing to let go of what has been in order to allow a new way of seeing and being to emerge. Through my own experience, I understand how daunting Ascension can be, but our angels are ever present, supporting us along the pathless path and encouraging us to trust that the unfamiliar is the creative space in which we can birth our dreams.

Rising in Grace

Archeia Constance, who is also the angel of time, reminds us that we never need to rush, strive, or control our spiritual development, for we're all headed in the same direction. Likewise, we don't need to suffer or make sacrifices in order to progress on our journey. Instead, Archeia Constance invites us to sync with grace, so we can easily ebb and flow in rhythm with our Divinity.

Just like the night sky, which is so reflective of Constance, our eternal essence can be calm and silent, but also ever changing, filled with colour, light, and multi-dimensional connections. By leaning into this grace, we learn to stay in the moment, to fully appreciate everything that's taking place. And by being present, we realize that we're forever in the right place at the right time. If we ever doubt this, we need only look at the many signs, symbols, and synchronicities reflecting in our reality for a reminder that our dreams are birthing and we are ascending.

As we expand into different dimensional frequencies, if we're inspired to rest, enjoy a massage, or go for a walk, we would do well to follow our guidance, no matter how busy we think we are, for the busier we feel, the greater the call to take time out! This requires removing the concept of "should" from our psyche (as in, "I *should* be doing this" or "I *shouldn't* be enjoying myself when I *should* be working!").

Constance guides us to replace "should" with trusting our inner guidance, so we can keep in Divine conversation with ourselves and feel good about addressing our needs. She inspires us to be mindful when we say things like, "I need to make a quick trip to the toilet" or "I'll be ready in a second", and instead enquire why we feel we need to rush. **Constance would love us to sip and savour each moment without having to defend or rationalize our time or pleasure**.

It's taken me a while to put this into practice, but as a result of shedding hand-me-down beliefs, I can happily share that some of my best ideas come to me while taking a bath or on the toilet! Even when my workload is high and there's housework galore to do, if I'm inspired to pause to receive guidance from my inner being and angels, I'll do so without question. If this resonates with you, too, do give yourself permission to answer the callings of your heart, soul, and Spirit. Let your path and your pleasure be one and the same.

Archeia Constance Revealed

Archeia Constance, whose name is derived from the Latin word *constantia*, meaning "standing firm", serves on the Diamond Ray of Universal Ascension and Sacred Geometry with her counterpart, Archangel Metatron. Other names for Constance include "Lady Constance" and "Sophia". Archeia Constance has a healing influence on the stellar gateway and soul star chakras, as well as the light body. Although she serves on the Diamond Ray, Constance often manifests as expressions of silver, purple, indigo, gold, and black Light.

As noted in the Introduction, Constance's image took over a month to produce because she inspired so many personal breakthroughs in me, and I needed time to integrate them before her form could fully emerge. She asked that the symbology of bees, DNA, stars, and sacred geometry be included in her depiction in order to reflect the constancy of life—that is, everything is always emerging, growing, and rebirthing in cyclical flow.

Constance and Metatron help us decode sacred geometric shapes and apply their wisdom in our everyday lives. Constance is connected to Metatron via "Metatron's Cube", the sacred symbol shown above her head. She's also linked with the Vesica Piscis that she holds between her hands. This seemingly simple shape of two overlapping circles has featured in the symbology of all the main religions and is particularly important in our current age.

Constance would gladly write an entire book about this magical symbol, but suffice to say, this geometry defines pure feminine power! Like a womb, it's a portal for non-physical energy to manifest into physical form. The iteration of the Vesica Piscis shown in Constance's image has been adapted according to her instruction and includes the Seed of Life at its core with a Divine nod to the All-Seeing Eye. While sacred geometry has been misused and abused in previous Golden Ages, Constance is helping us connect with its original purity, so we may use it to reclaim our Divine Innocence.

I regard Archeia Constance as the "Queen Bee" of our Universe, for her energy is vast, vital, brilliant, and brave. She is an incredible blend of strength and regal beauty. Constance reminds us that **the only limits are those we create and perpetuate. When we surrender these limits to Source, nothing can stop us!** She helps empower the rise of our inner femininity, no matter what gender we identify with, and can aid us by increasing our willpower and organizational skills when she is invited in.

Anchoring Your Light

Choosing to express and embody our inner spirituality has nothing to do with attaining anything in the external world. We don't need to attend retreats, buy yoga mats, gain certificates, or identify with anyone or anything outside of ourselves. Being spiritual is simply returning to our natural state.

This innate way of being inspires us to live in the moment, with two feet on the ground and a heart open and connected with all life. In this process, we can appreciate that Mother Earth is ascending, too. As she shifts into her embodied state of being, her grid systems, inner elements, and ley lines are adjusting, just as our inner systems, elements, and meridians are—all for the purpose of anchoring Light.

Now more than ever, our planet is receiving great increments of Light. During eclipse windows, Mother Earth receives huge downloads of energetic codes encrypted with information to accelerate her ascent (she also receives new codes during lunar phases, such as when the moon is full). Because we're linked with Earth through our body, sometimes our system can struggle to keep up with unpacking the new data. This is why many of us feel weighed down during eclipse windows. It's not that there's anything wrong with our physical body; it's just that we're trying to integrate new information.

If you find yourself experiencing "Ascension symptoms", give yourself time to just "be" while this inner process plays itself out. As Constance has already shared, rest when you're inspired. Fasting and time spent in nature also help if you feel exhausted and are struggling to keep up in your physical body.

The 13-Chakra System

We can enjoy a more graceful ascent by consciously connecting with the energetic centres of the body (aka our chakras), which process the uploading and downloading of Light. Although the frequency of this book and the Love within its ceremonies and images all help activate the chakras, the following meditation weaves together the Light of all the Archeiai to anchor your 13-Chakra system. These chakras were fully embodied during the times of Golden Atlantis and Lemuria, and this can be the case again through consciously integrating them.

This journey is simply Divine to do on a regular basis! Please drink plenty of water afterwards and give your body time to rest and receive the benefits of the meditation.

Integrating Your 13 Chakras

◊ Sitting in a comfortable place where you won't be disturbed, bring your hands into prayer pose at your heart centre, and close your eyes. Take a few moments to relax and come into a meditative state. See yourself held in a column of sparkling diamond Light that spans your aura, going 44 feet in all directions. Breathe in diamond Light . . . and breathe it out . . . sensing yourself connect to the centre of the Earth and the centre of the Sun. Your guardian angels approach, and stand either side of you. Feel their Love now. Breathe it in . . .

◊ Take your attention to your stellar gateway chakra (18 inches above your head), seeing it spin as a bright golden-orange ball. Feel yourself connect directly to Source . . . Archeia Constance begins to pour Light into your stellar gateway. As she does, she asks you to affirm aloud, *"No matter how life ebbs and flows, I trust the Light of my Divinity to guide me, for I am Constance."* Breathe in . . . breathe out.

◊ Sense your soul star chakra (6 inches above your head), seeing it spin as a deep magenta ball. Feel yourself connect with the heart of the Central Sun . . . Archeia Mercy begins to pour Light into your soul star. As she does, she asks you to affirm aloud, *"I embrace the vibrant, worthy Goddess within me. I am equal to all, and I love all, for I am Mercy."* Breathe in . . . breathe out.

◊ Focus on your causal chakra (3–4 inches above your head), seeing it spin as a glowing white ball. Feel yourself connect with pure divine Love . . . Archeia Charity begins to pour Light into your causal chakra. As she does, she asks you to affirm aloud, *"Every breath I take is a breath of Love. I am Love in flow, for I am Charity."* Breathe in . . . breathe out.

◊ Sense your crown chakra (at the top of your head), seeing it spin as a pearlescent gold ball. Feel yourself connect with your Higher Mind . . . Archeia Clarity begins to pour Light into your crown. As she does, she asks you to affirm aloud, *"I am not apart from God, or a part of God; I am God. He is me, and I am him. She is me, and I am her. I am All, for I am Clarity."* Breathe in … breathe out.

◊ Focus on your third eye chakra (in between the eyebrows), seeing it spin as a crystal-clear ball. Feel yourself connect with Infinite intuition . . .

Archeia Victory begins to pour Light into your third eye. As she does, she asks you to affirm aloud, *"I allow my Divine senses and instincts to be upgraded at the highest level, for I am Victory."* Breathe in . . . breathe out.

◊ Sense your throat chakra (at the centre of your neck), seeing it spin as an aqua-blue ball. Feel your Truth align with Source's Truth . . . Archeia Faith begins to pour Light into your throat. As she does, she asks you to affirm aloud, *"I am awake. I am here. I see Source in all, including myself, for I am Faith."* Breathe in . . . breathe out.

◊ Focus on your higher heart chakra (between your throat and heart centre), seeing it spin as a pink crystalline ball. Feel yourself as the embodiment of Divine Love . . . Archeia Virtue begins to pour Light into your higher heart. As she does, she asks you to affirm again, *"I am ready to feel good. As I let go of all resistance, Love fills me anew, for I am Virtue."* Breathe in . . . breathe out.

◊ Sense your heart chakra (at the centre of your chest), seeing it spin as a glowing white ball. Feel yourself as a beacon of Divine Love, radiating brilliance in all directions now . . . Archeia Joy begins to pour Light into your heart. As she does, she asks you to affirm again, *"I am a magnet for magic and miracles, for I am Joy."* Breathe in . . . breathe out.

◊ Focus on your solar plexus (2 inches above your belly button), seeing it spin as a bright golden ball. Feel yourself align with Source's Power . . . Archeia Grace begins to pour Light into your solar plexus. As she does, she asks you to affirm aloud, *"I am on the right path, and everything important to me is easily manifesting, for I am Grace."* Breathe in . . . breathe out.

◊ Sense your navel chakra (slightly under your belly button), seeing it spin as a bright orange ball. Feel your life and soul's path uniting as One . . . Archeia Freedom begins to pour Light into your navel. As she does, she asks you to affirm aloud, *"I am the Light within the dark. I am the solution to every problem. I choose to live life through a new lens, for I am free, I am Freedom."* Breathe in . . . breathe out.

◊ Focus on your sacral chakra (2 inches below your belly button), seeing it spin as an orange-pink ball. Let yourself feel how beautiful, complete, and whole you are . . . Archeia Purity begins to pour Light into your sacral chakra. As she does so, she asks you to affirm aloud, *"I am Divine perfection embodied. As I accept myself, I accept all, for I am Purity."* Breathe in . . . breathe out.

◊ Sense your base chakra (at the bottom of your spine), seeing it spin as a platinum ball. Feel yourself as the strong, steady Master you are . . . Archeia Serenity begins to pour Light into your base. As she does, she asks you to affirm aloud, *"I am Divine bravery in constant flow, for I am Serenity."* Breathe in . . . breathe out.

◊ Focus on your earth star chakra (12 inches below your feet), seeing it spin as a deep silver ball. Feel yourself connect with the heart of Mother Earth . . . Archeia Patience begins to pour Light into your earth star. As she does this, she asks you to affirm aloud, *"I trust the process of my path and marvel in its magic, for I am Patience."* Breathe in . . . breathe out.

◊ Feel all your chakras align in a column of diamond Light. Sense your DNA opening and anchoring Source energy, as it pulses through, from, and to you now. Breathe in

◊ Sovereignty . . . and breathe out Oneness . . . seeing everything in the cosmos and all of Earth bathed in pure Divine Love.

◊ Stay in this bliss for as long as you like before thanking all concerned and grounding yourself by drinking some water.

Rise Like an Angel

◊ "Integrating my 13-chakra system felt like . . ."

◊ "The chakras that felt most significant to anchor were . . ."

Please enjoy attuning to Archeia Constance to continue to soar, after first reading "How to Prepare for Attunements" in Chapter 2, page 50.

Archeia Constance Attunement

Feeling centred, sense yourself held in a column of sparkling Diamond and Purple Light. Breathe this blended Source Ray in and out. Allow it to fill every part of you, including your aura and wings, and then see it connect through you to the centre of the Earth and the centre of the Sun. Feel your guardian angels standing on either side of you, radiating their Love, which further expands your Light. When you're ready to invite in Archeia Constance, affirm aloud:

"Loving Archeia Constance, angel of Universal Ascension and Sacred Geometry and master of the Diamond Ray, may you now attune me to your vibration and consciousness, so that I am forever linked with you and may channel your energy. Thank you for inspiring me to stand firm in my Power, to recognize and express all I am, and to accelerate my Ascension in knowing when to act and when to rest. Thank you. And so it is."

Breathe in Sovereignty . . . and breathe out Oneness . . . as you merge with this Divine angel. Ask Archeia Constance what the highest and best guidance is for you at this time, and if there's anything you can support her with.

As you continue to attune to Constance, you can also channel her healing Light. If there's a part of your body you'd like to heal, bring your hands to that area now, or bring your hands to your soul star, a chakra that Constance influences. Sense the Diamond Ray, in all its colours and vibrancy, begin to pour into your upper crown chakras and then cascade around your aura as a brilliant waterfall of Light. Breathe in its radiance and breathe it out to bless your space . . . Continue this visualization for at least 10 minutes to receive this healing attunement to the Diamond Ray, as it raises and expands your frequency on all levels of being.

When you feel the energy beginning to wane, intend the attunement to be complete. Thank your guardian angels and Archeia Constance before opening your eyes and drinking some water to ground yourself.

Rise Like an Angel

◊ "Attuning to the depth of Archeia Constance felt like . . ."

◊ "Her guidance for me at this time is . . ."

◊ "I'll continue to invite in Archeia Constance to support me with . . ."

Daily Affirmation to Connect with Archeia Constance

"I trust in the bright new world that's emerging and the inherent goodness of humanity."

Crystal Allies

Azeztulite, blue sky fluorite, charoite

Plant Allies

Cornflower, mugwort, quince

Invite In Archeia Constance for . . .

Ascension, anchoring higher-dimensional energies, balancing and integrating the chakras, cosmic connection, light-body activation and expansion, organization, and willpower.

Chapter 17

ARCHEIA RADIANT
"I AM ready to shine"

Elevate How You See Yourself

As we come to meet the penultimate angel in our guidebook for personal and planetary thriving, we're invited to resolve any form of hiding our Light and lowering our standards. For through the eyes of our angels, we are perfect, healthy, abundant, worthy, capable, and loved beyond measure.

Whether you feel this way about yourself or not, know your angels never wish for you to identify with anything less than what you Divinely are. By consciously inviting Archeia Radiant into your life, any dulling tendencies can naturally dissolve. An ease of being seen and heard returns, and the stage door of life opens, welcoming you to boldly shine as your glorious Self.

It can be this simple. It is this easy.

Archeia Radiant Revealed

Archeia Radiant, whose name is derived from the Latin word *radiare*, meaning "to shine", serves on the Silver Ray of Illumination, Grace, and Self-Acceptance with her counterpart, Archangel Haniel. While the calming pale blue and silver presence of Haniel helps humanity to have self-belief through uncovering hidden gifts and talents, the prominent pink presence of Radiant de-mists illusions that arise through self-reflection. She helps us to accept every aspect of ourselves, so we can shine brightly, like the moon, the celestial being she's linked with.

Archeia Radiant takes what we feel are the ugly, messy, and imperfect aspects of ourselves and wears them as the most magnificent gown to mirror how beautiful we are. She guides:

Do not judge a book by the cover. Equally, do not hide behind the weight of perfectionism. Let yourself be you. No ifs nor buts, no falsehoods nor filters; just You.

Archeia Radiant has a healing influence over our heart and stellar gateway chakras. Other names for this angel include "Lady Radiant" and "Maryllisa".

When channelling Radiant's artwork, she came forward wearing the ritzy 1920s dress shown in her picture. And like the 1920s, a decade that was synonymous with political advancements such as giving women the right to vote, Radiant brings forth a sense of entitled equality, poise, and sophistication.

Just by being in Radiant's company, it's easy to feel more at ease in your skin and comfortable being the sole authority in your life. While everyone on Earth is Divine, many people don't act this way, and this can be particularly true on a personal level. Archeia Radiant can assist you to love and accept all people, regardless of bias, while heeding the reminder that you do not need to be liked or loved by anyone except yourself. Invite in Radiant to support you in finding ways to love the haters, quell the self-doubt, and make room for your Light to shine brightly.

Transforming Imposter Syndrome

Whatever self-limitations you identify as coming from your ancestry, culture, ethnicity, sexual orientation, or gender identification, lean into Radiant to help you transform them.

For example, Archeia Radiant shares that the core wound of self-doubt stems from not being believed and/or seen as a child. Maybe you identify as having been the "invisible child", the "rebel child", or the "bad child" in your family, school, or community growing up? Know such archetypes still live within you and most likely, are influencing your beliefs and actions, for when our parents and caregivers don't believe in us, we struggle to believe in ourselves.

In later life, this can develop into "imposter syndrome", whereby we believe we can't do things alone. This has the knock-on effect of stunting our personal, professional, and spiritual growth and drawing in people and circumstances that hold us back; for example, toxic mentors, colleagues, clients, and students—connections devoid of healthy boundaries that escalate to greater suffering for all concerned.

As we partner with Radiant, she makes us aware of the ways in which our wounded inner child is affecting how we see and express ourselves and the limiting beliefs we're empowering from our child brain rather than our adult brain. She guides us to reassure our younger aspects that it's safe to shine, to be seen, heard, and believed. This supports us to allow our inner child to grow and make more conscious choices, as opposed to being influenced by subconscious and unconscious memories and beliefs.

Through this process, we can cultivate the belief that we can do things alone; in fact, we can *excel* when we do things independently! By being willing to believe in ourselves, we allow accumulated conditionings to transform and reunite with the optimistic flow of our inner being. Then, whether we're going it alone, or as part of a group of shining souls, we remain authentic, radiating our true nature for the sheer joy of it!

Strut the Catwalk of Your Life

While you may see yourself in a mirror every day, Archeia Radiant inspires you to look closer in order to connect with your inner being. Despite mirror work being (at first) an awkward, embarrassing, strange, and even upsetting practice, it can be profoundly healing. Sitting quietly as we look at our reflection automatically illuminates the subconscious and unconscious core beliefs preventing us from improving our reality and enjoying a closer relationship with our body, with others, and ultimately, with our Self. Radiant guides you to incorporate the following ritual and alchemical visualization into your daily routine until you can look at yourself lovingly in the mirror without any inner (or outer) criticism getting in the way.

Reflective Radiance Ritual

◊ Choose a time and place where you won't be disturbed, and sit in front of a mirror. Follow the Four Essential Steps on page 75, and at the fourth step, welcome in your guardian angels, Archeia Radiant and her grounding Silver Ray, to envelop you. Breathe in this collective presence . . . and breathe out, as you release any less-than-worthy thoughts. Thank Archeia Radiant for helping you see, connect, and honour yourself.

◊ Place your hands on your heart, and look into your eyes. At first, uncomfortable feelings or thoughts may arise, for you are laying yourself bare. While it's important to embrace the emotions that surface, mentally recite an affirmation like "I am learning to love and accept myself", if the negative self-talk becomes too much. (At first, you may only feel comfortable to look at yourself for a few minutes, but keep extending the time until you can genuinely say, "I love and accept myself" in the mirror. In between your mirror practice sessions, journaling about your experiences will accelerate this process.)

◊ Close your eyes now, and continue to breathe deeply, inhaling Acceptance . . . exhaling Peace . . . Feel rooted into Mother Earth and cocooned in Radiant's Love in order to keep present as you flow into the second part of this practice.

◊ To quash inner and outer criticism and transform any related subconscious and unconscious beliefs, imagine yourself strutting confidently along a catwalk. Make this scene big, bright, and bold . . . Know yourself to be wearing the clothes that make you feel extra fabulous! Embroidered into the fabric are jewels representing each empowered Source Ray. Threads of Gold, Silver, and Diamond Fire are also woven into the material, fortifying you as you walk down the runway, saucily radiating your unique style of sass and sparkle!

◊ Feel the warm catwalk lights illuminating your path with all eyes on you. In the audience are those who represent criticism and those who represent praise. The haters are here; the fair-weather friends; the two-faced folks; the ghosts of your past, present, and future; bullies; mentors; family members; colleagues and friends; supporters; co-creators; lovers; kindred souls you've yet to meet; ethereal ones from your spirit team (guides, angels, elementals, animals, crystal and plant beings; aspects of your inner child; deity and ascended master consciousness; and star being and councils of Light aspects). All are looking at you as a reflection of your multi-dimensional Self.

◊ No matter how they look to you, S H I N E. No matter what they say to you, S H I N E. No matter if they try to influence you, S H I N E as you continue to strut the catwalk of your life. Affirm three times, "I am beautiful. I am safe. I am loved. I am free. I don't need to be like them, I just need to be me." This is your walk. Your life. Own it. Lead it. Open your wings, and set it ablaze!

◊ Stay in this blissful state for as long as you wish before reversing the Four Essential Steps and thanking the angel, then drinking some water to ground yourself and close the practice.

Rise Like an Angel

◊ "This empowering practice is meaningful for me because . . ."

◊ "Strutting the catwalk of my life feels . . . I'll use this visualization, coupled with opening my wings, anytime doubt creeps in."

Finery Is Your Birthright

Over the years, the Archeiai have shared that we all already sit upon a royal throne, albeit asleep to our Divinity until the moment we choose to wake up. As Divine queens, kings, and sovereign beings, we deserve to enjoy the kingdom we co-create with Source, filling our court with those whom we love and allowing in an overflow of abundance for all.

Archeia Radiant would like to remind you of this birthright, especially if you feel there's no current joy or nothing to look forward to in your life. If this resonates for you, perhaps work, family, and service take up all your attention? While this conveys the generosity of your innate angelic heart, Radiant would like you to spare a care for your own unconditional joy.

In the course of helping thousands of women tap into their Divine Feminine wisdom, I've found that many beauties get to a stage in their lives when they stop manifesting what Radiant calls "a sense of finery". By that she means, forms of magic and grandeur, such as eating at exquisite restaurants; attending red carpet events, galleries, concerts, and balls; or dressing up for the fun of it, whether staying home or going out—literally lavishing love on ourselves!

Here again, what gets in the way of us doing that is our belief that we can't enjoy finery alone and must have company in order to justify and be worthy of this joy; otherwise, people will think we're selfish or simply strange! While this outdated, patriarchal constraint is fading, it remains disabling for many people. What if we could surrender these beliefs and enjoy eating solo at the most fabulous restaurants? What if we cared about our wellbeing enough to cook a multi-course meal just for ourselves alone? What if we sang and danced our heart out at a gig and didn't care who was judging? What if we took ourselves to a ball and held our hearts high as the sovereign beauty we are? What if we gifted ourselves all (and more) of these pleasures, reclaiming our royal heritage and meeting our soul tribe along the way?

Express What You're Ready to Attract

While writing the first edition of this book my fiancé and I ended our relationship. Three years on, and after a lot of healing, I'm ready to meet a beloved. Working with the angel power combo that is Archeiai Radiant, Strength, and Charity, I've come to understand this beautiful Love won't just fall from the sky! I must first believe I'm worthy to receive him, then emulate the qualities I'm looking for in him within myself, and lastly, take myself back out into the world, instead of tucking myself away at home.

Echoing Archeia Radiant's teaching on manifesting finery, and doing my best by you, beautiful reader, I began to get myself "out there" while writing this chapter, surrendering similar beliefs to those shared earlier.

I've since enrolled in dance and singing lessons (my idea of finery), joined a cooking class to meet like-minded souls, and signed up to a dating app. For the first time in my life, I'm being 100 percent me in my profile—no censoring who I am in order to fit in, no pretending to be something I'm not; just simply and unapologetically shining, as the best Love draws in from a space that's no longer guarded, wounded, or conditional.

This is the happy side to being authentic and allowing yourself to be seen and heard as you are; you'll attract the same from life.

Rise Like an Angel

◊ "I appreciate that finery is my birthright. Finery for me means . . ."

◊ "I can be more conscious in manifesting these pleasures into my life by . . . "

When we intentionally draw this kind of magic into our life, excess stress, worry, and weight also melt away. Coupled with this, hormonal imbalances tend to harmonize, too. This is because the weight on the Spirit (from a lack of joy) becomes the weight on the body, and the repressed feelings become the imbalanced hormones. Everything is connected.

Advanced Spiritual Hygiene

Archeia Purity first introduced the concept of "spiritual hygiene" in Chapter 5 when she highlighted the importance of taking everyone we've connected with through the day out of our energy field before sleep.

As empaths, it's easy to carry the beliefs, feelings, wounds, and psychic imprints of not just other people in our energy field but also the vibrations of places, events, and objects. Over time, if we do not remove these frequencies, they compound and dim our Light. As they crystallize, they can incite mental, emotional, and physical dis-ease, as prefaced earlier.

Over the last few years, as my Awareness has heightened, and along with it, my sensitivity and visibility across social media platforms, I've found more people and energies trying to connect with me. I'm not alone in this, for, as the collective consciousness of humanity raises, so too does our level of empathy.

If you take nothing else from this book and apply only the Mirror Technique that follows, you'll see great changes in your life, for, in our current age, **99 percent of all dis-ease states manifest from a psychic**

or spiritual imprint we've picked up, aligned with, or bought into. When we consciously cleanse these attachments, they can't take hold and crystallize within our being. If you doubt this, try using the technique over the course of a few nights and see what changes appear for you in the coming days.

The Mirror Technique

◊ Before going to bed, immerse your feet in cold water for 15 seconds, as detailed in the Magic Nine for Sleep Divine (see page 162). As you cleanse your feet, affirm aloud:

"I surrender all people, places, events, objects, and interactions of my day that I've connected with consciously, unconsciously, and subconsciously, on a physical and non-physical level, to Source now.
Thank you. And so it is."

◊ Take a deep breath in . . . and as you exhale, see all copies of you coming out of everything and everyone. Plug yourself and these copies back into Source now.

◊ Take another deep breath in . . . and as you exhale, see all copies of others and unwanted energies coming out of you.

◊ Immediately after doing this, surround yourself with mirrors. Mirrors can only reflect outwards, so now, when someone or something attempts to psychically reengage you, no matter what their intentions are, they'll only see and connect with themselves. Set up your mirrors in such a way as to allow those in your circle of trust to still connect with you; for everyone and everything else, they will reflect only pure unconditional Love. In this way, you honour everyone, while having a peaceful, undisturbed slumber.

◊ You can reinforce this technique by intending your crown and ear chakras to close before going to bed (you can open them again in the morning) and by applying a "muggle overlay" over your home (as detailed on page 122).

Rise Like an Angel

◊ "After a few days of using the Mirror Technique, my sleep is . . . , my mood is . . . , my clarity is . . . , and overall, my vibration feels . . . "

To fully merge with the illuminated wisdom of Archeia Radiant, please enjoy attuning to her after first reading "How to Prepare for Attunements" in Chapter 2, page 50.

Archeia Radiant Attunement

Feeling centred, sense yourself held in a column of sparkling pink and silver Light. Breathe this blended Source Ray in and out. Allow it to fill every part of you, including your aura and wings, and then see it connect through you to the centre of the Earth and the centre of the Sun. Feel your guardian angels standing on either side of you, radiating their Love, which further expands your Light. When you're ready to invite in Archeia Radiant, affirm aloud:

"Loving Archeia Radiant, angel of Illumination, Grace, and Self-Acceptance and master of the Silver Ray, may you now attune me

to your vibration and consciousness, so that I am forever linked with you and may channel your energy, love, and teachings for the best for all concerned. Thank you for helping me shine my authentic Self, no matter what I'm doing, where I am, or who I'm with. No longer will I dull my sparkle or dim my Light, for I love and accept myself as I am. Thank you. And so it is."

Breathe in Acceptance . . . and breathe out Peace, as you merge with this Divine angel. Ask Archeia Radiant what the highest and best guidance is for you at this time, and if there's anything you can support her with.

As you continue to attune to Archeia Radiant, you can also channel her healing Light. If there's a part of your body you'd like to heal, bring your hands to that area, or rest your hands upon your heart (where Radiant influences the most). Breathe the Silver Ray and its feminine, lunar Love, and reflect upon the following questions: Where do I need to raise my standards? What would it take for me to try new things? Which qualities do I need to express to call in what I'm ready for? Radiant reminds you that in raising your standards, you've nothing to lose and everything to gain.

When you feel the energy beginning to wane, intend the healing and attunement to be complete. Thank your guardian angels and Archeia Radiant before opening your eyes and drinking some water to ground yourself. Continue this visualization for at least 10 minutes to receive this healing attunement to the Diamond Ray, as it raises and expands your frequency on all levels of being.

When you feel the energy beginning to wane, intend the healing and attunement to be complete. Thank your guardian angels and Archeia Radiant before opening your eyes and drinking some water to ground yourself.

Rise Like an Angel

◊ "Attuning to the brilliance of Archeia Radiant felt like . . . Her guidance for me at this time is . . . "

◊ "Where do I need to raise my standards . . . ? What would it take for me to try new things . . . ? Which qualities do I need to express to call in what I'm ready for . . . ?"

◊ "I'll continue to invite in Archeia Radiant to support me with this and . . . "

Daily Affirmation to Connect with Archeia Radiant

"I strut the catwalk of my life as the Royal Beauty I am!"

Crystal Allies

Hematite, Picasso jasper, rainbow moonstone

Plant Allies

Alpine lily, monkshood, violet

Invite In Archeia Radiant for . . .

Divine feminine connection; grace; self-acceptance, self-discipline, and self-esteem; sensitivity; transforming self-doubt; and understanding our deepest nature, cycles, and rhythms.

Chapter 18

ARCHEIA JOY
"I AM ready to play"

Time to Play, Beauty!

Throughout the book, you've met the most on-purpose Archeiai for our ascending age and discovered how they can help you heal and empower your life. Know every time you invite in an Archeia and weave her medicine into your life, you bless the entire world. New Earth doesn't dwell outside you but lives now, within your very breath. As you bridge to Heaven, so too do you bring Heaven to all.

The story of this book's creation is really a universal one, because let's face it, living our Truth isn't always easy. We all experience pain and setbacks, and have moments, if not days, where we just don't want to get out of bed; moments when life is suddenly filled with so many endings that we lose sight of our way and feel stranded and lost.

Amid the haziness of impossibility, as the old crumbles away to give way to the new, we can receive flashes of our potential, as reflected by our inner being and angels. Tiny glimmers of hope that herald how through breakdowns, breakthroughs emerge! These inception points ask us to dig deeper into our pain, fears, and doubts than ever before, so we can see through the limitations and rise again.

And so, radiant one, from my Truth to yours, may you use the setbacks, the hardships, and the judgements as fuel to birth all that's important to you, remembering that you are Creation and Creator in every moment.

If you've read this far without enjoying the attunements, meditations, and *Rise Like an Angel* exercises, please go back and do them in sequence—you'll be so glad you did! Plus, by the time you come to dive into your 30-Day Angel Play (which follows shortly), you'll be better prepared for the profound transformation that's available.

Having a daily angel practice is a form of energetic fitness that tones the mind, body, soul, and Spirit. It's a space to meet, merge, and grow your embodied divinity; not for attaining anything, but simply to honour the Source within you. Through this practice, fears and limitations transform and a greater flow of prosperity comes into your life.

By showing up consistently for 30 days, you'll rewire your brain by creating new pathways of positive habitual consciousness, helping make this a lifelong gift you give yourself. But before we unpack the daily practice, let's meet the last angel in our adventure, Archeia Joy.

Archeia Joy Revealed

Archeia Joy, whose name is derived from the Latin word *gaudium*, meaning "rejoice", serves on the Gold Ray of Blessings, Truth, and Unity with her counterpart, Archangel Barachiel. While Barachiel manifests with a vivid green glow, Joy comes forward with pink and golden hues.

This lesser-known angel joined Angel Healing® in April 2020, when the collective consciousness took another quantum leap forward. During this time, many beautiful souls began to awaken on their spiritual path, and a call was sent out to Archangel Barachiel, who helps us know who our guardian angels are, while strengthening our overall connection with Heaven. Archeia Joy is the underlying glue that fosters the growth of close angelic relationships. She helps us acknowledge that we also come from Heaven, and as an angelic soul, we have the capacity to uncover the underlying blessings within all things.

Together, Barachiel and Joy help lift the restrictive societal and religious conditionings we may feel tethered to, so we can live peacefully and comfortably with our own choices and not have to conform to the ideals of others. As a guiding angel for the LGBTQ+ community, they encourage us to love and accept ourselves as we are, living outside the lines, and doing so in ways that feel naturally good. They echo that the only validation we need is our own, for we weren't born to fit in; we came to Earth eager to make a difference and express our Light uniquely.

Joy, also known as "Lady Joy" and "Rosa", has a healing influence on the throat, heart, and solar plexus chakras. As a pure expression of Love, Joy reminds us to take ourselves lightly and to make our spiritual path of Ascension fun. She shares:

> Know yourself to be the artist of your life. Bring in colour, form, and feeling. Choose to make your path a masterpiece!

In her depiction, Archeia Joy is literally bursting with life! Per her request, she is surrounded by blooming flowers, symbolic of keeping ourselves open to pleasure and play. This is reiterated by her forearm tattoo, which reads, "Love is real." This echoes the teaching that **we're not here to be in servitude to anything external; our only service is to Love**, and we can serve best by both being Love and practising Love through our thoughts, words, actions, and contributions.

The Blessing of Thank You

In the following exercise, Archeia Joy invites you to bring greater thanksgiving into your everyday world. Saying thank you is the greatest portal to joy; the more you say it, the better you feel.

Embodying Joy

◊ As you wake each morning, begin with a smile. Appreciate being alive, praising this new dawn, and all the blessings currently in your life, and those you're magnetising. Affirm aloud, "I am worthy of my wildest dreams coming true and they are already here."

◊ Throughout the day, thank your water, food, home, plants, activities, places, people—everything and everyone, shower all with appreciation. Give yourself pleasure moments to stop and "smell the roses", savouring what you're doing, who you're with, and how you're feeling.

◊ Find the blessings in any uncertainty or challenges that may present. If something feels especially difficult, ask yourself, "How can I move through this, and do so with Joy?" By adding "and do so with Joy" you're sending a signal to your inner being to inspire you with the best course of action.

◊ Before going to sleep enjoy Magic Nine for Sleep Divine (see page 162) or say thank you for your bed, for shelter and warmth. Send a blessing out to the world, such as, "As everyone goes to sleep tonight, may they know how loved, cherished, and appreciated they are." As you give Joy so too, recognise that the Spirit of Joy lives within you.

The Blessing of Life

Archeia Joy, like all the Archeiai and Archangels, encourage us to live every day to the fullest, for life is a blessing, a fragile gift that hangs on a breath . . . literally!

Many people take life for granted, assuming it's always going to be here for them, but we never know when our last physical moment will be. Life doesn't come at some point in the future, when we've finally found the person, lost the weight, or have the level of financial freedom we want; it's happening NOW, and NOW, and NOW . . . a series of fleeting moments that we can have the Awareness of being in, as well as, observe.

When we focus only in and on the moment, everything becomes meaningful. The underlying blessings of all reveal themselves and we see that a full life is one that includes death, pain, adversity, limitation, and growth. Every moment becomes precious: every smile, every tear, every laugh, every kiss, every "I love you"—ALL of it. By appreciating every iota of life, we make all experiences joyful. This is both our work and play!

Expressing Joy through Art

If you decide to welcome Archeia Joy into your life, she'll inspire you to reflect and act upon the following questions: *What makes my heart sing? What tickles and delights me? What makes me feel most alive?* Whether you're inspired to sing, move, create more, make love more, bring your soul into all that you're in-joying! You'll lift and bless the space you're in, while charging your life force so you're always giving (and expressing) the best of yourself. You can elevate this more with the following angelic art session to intentionally express and mirror joy in your environment.

◊　Gather paper, card, or canvas and a variety of pens, chalks, or paints, along with any embellishments you wish to add to your art. Follow the Four Essential Steps (see page 75), and in the fourth step, welcome your guardian angels, Archeia Joy and Archangel Jophiel and their Gold Ray, to be with you. Breathe in their collective presence as you ask them to inspire your creativity to flow freely . . . and breathe out into Appreciation.

◊　Draw or paint a picture that either reflects your growth with the angels so far, or consider illustrating the growth you wish to see for yourself, your life, and/or New Earth as a whole. Allow the angels to move through you as you select the colours and embellishments that feel best. Symbols, angelic light-language, virtues, and words may also flow through for you to incorporate.

◊　You may be inspired to add your favourite quote or teaching from this book (or another one) so that your art reflects back to you and your space pure positive vibrations. (Since hanging my favourite quote, "She decided to live the life she always imagined", opposite my shower, I'm reminded each day to stay focused and accountable in my thoughts, choices, and actions to make this reality.)

◊ Frame and hang your picture somewhere you'll see it every day, and thank the angels for adding their magical support, too.

Rise Like an Angel

◊ ". . . makes my heart sing." ". . . tickles and delights me." ". . . makes me feel most alive."

◊ "My favourite empowering quotes are . . ."

◊ "I'll continue to experiment with angelic art, channelling Archeia/Archangel . . . next for the purpose of . . . "

Daily Angel Practice

To cultivate one-on-one time with your angels, please enjoy connecting with them for 30 consecutive days. First, decide on a start date. Beginning your practice at the start of a month or on a New Moon are ideal times. Secondly, set an intention for change. What do you want to transform, manifest, learn, grow, and give over the 30 days? Thirdly, set up an angel altar, a sacred space in your home where you can place both your written intention and this book, and adorn the space with flowers, crystals and your favourite angel cards or statues. Choose to devote at least 20 minutes per day to sitting in front of your altar and enjoying your angel play.

Doing your daily practice in the early morning is best, before anything can muddy or distract your natural Source flow. Keep your journal handy to record the insights and messages that reveal themselves.

If you feel any resistance or psychic interference getting in the way of enjoying your practice, observe what's emerging, and surrender it to the Archeiai.

Always begin each day with the Four Essential Steps (see page 75), and focus on your intention for change. If, for whatever reason, you miss a practice day, don't worry; just pick up the next day where you left off. Envision yourself completing the 30 days, and doing so with Joy in your heart. Let the magic and miracles flow!

30-Day Angel Play

Arriving at your angel altar (or another prepared sacred spot), affirm aloud:

> *"Thank you for this new day, a new way to be,*
> *a new way to see. I am awake. I am here.*
> *At One with Source and crystal clear."*

Sense yourself held in a column of swirling rose-gold Light that extends 44 feet around your aura. Breathe into this Light . . . and breathe it out. Follow the Four Essential Steps (see page 75), as you sense every part of you, including your wings and aura, showered in rose-gold Light. Enjoy how centred, grounded, and connected you feel.

Now enjoy the suggested practice for each day (as highlighted below), or open the book randomly and enjoy the exercise shown.

◊ Receiving Your Wings meditation (page 30)

◊ Birthing New Earth activation, plus Archeia Faith attunement (pages 48 and 51)

◊ Forgiveness Ceremony, plus Archeia Virtue attunement (pages 65 and 68)

◊ Writing with Hope exercise (page 82)

◊ Energy Drainers and Energy Raisers, plus Archeia Purity attunement (pages 95 and 102)

◊ Violet Flame Cleanse (page 99)

◊ Receiving Your Diamond Heart activation (page 108)

◊ Five Temple Steps of Angelic Feng Shui (page 116)

◊ Divine Alchemy Session (page 294)

◊ Archeia Charity attunement (page 155)

◊ Love Yourself Ritual (page 149)

◊ Sunnier Self-Talk exercise, plus Archeia Clarity attunement (pages 164 and 168)

◊ Magic Nine for Sleep Divine (page 162)

◊ Mirror Alchemy Session, plus Archeia Mercy attunement (pages 174 and 183)

◊ Love Your Body Ritual (page 176)

◊ Archeia Freedom attunement (page 197)

◊ Empower Your Sexuality activation (page 194)

◊ Tuning in to Harmony healing, plus Archeia Harmony attunement (pages 205 and 212)

◊ Ancestral Breathwork Healing (page 209)

◊ Uprooting Financial Beliefs, plus Archeia Patience attunement (pages 220 and 227)

◊ Money Alchemy Session (page 222)

◊ I AM Fearless list, plus Archeia Serenity attunement (pages 235 and 240)

◊ Unleash Your Inner Warrior ceremony (page 237)

◊ Four Pillars of Building Resilience exercise (page 294)

◊   Integrating your 13 Chakras (page 264)

◊   Reflective Radiance Ritual (page 276)

◊   The Mirror Technique, plus Archeia Radiant Attunement (pages 281 and 282)

◊   Embodying Joy exercise, plus Archeia Joy Attunement (pages 298 and 296)

◊   Expressing Joy through Art (page 291)

Reflect on your journey. Was your intention met? Was it surpassed? How have you grown over the last 30 days? What has been your greatest takeaway from the experience? Give thanks to the angels, and let your loved ones borrow this book to share the Love.

Rise Like an Angel

◊ "My intention for my 30-Day Angel Play is . . . "

◊ "On Day 1, I'm feeling . . . On Day 30, I'm feeling . . . "

◊ "My next adventure with the Archeiai is . . . "

To fully merge with the merriment of Archeia Joy, please enjoy attuning to her, after first reading "How to Prepare for Attunements" in Chapter 2, page 50.

Archeia Joy Attunement

Feeling centred, sense yourself held in a column of golden-pink Light. Breathe this blended Source Ray in and out. Allow it to fill every part of you, including your aura and wings, and then see it connect through you to the centre of the Earth and the centre of the Sun. Feel your guardian angels standing on either side of you, radiating their Love, which further expands your Light. When you're ready to invite in Archeia Joy, affirm aloud:

"Loving Archeia Joy, angel of Blessings, Truth, Unity and master of the Gold Ray, may you now attune me to your vibration and consciousness, so I am forever linked with you and may channel your energy, light, and teachings for the best of all concerned. Thank you for helping me see that life doesn't have to be serious and know that I need only be myself to serve Source in the best way. May you continue to show me the blessings and humour in every situation, and laugh, lighten, and awaken all that I am through pleasure and play. Thank you. And so it is."

Breathe in Bliss . . . breathe out Bliss, as you merge with this Divine angel. Ask Archeia Joy what the highest and best guidance is for you at this time, and if there's anything you can support her with.

As you continue to attune to Joy, you can also channel her healing Light. If there's a part of your body you'd like to heal, bring your hands to that area now, or place your hands on your throat, heart, or solar plexus (the chakras that Joy influences). As you relax into the healing, recount your happiest memory, and imagine that you are there reliving the moment. If this memory could be encapsulated into a colour and quality, what would the colour and quality be? Now sense yourself being bathed in these energies, perhaps feeling this sensation to be like a "golden hug". Any time you'd like to feel joyful in the future just remember this colour and quality, breathe it in . . . bathe in it . . . become Joy.

When you feel the energy beginning to wane, intend the healing and attunement to be complete. Thank your guardian angels and Archeia Joy before opening your eyes and drinking some water to ground yourself.

◊ "Attuning to the cheerfulness of Archeia Joy felt like . . . "

◊ "Her guidance for me at this time is . . . "

◊ "I'll continue to invite in Archeia Joy to co-create . . . "

Daily Affirmation to Connect with Archeia Joy

"I am eager to play, have fun, enjoy adventures, and live beyond limitation."

Crystal Allies

Blue amber, honey calcite, yellow quartz

Plant Allies

Sierra primrose, tiger lily, zinnia

Invite In Archeia Joy for . . .

Embracing personal evolution, inciting expansion, levity, appreciating the moment, understanding sensations of déjà vu, unity, and witnessing the underlying blessings within everyone and everything.

CONCLUSION

The aim of *The Female Archangels* was to share with you the loving, and profoundly life-changing teachings of the Archeiai from a tried and tested perspective. These incredible angels are here on purpose to empower you to reclaim the full potentiality of your heart, mind, soul, Spirit, and your ever-expanding body of Light, so you can joyfully live in greater wholeness with All that you are.

Know that every time you invite in an Archeia and weave her medicine into your life, you bless the entire world for this co-creation is truly a gift that keeps on gifting! You *are* a New Earth pioneer and part of co-creating New Earth for all to enjoy is to remember that this realm of greater possibility and freedom doesn't exist outside of you, but lives now, within your very breath. All you need to do is to engage with the fire of your Truth within to breathe this brand-new world into physical existence. As you bridge within to Heaven, so too do you bring Heaven to Earth.

As we come full circle together, there's an overflow of Love in my heart and Gratitude in my tears that are flowing onto this page. Sacred tears of pure appreciation for you, for me, for the richness of Heaven being here, within and around us. I have dedicated much of my adult life to introducing who the Archeiai are and sharing how we can partner with them. There have been times this sacred work has been repurposed, as can happen. Nevertheless, I am a firm believer in the original teachings this book and its accompanying oracle deck share; shining no matter any opposing forces as we collectively evolve what is known about the reality of Heaven and the realm of angels.

We could say that the story of the book's creation is really a universal one, because let's face it, living our Truth isn't always easy. We all experience pain and setbacks, and have moments, if not days, where we just don't want to get out of bed; moments where life is suddenly filled with so many endings that we can lose sight of our way and feel stranded, unwanted, or unworthy.

Amid the haze of impossibility, as the old crumbles to give way to the new, we can receive flashes of potential, as reflected by our inner being and angels. With tiny glimmers of hope that herald through breakdowns, breakthroughs emerge. These inception points ask us to dig deeper than ever before into our pain, fears, and doubts, until we see the layers are shed, the truth comes up and we rise again.

So, Shining One, from my Truth to yours, use the pain, the set-backs, and any inner and outer judgements as fuel to birth all that's important to you, remembering you are both Creator and Creation, shaping reality in every moment through your words, feelings, choices, and actions. Be brave enough to push through any opposition and let your authentic Light shine. Build your reality on a foundation of faith as you find yourself wiser, lighter, and freer than ever before.

To midwife and illuminate this path and process of divine alchemy, if you've read this far without diving into the angelic attunements, meditations, and exercises, please go back and enjoy them in sequence now. Trust me, you'll be so glad you gifted yourself the time, space, and integration to sip and savour these. Plus, by the time you come to enjoy your 30-Day Angel Play (in the last chapter), you'll be better prepared for the profound transformation that awaits!

Stay in touch and share your progress by using the hashtag *#TheFemaleArchangels*, and joining the Instagram page, *@TheFemaleArchangels*. I'd love to hear your insights of meeting, merging, and partnering with our celestial big sisters, and answering any questions you have that'll help further your connection. There is also a free book club community at *https://www.facebook.com/groups/ TheFemaleArchangels* to connect with fellow angel tribe and support one another in this incredible journey of divine remembrance and embodiment.

If you'd like to learn more about Angel Healing® and become a certified practitioner for you, your family, and wider community then send me a message via *https://www.CalistaAscension.com.*

Until we meet again, dearest heart, may you continue to see your greatest potential in the loving embrace of the angels. Let them raise you up and help you to **S H I N E** for the sheer joy of being authentically You!

I honour you. I love you. And I proudly walk beside you.

Your sis'star,

Calista

APPENDICES

APPENDIX I

Table 1: Angel Attributes

Archeia	Archangel	Source Rays Serving Upon	Colour Manifestation	Energetic Influence
Charity	Chamuel	Pink, Ruby, and Red Rays of Divine Love and Devotion	Pink, red, and gold	Higher heart, heart, and causal chakras
Clarity	Jophiel	Yellow and Gold Rays of Illumination, Beauty, and Wisdom	Like sunlight: white, gold, and yellow	Crown chakra
Constance	Metatron	Diamond Ray of Universal Ascension and Sacred Geometry	Orange, gold (mostly Metatron), silver, purple, indigo, and black (mostly Constance)	Stellar gateway and soul star chakras, Light-Body
Faith	Michael	Blue, Gold, and Sapphire Rays of Divine Will, Power, and Protection	Blue, gold (mostly Faith), indigo	Throat chakra
Freedom	Jeremiel	Orange Ray of Acceptance, Compassion, and Understanding	Orange, brown, and electric blues (mostly Freedom)	Throat, heart, navel, and sacral chakras
Grace	Uriel	Ruby Ray of Peace, Devotion, and Inspiration	Red, orange, gold, and purple (mostly Uriel)	Solar plexus chakra, auric field
Harmony	Raguel	Pale Blue Ray of Co-operation and Unity	Pale blue and sparkling white (mostly Harmony)	Solar plexus, heart, and throat chakras

Archeia	Archangel	Source Rays Serving Upon	Colour Manifestation	Energetic Influence
Hope	Gabriel	White and Crystalline Rays of Harmony, Purity, and Communication	Creamy pearlescent white and watery blues	Navel, sacral, and base chakras
Joy	Barachiel	Gold Ray of Blessings, Truth, and Unity	Bright green (mostly Barachiel), pink, and gold.	Throat, heart, and solar plexus chakras
Mercy	Azrael	Copper and Magenta Rays of Soul Ascension	Copper, deep metallic brown, peach, rose-gold, and magenta (mostly Mercy)	Soul star, throat, heart, and base chakras
Patience	Sandalphon	Rainbow Ray of Music, Manifestation, and Integration	Earthly browns and crystalline rainbow hues	Base and earth star chakras, auric field
Purity	Zadkiel	Violet Ray of Transformation and Surrender	Magenta, violet, silver, and gold	Soul star, crown, and sacral chakras, auric field
Radiant	Haniel	Silver Ray of Illumination, Grace, and Self-Acceptance	Like moonlight: silver, pale blue, and pink	Heart and stellar gateway chakras
Serenity	Cassiel	Black Ray of Transcendence and Potential	Black, grey, white (mostly Cassiel), pearlescent silver, and pink (mostly Serenity)	Crown, solar plexus, and base chakras
Strength	Ariel	Orange and Green Rays of Acceptance, Fortitude, and Nature	Lime green and orange	Solar plexus and base chakras

Appendix 1

Archeia	Archangel	Source Rays Serving Upon	Colour Manifestation	Energetic Influence
Victory	Raziel	Diamond Ray of Universal Ascension, Magic, and Wisdom	Rainbow colours, crystalline, and gold	Third eye, crown, and stellar gateway chakras
Virtue	Raphael	Green, Pink, and Emerald Rays of Healing, Truth, and Divine Love	Green, purple (mostly Raphael), and pink (mostly Virtue)	Third eye, higher heart, and heart chakras

Table 2: Archeia Messages and Allies

Archeia	Key Message	Guiding Affirmation	Crystal Allies	Plant Allies
Charity	Bring in Love	"I am loved, lovable, worthy, and wonderful."	"Heart of God Within", pink andara, rose quartz, ruby	Buttercup, harebell, mariposa lily
Clarity	Rest, Reflect, Recharge	"Resting is my new doing."	Natural citrine, solaris andara, yellow phenakite	Ash, fig flower, lemon flower
Constance	Bring Heaven to Earth	"I trust in the bright new world that's emerging and the inherent goodness of humanity."	Azeztulite, blue sky fluorite, charoite	Cornflower, mugwort, quince
Faith	Lead with confidence	"I rejoice in knowing that my life is by my design."	Elestial sapphire andara, golden topaz, Labradorite	Frankincense, sunflower, tall mountain larkspur
Freedom	Enliven your senses	"I am free, free to be me."	Carnelian, lemurian amber andara, tangerine aura quartz	Easter lily, hibiscus, walnut
Grace	More flow, less hustle	"Every moment of my life is a miracle to savour and enjoy."	Fire opal, mookaite, clear topaz	Ginger, hound's tongue, red poppy
Harmony	Bring in music	"I live in joyous co-creation with life, honouring its diversity and contrast while staying centred."	Brucite, blue lace agate, celestite	Grapefruit flower, lungwort, vervain

Archeia	Key Message	Guiding Affirmation	Crystal Allies	Plant Allies
Hope	Expect the best	"I am a lover of life and its Infinite possibilities!"	Aquamarine, blue calcite, chrysocolla	Calendula, trumpet vine, white lily
Joy	Prioritize play and pleasure	"I am eager to play, have fun, enjoy adventures, and live beyond limitation."	Blue amber, honey calcite, yellow quartz	Sierra primrose, tiger lily, zinnia
Mercy	Cherish your sacredness	"Body, you are a living, thriving genius, a work of art and a temple to adore. Thank you, for everything you do. I love you. I honour you."	Cuprite, garnet, magenta Vesuvianite	Freesia, hawthorn, rose
Patience	Trust the process	"Within my world there's an overflow of abundant prosperity for all to enjoy."	Cinnabar, Raspberry garnet, tsavorite	Baby blue eyes, trillium, white daisy
Purity	Cleanse and detoxify	"Keeping my energy bright and buoyant empowers me to create and live my best life."	Auralite 23, sugilite, violet flame opal	Lavender, St. John's wort, yarrow
Radiant	Raise your standards	"I strut the catwalk of my life as the Royal Beauty I am!"	Hematite, Picasso jasper, rainbow moonstone	Alpine lily, monkshood, violet

Archeia	Key Message	Guiding Affirmation	Crystal Allies	Plant Allies
Serenity	Weave a new story	"Thank you, fear, for showing me where I need to let the Light in. As I relax, all softens, for I am Serenity."	Cosmic ice andara, larimar, shungite	Chamomile, star of Bethlehem, violet
Strength	Unleash your magic	"I am magical, and I use my Magic to conjure spells of worthiness, strength, determination, and love. I embrace sacred action and the positive change that's unfolding."	Amazonite, fluorapatite, orange calcite	Borage, dandelion, star thistle
Victory	Raise your vibration	"I delight in knowing that my invincibility, like my vibrational alignment, is within my control."	Angel aura clear quartz, diamond, silver quartz	Larch, magnolia, star tulip
Virtue	Open your heart	"It is safe for me to open my heart to Love and be loved in return."	Emerald, petalite, rhodochrosite	Daffodil, hyssop, willow

APPENDIX II

A–Z Angel Healing® Prescription Guide

Angels never assume we need "healing", for they see us in their highest Light. Yet, they understand that living a physical life with free will brings conditioning and challenges that promote a sense of separation from Source. This separation can in turn cause a build-up of resistance and dis-ease to manifest in our body.

Angels (especially the Archeiai) help unearth the root cause of disease, so we can enjoy radiant health and wellbeing. When we invite in the angels for the purpose of healing, their angelic frequencies flow to to where they are needed in alignment with the wisdom of our inner being; therefore, angels can assist with any healing intention.

The following A–Z Angel Healing® Prescription Guide is a unique multi-purpose directory based upon a decade of Angel Healing® practitioner and client breakthroughs and includes close to **400 dis-ease symptoms and the best angels to invite in to resolve them**. You'll notice that sometimes more than one angel is listed for an ailment. This is because certain angels will focus their energy on addressing the symptoms of the dis-ease and others on transforming their underlying root cause. Please invite in the angels in the order they appear, unless your intuition guides you to do otherwise.

For ease, I have grouped ailments into those concerned with the physical body (including the main organs, tissues, and systems), the emotional and mental body, and the spiritual/energetic body (including the chakras, auric field, and light-body). The directory is in no way definitive, so please add to it as you deepen your angelic skillset. Remember, your healing is ultimately in your hands, but when you open yourself to the vibrational support of angels and believe in the template of wellbeing they hold for you, you'll return to wellbeing far faster. Give thanks to the angels for their assistance each time you partner with them, and do share this guide with others.

How to Use the Directory

1.   Match your ailment to the appropriate angel(s).

2.   Follow the Four Essential Steps on page 75. At step 4, invite in
     your guardian angels and affirm aloud (inserting the names of
     the appropriate angels):

     "Loving Archeia _____ and / or Archangel _____, may
     you now come forward and channel your healing Light through
     me and into me, for the highest and best of all concerned.
     Thank you. And so it is."

For healing another, please gain their permission first then affirm aloud:

     "Loving Archeia _____ and / or Archangel _____, may
     you now come forward and channel your healing Light through
     me and into _ (inserting the person's name)__ , for the highest
     and best of all concerned. I ask this under the Law of Grace.
     Thank you. And so it is."

3.   Place your hands on your heart or on the area where you sense
     the root of the dis-ease is. Relax as the LoveLight moves through
     you. (The speed, flow, and depth of the vibrational frequencies
     you experience will vary depending on the angels you're part-
     nering.) Stay open to any guidance that comes to you during
     the healing, such as taking a certain action or making a lifestyle
     change. Envision the highest resolve of what you and the angels
     are bringing healing, love, andempowerment to.

4.   Enjoy the treatment for as long as you're guided. To close, reverse
     the *Four Essential Steps*, giving thanks to the angels and ground-
     ing your Awareness back in your body.

1. Angel Prescriptions for the Physical Body

A

Abdomen ailments: Archangel Uriel, Archangel Michael, Archeia Patience

Abortion (healing of): Archangel Gabriel, Archeia Faith, Archeia Mercy, Archeia Charity

Acidity: Archeia Joy, Archangel Gabriel, Archeia Grace

Aches and pains: Archangel Uriel, Archangel Raphael, Archeia Radiant

Acne: Archeia Purity, Archangel Raphael, Archeia Virtue

Ageing (to slow effects of): Archeia Charity, Archangel Metatron, Archeia Grace

AIDS: Archeia Freedom, Archeia Charity, Archeia Purity, Archangel Michael

Allergies: Archeia Purity, Archangel Gabriel, Archeia Charity

Altitude sickness: Archangel Jophiel, Archangel Barachiel, Archangel Chamuel

Anaemia: Archangel Ariel, Archangel Gabriel, Archeia Hope

Angina: Archangel Chamuel, Archangel Raphael, Archeia Virtue

Arteriosclerosis: Archangel Chamuel, Archeia Mercy

Arthritis: Archangel Cassiel, Archeia Serenity, Archeia Virtue, Archeia Freedom,

Asthma: Archeia Charity, Archeia Freedom, Archangel Raphael, Archangel Raguel

Autoimmune disease: Archeia Freedom, Archangel Zadkiel, Archangel Michael, Archeia Charity

B

Back pain: Archangel Sandalphon, Archeia Patience, Archangel Jophiel

Bacterial infections: Archangel Zadkiel, Archeia Purity, Archangel Raphael, Archangel Michael

Bad breath: Archeia Purity

Bile duct blockages: Archeia Freedom, Archangel Uriel, Archangel Cassiel

Bladder issues: Archeia Freedom, Archangel Raphael

Blistering: Archangel Chamuel, Archangel Raphael

Bloating: Archangel Gabriel

Blood issues: Archangel Ariel, Archangel Gabriel, Archeia Hope

Blood pressure (high): Archangel Gabriel, Archeia Grace, Archeia Patience

Blood pressure (low): Archangel Ariel, Archeia Strength

Boils: Archangel Cassiel, Archeia Virtue, Archeia Freedom, Archeia Faith

Bones (issues and fractures): Archeia Strength, Archangel Uriel, Archangel Sandalphon

Breastfeeding: Archangel Gabriel, Archeia Mercy

Bronchitis: Archeia Charity, Archeia Freedom, Archangel Raphael, Archangel Raguel

Bruises: Archangel Michael, Archangel Raphael, Archangel Gabriel, Archeia Joy

Burns: Archangel Gabriel, Archangel Raphael, Archangel Chamuel

Calcium deficiency: Archangel Uriel, Archeia Clarity

Cancer-related diseases: Archangel Michael, Archangel Zadkiel, Archangel Chamuel, Archeia Charity

Cell rejuvenation: Archangel Raphael, Archeia Virtue, Archangel Michael, Archangel Jophiel

Cellulite: Archangel Haniel, Archeia Radiant, Archeia Charity, Archeia Freedom

Chemotherapy: Archangel Michael, Archeia Strength, Archeia Radiant, Archangel Zadkiel

Chickenpox: Archangel Zadkiel, Archangel Raphael, Archeia Purity

Childbirth: Archeia Virtue, Archangel Gabriel, Archeia Constance, Archeia Mercy

Cholesterol (to lower): Archangel Raphael, Archeia Charity, Archeia Mercy

Chronic illness: Archangel Raphael, Archangel Zadkiel, Archangel Jeremiel

Circulation (to boost): Archangel Michael, Archeia Freedom, Archangel Raphael

Claustrophobia: Archangel Michael, Archangel Cassiel, Archeia Grace
Colic: Archangel Gabriel, Archangel Metatron, Archeia Constance, Archeia Hope
Colour blindness: Archangel Uriel, Archangel Raphael, Archeia Virtue
Cramp: Archangel Chamuel, Archeia Hope, Archangel Michael, Archeia Virtue

D

Depression: Archeia Virtue, Archangel Raphael, Archeia Faith, Archangel Michael
Detoxification: Archeia Purity, Archangel Gabriel, Archangel Zadkiel
Diabetes: Archangel Jeremiel, Archeia Constance
Diarrhea: Archangel Sandalphon, Archeia Hope, Archeia Freedom
Digestive problems: Archangel Cassiel, Archeia Patience, Archeia Grace
Dizziness: Archangel Sandalphon, Archeia Clarity
Drunkenness: Archangel Sandalphon, Archeia Clarity, Archeia Purity
Dyslexia: Archangel Michael, Archangel Raguel, Archeia Harmony

E

Ear problems: Archangel Uriel, Archangel Raphael, Archangel Raziel
Eating disorders: Archeia Radiant, Archeia Charity, Archeia Mercy
Eczema: Archangel Michael, Archangel Raphael, Archangel Gabriel, Archeia Joy
Epilepsy: Archangel Michael, Archeia Purity, Archangel Metatron
Excess acid: Archangel Gabriel
Excess adrenaline: Archeia Harmony, Archangel Raguel
Eye problems: Archangel Raphael, Archeia Virtue, Archangel Raziel

F

Fatigue: Archeia Joy, Archeia Strength, Archangel Michael
Fertility: Archangel Gabriel, Archeia Mercy
Fever: Archangel Raphael, Archeia Virtue, Archangel Gabriel, Archeia Hope
Foot ailments: Archangel Sandalphon, Archeia Purity, Archangel Cassiel

Forgetfulness: Archeia Clarity, Archangel Jophiel, Archangel Raziel

Fractures: Archangel Michael, Archangel Jophiel, Archeia Strength

Frigidity: Archeia Patience, Archeia Mercy, Archangel Gabriel, Archangel Jeremiel

Fungal ailments: Archangel Michael, Archangel Jeremiel, Archeia Purity

G

Glands, swollen: Archangel Gabriel

Gout: Archangel Gabriel, Archeia Hope

H

Haemorrhoids: Archeia Freedom, Archeia Joy

Hair problems: Archangel Michael, Archangel Raphael, Archeia Radiance

Hangover: Archangel Zadkiel, Archeia Clarity, Archeia Purity

Headache (and migraines): Archangel Zadkiel, Archeia Purity, Archangel Gabriel

Hearing problems: Archangel Uriel, Archangel Raphael, Archangel Raziel

Heart problems: Archeia Charity, Archangel Chamuel, Archangel Jeremiel

Hormone imbalance: Archangel Raphael, Archangel Gabriel, Archeia Virtue, Archeia Hope

Hot flushes: Archangel Gabriel, Archeia Mercy, Archeia Serenity

I

Immune system deficiencies: Archeia Freedom, Archangel Zadkiel, Archangel Michael, Archeia Charity

Impotence: Archangel Sandalphon, Archeia Patience, Archangel Jeremiel

Infection: Archangel Zadkiel, Archangel Chamuel, Archeia Purity

Infertility: Archangel Gabriel, Archeia Mercy

Inflammation: Archangel Michael, Archangel Raphael, Archeia Virtue

Influenza (and colds): Archangel Raphael, Archeia Charity, Archangel Raguel

Insomnia: Archeia Purity, Archangel Zadkiel, Archangel Raphael, Archeia Virtue

Intestinal issues: Archangel Uriel, Archangel Ariel, Archangel Raguel, Archangel Cassiel

Intestinal parasites: Archangel Zadkiel, Archeia Purity

Irritable bowel syndrome: Archangel Gabriel, Archeia Hope, Archeia Freedom

K

Kidney problems: Archeia Freedom, Archangel Zadkiel, Archeia Constance, Archangel Michael

L

Lactation (to boost): Archangel Gabriel, Archeia Hope, Archeia Grace

Laryngitis: Archangel Michael, Archeia Patience, Archeia Freedom

Learning difficulties: Archangel Metatron, Archeia Constance, Archangel Michael

Libido (to boost): Archangel Michael, Archeia Virtue, Archeia Grace, Archeia Mercy

Ligaments, torn: Archangel Michael

Liver problems: Archeia Grace, Archangel Ariel, Archeia Harmony

Lung problems: Archeia Charity, Archeia Freedom, Archangel Raphael, Archangel Raguel

Lupus: Archangel Raphael, Archangel Zadkiel, Archangel Michael, Archeia Charity

Lymphatic ailments: Archeia Freedom, Archangel Zadkiel, Archangel Michael, Archeia Charity

M

Malabsorption of vitamins and minerals: Archangel Uriel, Archeia Strength, Archeia Patience

Malaria: Archeia Purity, Archangel Raphael

Menopause: Archeia Mercy, Archeia Purity, Archeia Freedom, Archeia Joy

Menstrual disorders: Archeia Mercy, Archeia Purity, Archeia Freedom

Metabolic dysfunction: Archangel Raphael, Archangel Raziel, Archeia Victory

Mouth ailments: Archangel Michael, Archeia Freedom, Archangel Raphael

Muscle spasms: Archangel Raphael, Archangel Michael

Myalgic encephalomyelitis (ME): Archangel Raphael, Archeia Joy, Archeia Strength, Archangel Michael

Nail problems: Archangel Raphael, Archeia Serenity

Nervousness: Archeia Harmony, Archeia Faith, Archeia Clarity

Neuralgia: Archangel Michael, Archangel Raphael, Archangel Zadkiel, Archeia Virtue

Osteoporosis: Archangel Uriel, Archangel Sandalphon, Archangel Cassiel, Archangel Jophiel

Pain: Archangel Michael, Archangel Raphael, Archangel Zadkiel, Archeia Virtue

Pancreatitis: Archangel Raguel, Archeia Serenity

Panic attacks: Archeia Charity, Archeia Serenity and Archangel Michael

Parkinson's disease: Archangel Chamuel, Archeia Virtue, Archangel Raphael

Poisoning (and poisonous bites): Archeia Purity, Archangel Raphael

Premenstrual tension: Archeia Mercy, Archeia Purity, Archeia Freedom

Radiation-related illness: Archeia Purity, Archangel Gabriel

Respiratory tract: Archeia Freedom, Archangel Raphael, Archangel Raguel

Rheumatism: Archangel Chamuel, Archeia Virtue, Archangel Raphael

Rheumatoid arthritis: Archangel Uriel, Archeia Virtue, Archangel Raphael

Scalds: Archangel Gabriel, Archangel Raphael
Sciatica: Archangel Chamuel, Archeia Hope, Archangel Michael, Archeia Virtue
Sick building syndrome: Archangel Azrael, Archangel Raphael, Archangel Michael
Sinusitis: Archeia Charity, Archangel Raguel, Archeia Harmony
Skin conditions: Archangel Michael, Archangel Raphael, Archangel Gabriel, Archeia Joy
Sleeplessness: Archeia Purity, Archangel Zadkiel, Archangel Raphael, Archeia Virtue
Smell (loss of): Archeia Charity, Archangel Raguel, Archeia Harmony
Sores: Archangel Raphael, Archeia Virtue
Spine: Archangel Jophiel, Archeia Strength, Archangel Raziel, Archangel Zadkiel
Stammer: Archeia Victory, Archeia Freedom, Archeia Mercy
Stiff neck: Archangel Raguel
Stomach ailments: Archeia Joy, Archangel Gabriel, Archeia Grace
Swelling: Archangel Raphael, Archangel Zadkiel

Taste (loss of): Archangel Raphael, Archeia Joy
Throat issues: Archangel Michael, Archeia Faith, Archangel Gabriel
Thyroid issues: Archangel Michael, Archeia Faith, Archeia Mercy
Tired eyes: Archangel Raphael, Archangel Raziel, Archeia Virtue
Tissue degeneration: Archangel Raphael, Archeia Virtue, Archangel Michael
Tonsillitis: Archeia Freedom, Archangel Michael
Tooth pain: Archeia Clarity, Archangel Michael, Archangel Uriel, Archangel Raphael
Tumour: Archangel Raphael, Archeia Virtue, Archangel Zadkiel, Archeia Purity

Ulceration: Archangel Raphael, Archeia Virtue, Archeia Clarity

Varicose veins: Archangel Michael, Archeia Freedom, Archangel Raphael

Vertigo: Archangel Barachiel, Archangel Chamuel

Water retention: Archangel Gabriel, Archeia Serenity

Weight loss: Archeia Clarity, Archangel Uriel, Archangel Michael, Archeia Radiant

Whooping cough: Archeia Charity, Archeia Freedom, Archangel Raphael, Archangel Raguel

Wounds: Archangel Raphael

Wrinkles: Archeia Charity, Archeia Radiant, Archangel Jophiel

X-ray, effects of: Archangel Chamuel, Archeia Charity

Yeast infection: Archangel Azrael, Archeia Mercy, Archangel Gabriel, Archeia Virtue

Angels for Supporting the Organs/Main Tissues

Adrenal glands: Archeia Purity, Archangel Zadkiel, Archangel Raphael, Archeia Virtue

Bile duct: Archeia Freedom, Archangel Uriel, Archangel Cassiel

Bladder: Archeia Freedom, Archangel Raphael

Bowels: Archangel Sandalphon, Archeia Hope, Archeia Freedom

Brain: Archangel Jophiel, Archangel Michael, Archangel Raziel

Cells: Archangel Raphael, Archeia Virtue, Archangel Metatron

Colon: Archangel Uriel, Archangel Ariel, Archangel Raguel, Archangel Cassiel

Eyes: Archangel Raphael, Archeia Virtue, Archangel Raziel

Gall bladder: Archangel Uriel, Archangel Cassiel, Archeia Freedom

Heart: Archeia Charity, Archangel Chamuel, Archangel Jeremiel

Intestines: Archangel Uriel, Archangel Ariel, Archangel Raguel, Archangel Cassiel

Kidneys: Archeia Freedom, Archangel Zadkiel, Archeia Constance, Archangel Michael

Larynx: Archangel Michael, Archeia Faith

Liver: Archeia Grace, Archangel Ariel, Archeia Harmony

Lungs: Archeia Charity, Archeia Freedom, Archangel Raphael, Archangel Raguel

Pancreas: Archangel Raguel, Archeia Serenity

Reproductive: Archeia Freedom, Archeia Mercy, Archangel Gabriel, Archeia Virtue

Sinuses: Archeia Charity, Archangel Raguel, Archeia Harmony

Skin: Archangel Michael, Archangel Raphael, Archangel Gabriel, Archeia Joy

Spleen: Archeia Grace, Archeia Joy, Archangel Gabriel

Stomach: Archeia Joy, Archangel Gabriel, Archeia Grace

Angels for Supporting the Systems

Circulatory: Archangel Michael, Archeia Freedom, Archangel Raphael

Digestive (and excretory): Archangel Uriel, Archangel Michael, Archeia Patience

Endocrine: Archangel Raphael, Archangel Gabriel, Archeia Virtue, Archeia Hope

Haematopoietic: Archangel Ariel, Archangel Gabriel, Archeia Hope

Immune (including lymphatic system): Archeia Freedom, Archangel Zadkiel, Archangel Michael, Archeia Charity

Integumentary: Archangel Michael, Archangel Raphael

Muscular: Archeia Strength, Archangel Michael, Archeia Freedom

Nervous: Archangel Raphael, Archeia Clarity, Archangel Jophiel, Archeia Radiance

Renal: Archeia Freedom, Archangel Zadkiel, Archeia Constance, Archangel Michael

Reproductive: Archeia Freedom, Archeia Mercy, Archangel Gabriel, Archeia Virtue

Respiratory: Archeia Freedom, Archangel Raphael, Archangel Raguel

Skeletal: Archangel Uriel, Archangel Cassiel, Archangel Jophiel

2. Angel Prescriptions for the Emotional and Mental Bodies

A

Abandonment: Archangel Michael, Archeia Strength, Archeia Grace

Accident-prone: Archangel Cassiel, Archangel Sandalphon

Addictions: Archeia Strength, Archeia Purity, Archeia Freedom, Archangel Gabriel

ADHD (Attention Deficit Hyperactivity Disorder): Archangel Gabriel, Archeia Harmony, Archeia Serenity, Archeia Freedom

Aggression: Archeia Harmony, Archeia Mercy, Archeia Charity

Alcoholism: Archangel Jeremiel, Archangel Gabriel, Archeia Hope

Alienation: Archangel Haniel, Archeia Radiant, Archangel Michael

Alzheimer's disease: Archangel Chamuel, Archeia Charity, Archangel Jeremiel

Anger: Archangel Cassiel, Archeia Virtue, Archeia Grace, Archeia Faith

Anxiety: Archangel Jeremiel, Archangel Barachiel, Archeia Harmony, Archangel Raguel

Apathy: Archeia Clarity, Archeia Strength

Autism: Archangel Gabriel, Archeia Grace Archangel Metatron, Archangel Michael

B

Binge-eating: Archeia Serenity, Archangel Sandalphon, Archeia Virtue

Bipolar disorder: Archangel Michael, Archangel Jophiel, Archeia Clarity

Body image: Archeia Mercy, Archeia Radiant, Archeia Charity

Boundaries (to create): Archangel Zadkiel, Archeia Purity, Archangel Michael

Burn-out: Archeia Constance, Archeia Patience, Archangel Raphael, Archeia Grace

Change (to flow with): Archeia Grace, Archangel Azrael, Archeia Harmony

Co-dependency: Archangel Raguel, Archeia Harmony, Archeia Charity

Communication: Archeia Hope, Archangel Gabriel

Confidence: Archangel Michael, Archeia Strength, Archeia Faith, Archeia Freedom

Courage: Archangel Ariel, Archangel Michael, Archeia Faith

Creativity: Archeia Freedom, Archangel Gabriel, Archeia Constance

Criticism: Archeia Victory, Archangel Azrael

D

Daydreaming: Archangel Sandalphon

Decision making: Archangel Uriel, Archangel Zadkiel, Archeia Clarity

Delusions (to remove and understand): Archangel Michael, Archangel Raziel, Archeia Clarity

Denial: Archangel Chamuel, Archeia Mercy

Depression: Archeia Purity, Archeia Mercy, Archeia Freedom, Archangel Haniel

Despair: Archangel Cassiel, Archeia Serenity, Archeia Freedom

E

Emotional abuse: Archeia Freedom, Archeia Mercy, Archangel Jeremiel, Archangel Michael

Emotional baggage (to remove): Archangel Raguel, Archeia Harmony

Emotional balance: Archeia Harmony, Archeia Serenity, Archangel Gabriel, Archeia Hope

Emotional blackmail: Archangel Michael, Archangel Jeremiel

Emotional eating: Archeia Serenity, Archangel Sandalphon, Archeia Grace

Emotional hooks (to remove): Archangel Michael, Archangel Raphael, Archeia Virtue

Emotional shock: Archangel Jeremiel, Archeia Serenity, Archangel Cassiel

Emotional stress: Archangel Jeremiel, Archeia Harmony, Archeia Virtue

Endurance (to boost): Archangel Metatron, Archeia Strength

Energy (to boost): Archangel Michael, Archeia Victory, Archeia Strength

Envy: Archangel Chamuel, Archeia Charity, Archeia Mercy

Fearfulness: Archeia Strength, Archangel Cassiel
FOMO (Fear of missing out): Archeia Serenity, Archeia Radiant, Archeia Grace
Forgiveness: Archeia Virtue, Archangel Zadkiel
Frustration: Archangel Raguel, Archeia Harmony, Archeia Patience

Guilt: Archeia Virtue, Archeia Mercy, Archeia Freedom
Gratitude: Archangel Barachiel, Archeia Joy
Grief: Archeia Mercy, Archangel Azrael, Archangel Chamuel

Habits (to change): Archeia Grace, Archeia Freedom, Archeia Purity, Archeia Clarity
Happiness: Archangel Jophiel, Archeia Joy, Archangel Barachiel
Heartache: Archeia Mercy, Archeia Charity
High Sensitivity (especially in children): Archangel Metatron, Archangel Gabriel, Archeia Virtue
Hoarding: Archeia Purity, Archeia Victory, Archeia Grace
Hyperactivity: Archangel Gabriel, Archeia Harmony, Archeia Serenity, Archeia Freedom

Impatience: Archeia Patience, Archangel Sandalphon
Imposter syndrome: Archeia Radiant, Archeia Strength, Archeia Faith
Indecisiveness: Archangel Uriel
Inertia: Archangel Michael, Archeia Strength
Insecurity: Archeia Radiant, Archeia Faith, Archeia Strength

Jealousy: Archeia Purity, Archeia Virtue, Archeia Radiant
Joy: Archeia Joy, Archeia Constance

L

Letting go: Archeia Freedom, Archeia Mercy, Archeia Serenity
Loneliness: Archeia Patience, Archeia Virtue, Archeia Mercy
Love: Archeia Charity, Archeia Virtue, Archangel Chamuel

M

Mania: Archeia Grace, Archangel Gabriel, Archeia Hope
Mid-life crisis: Archangel Jeremiel, Archeia Freedom, Archeia Virtue
Money issues: Archeia Patience, Archangel Ariel, Archangel Barachiel
Mood swings: Archangel Gabriel, Archangel Jeremiel, Archeia Joy

N

Negative thoughts (to alleviate): Archeia Clarity, Archeia Hope, Archangel Zadkiel

O

Obsessive compulsive disorder: Archangel Jophiel, Archangel Barachiel, Archeia Grace
Overwhelm: Archeia Grace, Archeia Patience, Archangel Sandalphon

P

Panic attacks: Archangel Uriel, Archangel Raguel, Archeia Serenity
Paranoia: Archangel Michael, Archangel Raphael, Archangel Raziel
Patience: Archeia Patience, Archeia Grace
Perfectionism: Archeia Mercy, Archeia Freedom, Archeia Constance
Personality disorders: Archangel Michael, Archangel Haniel
Phobias (and fears): Archangel Michael, Archeia Faith, Archangel Zadkiel
Postnatal depression (and perinatal issues): Archangel Gabriel, Archangel Michael, Archeia Faith, Archeia Grace, Archeia Hope
Psychosexual problems: Archangel Gabriel, Archeia Mercy, Archeia Freedom
Psychosis: Archangel Michael, Archangel Raphael, Archangel Azrael
PTSD (Post-traumatic stress disorder): Archangel Jeremiel, Archeia Harmony, Archeia Serenity, Archangel Raguel

R

Rejection: Archangel Raphael, Archeia Virtue, Archeia Mercy
Relaxation: Archangel Raphael, Archeia Virtue, Archeia Patience
Repressed emotions: Archangel Jeremiel, Archeia Serenity, Archeia Freedom
Resentment: Archangel Uriel, Archangel Sandalphon, Archeia Virtue
Resilience: Archeia Strength, Archangel Michael

S

Sadness: Archeia Joy, Archangel Gabriel, Archangel Cassiel
Schizophrenia: Archangel Michael, Archeia Faith, Archangel Azrael
Seasonal affective disorder: Archangel Ariel, Archeia Radiant, Archeia Joy, Archangel Jophiel
Self-acceptance (and self-love): Archeia Charity, Archeia Radiant, Archangel Haniel
Self-esteem: Archangel Michael, Archeia Strength, Archeia Faith, Archeia Freedom
Self-expression: Archeia Freedom, Archeia Mercy, Archeia Constance
Self-harm: Archangel Michael, Archeia Virtue, Archeia Mercy
Self-healing: Archangel Raphael, Archeia Virtue, Archangel Michael, Archeia Faith
Self-worth: Archangel Haniel, Archeia Radiant, Archeia Charity, Archeia Freedom
Senile dementia: Archangel Chamuel, Archeia Charity, Archangel Jeremiel
Sexual abuse/trauma: Archeia Freedom, Archeia Mercy, Archangel Jeremiel, Archeia Virtue
Shyness: Archangel Ariel, Archeia Strength
Sleep problems: Archeia Purity, Archangel Zadkiel, Archangel Raphael, Archeia Virtue
Smoking cessation: Archeia Clarity, Archangel Michael, Archeia Faith, Archeia Grace
Social media comparison: Archeia Charity, Archeia Virtue, Archeia Clarity
Social media masking (projecting a false version of yourself): Archeia Radiant, Archeia Charity, Archeia Freedom

Stamina: Archangel Ariel, Archeia Strength, Archangel Michael, Archangel Zadkiel

Stress: Archeia Purity, Archangel Zadkiel, Archangel Raphael, Archeia Virtue

Suicidal feelings: Archangel Michael, Archangel Azrael, Archeia Virtue, Archeia Faith

Trauma: Archeia Faith, Archeia Freedom, Archeia Charity, Archangel Jeremiel

Vitality (to boost): Archangel Michael, Archangel Raphael, Archeia Faith, Archeia Strength

Waiting for the other shoe to drop: Archeia Clarity, Archeia Freedom, Archeia Faith

Willpower: Archeia Clarity, Archeia Faith, Archeia Victory

Worrying: Archeia Purity, Archangel Zadkiel, Archeia Freedom, Archeia Virtue

3) Angel Prescriptions for the Spiritual (Energetic) Body

Angels for Supporting the Chakras

Earth star: Archeia Patience, Archeia Strength, Archangel Sandalphon

Base: Archeia Serenity, Archeia Patience, Archeia Mercy, Archangel Gabriel

Sacral: Archeia Purity, Archeia Freedom, Archangel Zadkiel

Navel: Archeia Freedom, Archeia Strength, Archangel Gabriel

Solar plexus: Archeia Grace, Archangel Uriel, Archeia Serenity

Heart: Archeia Charity, Archeia Virtue, Archeia Mercy, Archeia Freedom

Higher heart: Archeia Charity, Archeia Virtue, Archangel Chamuel

Throat: Archeia Faith, Archeia Mercy, Archeia Freedom, Archangel Michael

Third eye: Archeia Virtue, Archangel Raphael, Archangel Raziel

Crown: Archeia Clarity, Archeia Serenity, Archangel Cassiel, Archeia Purity

Causal: Archeia Charity, Archangel Chamuel,

Soul star: Archeia Mercy, Archeia Constance, Archeia Purity, Archangel Azrael,

Stellar gateway: Archeia Constance, Archangel Metatron

To activate and align all chakras to Source: Archeia Constance, Archangel Metatron

Angels for Supporting the Auric Field

Align aura with the emotional body: Archeia Harmony
Align aura with the mental body: Archeia Clarity
Align aura with the physical body: Archeia Mercy
Align aura with the spiritual body: Archeia Constance
Balance: Archeia Serenity
Cleanse: Archeia Purity
Energize: Archeia Patience
Energy drainage (to stop): Archeia Purity, Archeia Grace
Entity removal: Archeia Serenity, Archangel Michael, Archangel Azrael
Protecting: Archeia Serenity, Archeia Faith
Strengthen (and expand): Archeia Grace, Archeia Radiant
Weakness (to stop): Archeia Purity, Archeia Faith

Angels for Supporting Spiritual Embodiment

Acceptance of divine nature: Archeia Mercy, Archeia Constance, Archeia Clarity

Ancestral healing (of cosmic timelines): Archangel Metatron, Archeia Constance, Archangel Michael, Archangel Raphael

Ancestral healing (of planet Earth timelines): Archangel Sandalphon, Archeia Patience, Archeia Virtue

Angelic communication (in general): Archeia Hope, Archangel Barachiel, Archangel Gabriel, Archangel Uriel

Ascension (to aid and understand): Archeia Constance, Archangel Metatron, Archeia Mercy

Astral projection: Archangel Azrael, Archangel Zadkiel

Centring: Archeia Harmony, Archeia Hope, Archeia Charity

Channelling (to develop): Archangel Michael, Archangel Uriel, Archangel Gabriel

Clearing limiting beliefs: Archeia Clarity, Archangel Raphael, Archangel Jophiel

Cosmic connection and journeying: Archangel Metatron, Archeia Constance, Archangel Raziel, Archeia Clarity

Crystal communication: Archeia Patience, Archangel Gabriel, Archangel Ariel

Curses (removing): Archangel Michael, Archangel Azrael, Archangel Raphael, Archeia Serenity

D

Development of clairaudience: Archeia Clarity

Development of claircognizance: Archangel Uriel, Archeia Faith

Development of clairsentience: Archeia Charity

Development of clairvoyance: Archangel Raziel, Archeia Victory

Development of intuition (in general): Archangel Uriel, Archangel Gabriel, Archangel Metatron, Archangel Raziel, Archeia Victory

Development of mediumship: Archangel Azrael, Archeia Mercy, Archangel Michael, Archeia Faith

Development of mindfulness and heartfulness: Archangel Metatron, Archeia Clarity, Archeia Grace

Dream recall and interpretation: Archangel Uriel, Archangel Raziel, Archeia Clarity, Archangel Jeremiel

E

Elemental communication (Air): Archangel Raphael, Archeia Harmony

Elemental communication (Earth): Archangel Uriel, Archeia Strength

Elemental communication (Fire): Archangel Michael, Archeia Grace

Elemental communication (Spirit): Archangel Raziel, Archeia Constance

Elemental communication (Water): Archangel Gabriel, Archeia Serenity

Extraterrestrial communication: Archangel Metatron, Archeia Constance, Archangel Raziel, Archeia Victory

F

Feng Shui (to aid): Archeia Victory, Archeia Purity, Archangel Gabriel

G

Geopathic stress: Archangel Sandalphon, Archangel Ariel, Archeia Victory

Grounding: Archangel Sandalphon, Archangel Ariel, Archeia Faith

Guardian angel (meeting of): Archangel Barachiel, Archangel Gabriel

H

Healing (in general): Archeia Virtue, Archangel Raphael

I

Inner child (connecting to and healing): Archeia Hope, Archangel Gabriel, Archangel Metatron, Archeia Virtue

Inner wounding of the Divine Feminine: Archeia Freedom, Archeia Mercy, Archeia Virtue

Inner wounding of the Sacred Masculine: Archeia Clarity, Archangel Jophiel, Archangel Michael

K

Karmic dis-ease: Archeia Purity, Archeia Grace, Archangel Zadkiel, Archangel Metatron

Karmic ties (unravelling and severing): Archeia Faith, Archeia Purity, Archeia Grace

L

Light-body activation: Archeia Constance, Archangel Metatron, Archangel Zadkiel

M

Magic (connecting to Mother Earth's magic): Archangel Raziel, Archeia Victory, Archangel Ariel

Magic (connecting to our inherent magic): Archangel Raziel, Archeia Victory, Archeia Strength

Manifesting: Archangel Ariel, Archangel Barachiel, Archeia Joy

Meditating (to boost quality of): Archangel Raphael, Archeia Virtue, Archeia Clarity

P

Past life (cord-cutting): Archeia Serenity, Archangel Michael, Archangel Metatron, Archangel Zadkiel

Past life (healing): Archeia Grace, Archeia Patience, Archangel Metatron, Archeia Purity

Past life (regression): Archeia Constance, Archangel Metatron, Archeia Charity

Planetary healing (to aid): Archangel Ariel, Archangel Sandalphon, Archeia Virtue

Protection: Archeia Serenity, Archangel Cassiel, Archangel Michael, Archeia Faith

Psychic attack (healing of): Archeia Serenity, Archangel Michael, Archangel Azrael, Archeia Purity, Archeia Virtue

Psychic surgery aid: Archeia Virtue, Archangel Raphael, Archeia Clarity

Q

Quantum energy healing: Archangel Metatron, Archeia Constance

R

Rebirthing: Archeia Mercy, Archeia Freedom, Archangel Gabriel, Archeia Virtue

Releasing negative attachments/cord-cutting: Archangel Michael, Archangel Zadkiel, Archeia Purity, Archeia Freedom

S

Self-care: Archeia Charity, Archeia Freedom, Archeia Joy, Archeia Purity

Shadow integration (of dense/dark shadows): Archeia Serenity, Archeia Purity, Archeia Grace, Archeia Freedom

Shadow integration (of light/golden shadows): Archeia Serenity, Archeia Clarity, Archeia Freedom, Archeia Joy

Shamanic journeying: Archeia Clarity, Archangel Sandalphon, Archangel Ariel

Shielding: Archangel Michael, Archeia Strength, Archangel Zadkiel, Archeia Purity

Soul healing: Archangel Zadkiel, Archeia Purity, Archangel Chamuel

Soul retrieval: Archangel Raziel, Archangel Metatron, Archeia Constance, Archeia Victory

Space cleansing: Archeia Victory, Archangel Zadkiel, Archeia Purity, Archangel Gabriel

Star-seed awakening & development: Archangel Raziel, Archeia Victory, Archeia Constance, Archangel Metatron

T

Timeline healing: Archeia Charity, Archangel Metatron, Archeia Constance

Twin flame/soul mate union: Archangel Chamuel, Archeia Charity

Y

Yin/Yang energies (to balance): Archeia Freedom, Archeia Serenity, Archeia Radiant

LIST OF PRACTICES, MEDITATIONS, AND CEREMONIES

BIBLIOGRAPHY

Books

Bhajan, Yogi, Ph.D. *The Aquarian Teacher*™: KRI International Kundalini Yoga Teacher Training Level 1 Yoga Manual. First ed. Santa Cruz, NM: KRI, 2003.

Brown, Brené. *Daring Greatly.* New York: Gotham Books, 2012.

Calista. *Angel Healing® Student, Teacher, and Practitioner Manuals.* Self-published. Scotland: 2009.

Calista. *The Female Archangels: Evolutionary Teachings to Heal and Empower Your Life.* London: That Guy's House, 2020.

Calista. *Unicorn Rising: Live Your Truth and Unleash Your Magic.* London: Hay House UK, 2018.

De-Gaia, Susan. *Encyclopedia of Women in World Religions: Faith and Culture across History.* Santa Barbara, CA: ABC-CLIO, 2018.

Fischer, Lynn. *Angels of Love and Light: The Great Archangels & Their Divine Complements, the Archeiai.* Southern Pub Group, 1997.

Hall, Judy. *Crystal Prescriptions: The A–Z Guide to Over 1,200 Symptoms and Their Healing Crystals.* Winchester, UK: John Hunt Publishing, 2010.

Hargreaves, Hilary Jane. *Walking with Archangels.* Cardigan, Wales, UK: Unity Consciousness Books, 2017.

Hay, Louise. *Heal Your Body: The Mental Causes for Physical Illness and the Metaphysical Way to Overcome Them*. London: Hay House UK, 2004.

Joseph, Sonya. *Sound Healing Using Solfeggio Frequencies*. BA Thesis. American College of Healthcare Sciences, Dept. of Nutrition, June 2019.

Olivia, Keeley. *Unleashing the Female O: Discover Your Orgasmic Potential and Start Having the Sex You Crave*. Self-published. pdfcoffee.com, 2018.

Journals

Akimoto, Kaho, Ailing Hu, Taguji Yamaguchi, and Hiroyuki Kobayashi. "Effect of 528 Hz Music on the Endocrine System and Autonomic Nervous System." *Health 10*, no. 9 (September 2018).

Buijze. Geert A., Inger N. Sierevelt, Bas C.J.M. Van de Heijden, Marcel G. Dijkgraaf, Monique H.W. Frings-Dresen. The Effect of Cold Showering on Health and Work: A Randomized Controlled Trial. *PLOS ONE 13*, no. 8 (Sept. 15, 2016), https://journals.plos.org/plosone/article?id=10.1371/journal.pone.0161749.

ACKNOWLEDGEMENTS

Thank you, dear reader, for showing up to be, do, and enjoy this sacred work. Through you, all is truly possible, and more so if you embrace the teachings of the Archeiai and all that Heaven is constantly helping you rekindle and express.

Gratitude and grace to my dear sis'star and Angel Healing® Practitioner Marie-Joe Fourzali, who brought to life the channelled visions of the Archeiai. Your talent, love, magic, and mischief know no bounds! And to our extended family, the radiant ones of Angel Healing® (and Unicorn Healing®)—thank you for asking for this book, and for your continued support in sharing the Light of the Archeiai and the Archangels far and wide.

To my friends, family, and social media tribes, thank you! I am blessed to walk through life beside you. A deep bow especially for my mama Janice, for all your help with the kids; Ash, for your divine cacao, which fuelled many of these pages; and Jewel, for your regular check-ins and love to push through the obstacles that presented while writing this book.

Special thanks to Sean at That Guy's House for publishing the first edition and to Sabine at Findhorn Press and Inner Traditions for publishing the second edition and *The Female Archangels Oracle* deck. To all who endorsed the oracle and the editions of the book—thank you, shining ones.

Lastly, heartfelt appreciation to the Archeiai, the Elohim, my spirit team, angels, and ancestors, the new farmhouse and land spirits, that midwifed this new edition; and to the best kids (and teachers!) a mama could ask for: Rowan, Eden, and Amaya. You are my world. I love you all-ways, and in every way.

ABOUT THE ARTIST

Photo by Hala El-Khoury Blackman

Since early childhood, **Marie-Joe Fourzali** has turned to drawing and art as her main means of self-expression. Supported and encouraged by Calista—who she met while studying for her Angel Healing® degrees—she developed her talent further, allowing the purest presences to channel through her and co-create the images of this book as well as the art within *Unicorn Rising: Live Your Truth and Unleash Your Magic* and *The Female Archangels Oracle*. Marie-Joe lives in Spain and continues to bridge Heaven and Earth within her art and creative projects.

www.instagram.com/mariejoefourzali/

ABOUT THE AUTHOR

Photo by Kelly McIntyre

Calista first met her guardian angel when she was six years old during a time of personal crisis. Ever since, she has developed her relationship with angels, creating the popular hands-on therapy system Angel Healing® in 2009 and travelling the world attuning thousands of souls to Heaven. She is well known for her work with unicorns, elementals, Ascension, and supporting people to gain personal freedom and spiritual sovereignty.

Calista was the first to fully explore who the Archeiai are and which gifts they hold for humankind. She is the author of *The Female Archangels Oracle* as well as the award-winning book *Unicorn Rising: Live Your Truth and Unleash Your Magic*. She teaches her certified modalities Angel Healing® and Unicorn Healing® globally and believes that by empowering our lives, we help all of Creation to thrive. Calista lives in the wilds of the Scottish countryside with her three young children and magical cat Luna.

www.CalistaAscension.com

Other Works by Calista

Books and Card Decks

Unicorn Rising: Live Your Truth and Unleash Your Magic
The Female Archangels Oracle
Celestial Unicorn Tarot

Audio CDs and Downloads

Activating Your Light-Body
Align to Your Divine Self
Angel Healing® Meditation series (including recordings of many of the
    journeys and exercises from this book)
Awaken to Atlantis
Become Self-Empowered
Connecting to Your Inner Child
Discover Your Other Lives
Embracing Oneness
Falling in Love with You
Ignite Your Light
Into the Heart of Gaia
Journey of Awakening
Living in Your Heart
Loving Your Body
*Meet the Elementals; Meet the Mermaids; Meet Your Dragon Guide; Meet
    Your Guardian Angel; Meet Your Spirit Guide*
Sacred Aura Breath™
Soul Healing with Your Unicorn
Unicorn Healing® Meditations
Unicorn Rising book journeys
Valley of Abundance

Courses and Events

Angel Healing® Level 1 and 2 Practitioner Degrees, plus, Level 3
Teacher Training online and in-person
Unicorn Healing® 12-week online Practitioner degree
Monthly Ascension Zoom workshops and retreats

Rise and become Infinite!

You are the One you've been waiting for.

If you'd like to know more about the Archeiai or to become an Angel Healing® Practitioner connect via…

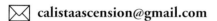 **calistaascension@gmail.com**

 **@CalistaAscension**

 **@CalistaAscension**

 **@CalistaAscension**

We'd love to hear your experiences of meeting and merging with the Female Archangels. Let us know with an Amazon review. Your feedback matters.

Parting Gift . . .

To receive your free recording of "Attuning to Angels", to merge with the vibration and consciousness of the 17 Archeiai of this book and their Divine masculine Archangel counterparts, plus receive a selection of other angel goodies, visit **CalistaAscension.com** and sign up for Calista's newsletter.

INDEX

Also by This Author

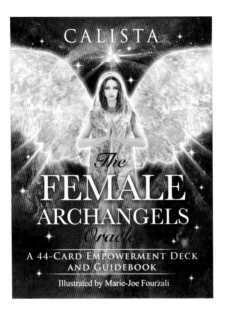

The Female Archangels Oracle

by Calista

An evolutionary oracle inspired by the Divine Feminine Archangels, the Archeiai, the female twins to the male Archangels.

Transmitting the unique frequencies of each Archeia and Archangel, the cards are embedded with vibrational keys of angelic energy, sacred geometry, crystalline Light-codes, and alchemical fires, creating a direct bridge into angelic consciousness. The deck includes 17 female Archangel cards, 17 male Archangel cards, and 10 cards with universal, powerful symbols.

ISBN 9–781–64411–580–0

FINDHORN PRESS

Life-Changing Books

Learn more about us and our books at
www.findhornpress.com

For information on the Findhorn Foundation:
www.findhorn.org